2

D1276317

WITHDRAWN

# Herbart and Herbartianism

370.15
D921h

# Herbart and Herbartianism: An Educational Ghost Story

## Harold B. Dunkel

The University of Chicago Press · Chicago & London

Standard Book Number: 226–17219–8
Library of Congress Catalog Card Number: 77–98126
The University of Chicago Press, Chicago 60637
The University of Chicago Press, Ltd., London
© 1970 by The University of Chicago
All rights reserved. Published 1970
Printed in the United States of America

To Mary Lou and Louise

186924

"Prolonged involvement with the works of a great man is the kind of honor he deserves; he can dispense with any other."
—Herbart on Kant

"Surely anything which is heralded and pursued with great exaggeration and enthusiasm necessarily declines. It has done its work once it has changed the inertness and indolence which it originally encountered into activity and concern."
—Herbart on Pestalozzi

# Contents

# A Personal Note

I hope only that the reader will find this book even one-tenth as interesting to read as I have found it fascinating to write. Authors of fiction and drama frequently remark that their characters take over the work and produce a final product quite different from what the author originally intended. Something of the same sort has happened here.

My interest in Herbart was first aroused almost twenty years ago when I taught a course entitled "Basic Contributions to Educational Thought," in which Herbart was one of the authors covered. While doing the reading necessary to choose the selections and handle the discussion of them, I became increasingly aware of the general sort of question presented in chapter 1 of this volume; I likewise became increasingly dissatisfied with the answers I was giving myself and my students.

When actual work was begun on this volume about eight years ago, I felt I was fairly well read in the literature by and about Herbart and, to a less degree, in that of the Herbartians. Still, though there were a number of excellent books and articles, the material I had read did not seem to me to shed any very intense light on what struck me as the intriguing questions about the rise and fall of Herbartianism, particularly the American portion of the saga where parts of the story appear most starkly. Nonetheless, at the outset I believed I had a fairly clear idea what the right questions were and what the probable answers would be. I was wrong. The more I have read and thought and written, the more the formulations of both questions and answers have changed.

During the academic year 1965–66, when through the kindness of Ralph W. Tyler, director of the Center for Advanced Study in the Behavioral Sciences, and of Roald F. Campbell, chairman of the Department of Education at the University of Chicago, I was able to devote full time at the center to completing this book, the modifications became even more frequent and drastic. The material is voluminous; the issues are complicated.

A few examples will indicate the kind of shift. Some years ago, I used to be distressed at the lack of success my students and I had in making sense out of the *Science of Education,* the Felkins' translation of the *General Pedagogy.* Then, as I read more widely in the German literature, I found that we were not the first to be baffled by the obscurity of this volume; ultimately, in the process of reading all Herbart's works, I discovered his own reservations about this book—his realization when he published it that it was puzzling and incomprehensible. Another instance is of a rather different sort. I began by taking a rather dim view of the metaphysics, became more impressed with its cleverness as I worked with it, but finally reached the conclusion that it is impossible. On the contrary, although initially unimpressed by Herbart's psychology, I have become convinced that he has nearly always been criticized for the wrong reasons and that few of his readers and critics have been prepared to take him seriously and honestly on his own terms. This is not to say that I now feel the future of psychology lies in revitalizing Herbart's doctrine; but his psychology was a greater intellectual achievement than has usually been acknowledged. Let me give a final example. Originally working with English translations for use in class, I wondered how such wretched jobs could even have been published and I muttered under my breath the old Italian chestnut about translators being traitors. Now that I have read the originals and have made the translations for this volume, I am completely sympathetic with the translators' dilemma of whether to produce a readable, comprehensible prose or whether to be true to Herbart's original—a problem to which there can be no good answer.

However much my assessments of Herbart as a philosopher and pedagogue have fluctuated, I have never lost my sympathy for Herbart the man; his determination to be true to himself and to the truth as he saw it still commands my admiration. ("The opposition I have encountered . . . is evident in the public journals. Without regard for external difficulties, I will continue my work as far as lies within my powers." [SW 15: 36]). Among the Herbartians, I have recast both heroes and villains from time to time as my knowledge expanded.

The following pages incorporate the best judgments I have finally been able to make. Although drastic simplification has been necessary to reduce the volume to reasonable bulk, I trust that the reader will get not merely my questions, my answers, and the evidence on which the latter are based, but also some insight into the problems involved in reaching decisions at all.

The translations, except for the half dozen specifically attributed to others, are mine.

For the typing of the manuscript at various stages I am indebted to Miss Mary Ellen Bell, Mrs. Helena Smith, Mrs. Dolores Ford, and Miss Pamela Lamport.

# Herbart and Herbartianism

# 1

## Up like the Rocket;
## Down like the Stick

The question, "Who was Johann Friedrich Herbart?" directed to even the educated man on the suburban street is sure to be answered with nothing more than a blank stare. Little more will probably be gleaned from similar inquiry at the local PTA, whose members are probably well versed in the dicta of Conant and Rickover, are experts on the McGuffey readers, and may even have some feeling of recognition when Montessori or even Pestalozzi is mentioned. In response to the same question, trained and practicing teachers, though they will be haunted by a dim memory that Herbart is a great name in education, will probably be able to do little more than say "Oh, he was the man with the 'five steps,'" or recall a few phrases like "the apperceptive mass" or "the threshold of consciousness."

Fame is usually fleeting, but oblivion has engulfed Herbart with unusual speed. Little more than fifty years ago his doctrines, or at least views passing as his, were a major force in educational theory and practice; now even his name is scarcely recognized by students and practitioners in the field. The man often called the "father of the scientific study of—

education" has become almost an unknown during the very period when the scientific study of education has been proliferating in universities and normal schools throughout the civilized world. Something obviously happened.

This rapid extinction of Herbart's reputation is not the only striking thing about his fame. He had been dead for about twenty-five years before he ever became famous. Thus, to any questions we have on why this fame ultimately ended so abruptly, we must add others concerning why it ever began and why it came so late. What led to this tardy, posthumous resurrection of his views, or at least of his name?

How this fame blazed up like a meteor and meteorlike was extinguished can be briefly sketched. Herbart was born in 1776, and, after training in philosophy at Jena, taught at the universities of Göttingen and Königsberg, then again at Göttingen. He wrote about a dozen volumes on philosophical and pedagogical topics, and during his twenty-four years at Königsberg conducted a pedagogical seminar. Although he was always a popular lecturer and had served on public and private boards and commissions concerned with education, his death seemed to mark the close of a mainly professorial career—successful, but not so distinguished as to merit international fame.

Putting exact dates to the beginning of historical movements is always precarious, but the Herbartian revival is usually dated from the publication in 1865 by Tuiskon Ziller, a Leipzig professor, of the book *Foundation of the Doctrine of Educative Instruction*,[1] which was intended to develop some of Herbart's ideas.

But Ziller, to suit his immediate purposes, omitted much of Herbart and added much that was his own. As a result, Herbartianism, from its very beginnings in Ziller's work, had only a partial connection with Herbart's own theories. A German society for the scientific study of education along Herbartian lines (Verein für wissenschaftliche Pädagogik) was

1. *Grundlegung zur Lehre von erziehenden Unterricht* (Leipzig: L. Prenitzsch, 1865).

formed in 1868 and became the prototype of similar organizations in other countries. From this time on Herbartianism flowered, especially after 1885, when Wilhelm Rein, who had been a student of Ziller's, became director of the pedagogical seminary and practice school at Jena. Jena then became the Mecca for teachers from all over the world who wished to be at the cutting edge of educational inquiry. Herbartian literature appeared in all the languages of Europe (including Armenian, Croatian, and Romanian),[2] and Herbartianism became an international educational movement from America in the West to Japan in the East.

In the United States, Charles DeGarmo published his *Essentials of Method* in 1889; Charles McMurry published his *General Method* in 1892 and collaborated with his brother, Frank, in writing *Method of the Recitation* in 1897. These volumes were the Bibles of American Herbartianism. The writings and other activities of these three men, who were the leading American Herbartians, made the movement a major force in the instruction of the growing mass of teachers being recruited and trained to staff the ever-expanding American schools, as well as a major influence on educational thinkers and writers. Herbartianism was the outstanding educational movement if only because it was more precise, coherent, and comprehensive than its potential competitors, such as "child study." As Colonel Francis Parker, no Herbartian, said in 1895, "No subject was ever brought into the American schools that furnished so much food for thought and such abundant means for discussion as the subject we call Herbartianism."[3] When, in 1895, the Herbart Club was expanded into "The National Herbart Society for the Scientific Study of Teach-

2. Extensive, though incomplete, listing of this literature at the acme of the movement can be found in A. Rudd, "Die Litteratur der Pädagogik Herbarts and seiner Schule," in Thilo, Flügel, Rein, and Rude, *Herbart und die Herbartianer* (Langensalza, 1897), pp. 52–154. See also F. Bartholomäi, "Johann Friedrich Herbarts Leben" in his *Joh. Friedr. Herbarts Pädagogische Schriften,* 7th ed. by E. von Sallwürk (Langensalza, 1903), 1: 116–17.
3. F. W. Parker, "Discussion," in *First Year Book of the Herbart Society,* ed. C. A. McMurry (Normal, Illinois, 1895), p. 153.

ing," the McMurrys and DeGarmo were, of course, the leading spirits in its formation; but figures like John Dewey and Nicholas Murray Butler also appeared on its original executive council.[4] The Herbartian bandwagon was rolling.

But then once more came change. Seven years after the organization of the society (one is inclined to write "seven *short* years"), the group reorganized as the "National Society for the Scientific Study of Education."[5] Clearly the name "Herbart" had lost its magic. Another bit of evidence on the decline of Herbartianism appears in A. F. Lange's translation of Herbart's *Outlines of Pedagogical Lectures*,[6] published in 1901 with preface and annotation by DeGarmo. A fundamental principle of Herbart's psychology was that "ideas" or "presentations" are not merely the building blocks of mind, but are also the basic elements in the formation of the desires and the will. This psychological view was the major warrant for the great claim of Herbart's educational theory—that education, by implanting the right ideas and building the proper circle of thought, could form the moral character. The only kind of education in which Herbart was interested was moral education, and for Herbart the possibility of moral education rested on the premise of the development of the good will through proper manipulation of the circle of thought. Moreover, it was precisely this possibility which had originally drawn Ziller to Herbart's theories and had thus given rise to Herbartianism. The reader of DeGarmo's notes is, consequently, brought up short by the statement:

> The reader will avoid all contradictions in educational theory by accepting the modern view of the primacy, not of ideas, but of what may broadly be termed the *will*. . . . The latter view is in accord with biological and historical science.[7]

4. Ibid., p. 204.
5. *First Yearbook of the National Society for the Scientific Study of Education* (1902), p. 70.
6. A. F. Lange, *Herbart's Outlines of Pedagogical Doctrine* (New York: Macmillan Co., 1901).
7. Ibid., p. 63.

To deny in this fashion the priority of the ideas is to negate most of Herbart's psychology and pedagogy, and much of Herbartianism.

DeGarmo can scarcely have been so naive as to think that if this fundamental principle was contradicted, Herbart's *Outlines* could still have much validity or utility for American educators—at least without much more extensive and profound revision than DeGarmo was apparently prepared to offer in his notes. His entire annotation was, in fact, an interesting commentary on the attitudes of a man who, for the preceding decade or so, had been the leading Herbartian in this country. He was certainly no longer taking Herbart's theories seriously, if he ever had. Yet, if his brand of Herbartianism had so little to do with Herbart, it seems odd, at least, that he was a party to this publication of Herbart's *Outlines*.

At any rate, Herbartianism in America was dying. From the years following 1905 it is hard to find an article on Herbart or Herbartianism which treats either as an active influence, rather than looking back on them purely historically. Once more, something had happened.

This history may be roughly summarized as follows: 1776–1841—the writings and educational activity of Herbart himself leave little apparent impress; 1842–1864—relative quiescence; 1865–1905—Herbartianism becomes a major international educational movement; 1906 to the present—decline into almost complete obscurity.

Why did Herbart become famous? Why did fame come so late? Why did fame, having come, depart so rapidly and completely as it did? To ask these questions, as I did a decade or so ago, is simply to generate a longer series of more specific inquiries. What did Herbart himself have to offer as an educational doctrine? Why did he have so little prominence and influence during his own lifetime? Then, since Herbart's influence on education is so clearly the consequence of the activities of his later followers, what is the relation between Herbart's own views and those which the Herbartians ascribed to him or spread under his aegis? Did his followers simply revive the original doctrine at more propitious times and places? Did they merely give it a more persuasive exposition? Or did they make certain necessary, though relatively minor, modifications, without which it could never have been effective? Or did they modify the doctrine to the point of distortion so that the rise and the fall of Herbartianism have essentially nothing to do with Herbart himself? If the last is true, do Herbart's own writings still have something to say to us, if we ignore the intervening aberrations of the Herbartians? Or has Herbart's thought become so much a part of the total structure of educational thinking and practice that what was good in it can no longer strike us as new and the points that seem novel are only falsities and eccentricities of the doctrine, now glaringly revealed by the light of later knowledge?

However intriguing questions of this sort may be for some of us, they may, like "what song the Sirens sang and what name Achilles bore when he was hidden among the women," seem of limited significance and interest, except to those who have acquired the taste. But Herbart has been a major figure in the development of the scientific study of education too recently to be dismissed cavalierly. Herbart and Herbartianism were so intimately connected with the rise of scientific education, and loomed so large in the training of the generation of scholars and teachers just preceding our own, that any light shed on the movement reflects on the present state of education as an area of study. Furthermore, some morals for current workers in the field may well be latent in the account of the rise and fall of Herbartianism. Partial answers to some of these questions can be sketched here, to be documented and developed more fully in the following chapters.

Herbart, in accordance with the custom of German university students of the time (a custom which received its classical statement in Schelling's "Lectures on the Method of Academic Study" of 1802), developed a general philosophic system. This plan divided the total domain of philosophy into three main parts: logic, metaphysics, and aesthetics. Metaphysics and aesthetics, in addition to their "general" portions, also had "applications," of which the most important for our purposes were psychology, as an applied branch of metaphysics, and ethics, as an application of aesthetics. Pedagogy was tightly enmeshed in this system, finding its ends in ethics (as derived from aesthetics) and its means and hindrances in psychology (as based on metaphysics).

This interlocking system had two general characteristics which had major consequences for Herbart and the Herbartians. First, this extensive, intertwined system was so cumbersome that it was almost impossible for Herbart or anyone else to explicate and use a part of it satisfactorily. In writing a book on psychology or pedagogy, say, he could not bring in the entire system, of which the topic under discussion was only a small piece; but the necessary bypassing of the total context of his thought tended to render the exposition of each section unintelligible to contemporary readers and reviewers. His attempts to write a one-volume conspectus of his whole system were equally unsuccessful. This unwieldiness of the system was a major reason that Herbart could not make his ideas understandable and useful to his contemporaries, especially his fellow-educators, and it kept him from acquiring much fame or influence during his lifetime. This clumsiness of the system likewise led the later Herbartians to abandon more and more of it.

The second characteristic of the system was the weakness of many of the individual parts. Herbart's logic is not at issue here. Herbart never had any particular interest in logic, and his *Chief Points of Logic* is merely a conventional handbook developed for the use of his students. But his ethics, metaphysics, psychology, and pedagogy all presented difficulties, both inherently and in relation to the times.

Herbart himself explicitly argued that his ethics was no new deliverance but was rooted in the long tradition of ethical thought since the Greeks. It was, in fact, more novel than Herbart claimed; and though it may seem old-fashioned with its talk about "the will," it is in many respects the least dated of any of the parts of Herbart's system. For our present interests, however, its most important feature was that it did not have a religious base. Herbart considered himself a religious man, but certainly not in the credal or dogmatic sense. In addition to having reservations about religion in its revealed and institutionalized forms, he was too much the rationalist to feel happy with any mystical aspects. Ignoring the details for the present, we easily see that Herbart's ethics would prove unattractive in the nineteenth century, which was marked by religiosity if not religiousness.

In addition to the effect of this general social climate, there was later the fact that the Herbartians were trying to introduce the doctrine into schools conducted by the Lutheran and Catholic churches. Accordingly, it is scarcely surprising not merely that Herbart's ethical doctrine was unpopular during his lifetime but also that the Herbartians, both German and American, should feel that the less they said about it the better. Therefore, though the Herbartians kept quoting Herbart's dictum that morality is the end of education, they were careful not to state what they meant by it, implying agreement with whatever views were held by the reader or hearer of the moment. Through this kind of attrition, ethics, as anything but the bare word, largely disappeared from the system of the Herbartians.

The situation in regard to metaphysics is more complicated. As the student of Fichte, the successor to Kant, and the contemporary of Schelling and Hegel, Herbart was competing in a philosophic major league, and at this acme of German idealism his adherence to realism was sufficient to put him outside the mainstream of German philosophy. But his metaphysics, quite apart from the fact that its general kind was unpopular at that time and place, had certain grave defects. It was ingenious, but in the last analysis it failed in its effort to describe and explain human experience in terms of his postulated world of simple "reals" or monads.

Its greatest relevance to education lay in its furnishing a basis for psychology, a task which it performed only with considerable logical difficulty. These shortcomings of the metaphysics limited the popularity and influence of this part of Herbart's system during his lifetime and in themselves would probably have been adequate reasons for his followers near the end of the century to minimize the importance of the metaphysics and its relations to the other parts of the system.

Additional factors were also operating at this later period. First, metaphysics in any form had grown unpopular. Second, Drobisch, Herbart's closest and most devoted follower within the field of psychology, had shown that the principles of Herbart's psychology could be reached from starting points other than Herbart's metaphysics, thus depriving the metaphysics of whatever significance it gained as a basis for psychology and, through it, for pedagogy. For all these reasons, the German and (even more so) the American Herbartians came to act rather as if Herbart's metaphysics had never existed.

Psychology was the philosophic field to which Herbart was most devoted, an attitude reinforced by his pedagogical view that an adequate educational technology could rest only on a truly "scientific" psychology. As with metaphysics, Herbart attempted to break new ground.

Rejecting the theories which saw mind as a set of faculties or functions, Herbart conceived the structure of mind as built up out of the "presentations" or simple ideas which arose in it. As a result it was impossible, he believed, to talk about mind "in general." Each individual mind was the unique product of those particular presentations which it itself had experienced, although not a mere aggregation of those specific presentations. The structure of this "circle of thought" or "apperceptive mass" was modified to some degree by each new presentation which entered it, and, conversely, the effect of each new presentation was conditioned by the precise nature of that particular apperceptive mass which it encountered. As Herbart saw it, the task of a scientific psychology was to discover the laws governing the interactions between presentations and groups of presentations. Accordingly, taking his model from physics, he sought to develop an analogous "statics and mechanics of mind." Since he saw that physics and astronomy had advanced by postulating "fictitious" laws and then testing their capacity to describe the relevant phenomena in the natural world, Herbart's psychological investigations consisted in large part of efforts to formulate mathematically these interactions between and among presentations.

Because many of these formulations embodied truisms taken from the principles and practices of philosophy, psychology, and education, the formulations and their applications often possessed considerable plausibility and surface validity. But partly because they lacked an adequate empirical base in a "natural history" of mind, partly because they did not lend themselves easily to empirical testing, and partly because Herbart concentrated on developing the formulations rather than on testing them, the theory remained largely what Herbart would have called in the work of others a "mythology." Still, a portion of Herbart's psychology, developed as "the theory of apperception," fascinated Herbart's later followers because of its plausibility at the gross level; and this part, often much "corrected" and "revised," tended to usurp the place of Herbart's entire psychological theory among the Herbartians.

This resulted in some measure from the fate of some other parts of Herbart's psychological theory. One important element in that doctrine had been the view already mentioned, that presentations were not merely the basic elements of conceptual thought but were the ultimate origin of the desires and the will as well. As we have seen, the belief that control of the presentations gave the psychologist or the educator considerable indirect control over the formation of the child's desires and will was the very cornerstone of Herbart's plan for a *moral* education directed toward fashioning the *good* will within the child. In addition to the psychological difficulties which this view involved, however, its "deterministic" or "mechanistic" nature ran directly counter to the moral and religious views of the time. As a result, despite the obvious appeal this theory had for teachers, on whom it conferred considerable power in shaping the intellectual and moral life of their pupils, the later Herbartians often ignored or contradicted this major portion of the psychology. And it disappeared into oblivion along with the parts of the pedagogy directly related to it.

The remaining important division of Herbart's doctrine, pedagogy, had weaknesses of its own in addition to those troubles caused by its involvement with the rest of the total system. The chief shortcoming of Herbart's pedagogical theory was that he took as the paradigm for his moral education the work in a private home of a tutor with two or three children in his charge. So, for example, one of his three major divisions of pedagogy, "discipline" (*Zucht*), rests fundamentally on extremely close personal relations and interactions between teacher and pupil. Likewise, the full development of his educative or moral "instruction" (*Unterricht*) is possible only if the teacher can build, bit by bit, the circle of thought of the individual child, taking careful account of the precise structure of that particular child's mind at each point. As a result, there was always a well-grounded suspicion among the Prussian officialdom of Herbart's day that his pedagogical seminar at Königsberg was primarily training tutors for private families, not teachers for the Prussian schools. His later followers ignored most of this individualized pedagogy as inapplicable in their situations. Individualization of this sort was definitely not going to occur in the schools of Herbart's time, with their classes of twenty-five to thirty pupils, and it was equally impossible in the German and American public schools with which his later followers had to work.

Similarly, the fact that Herbart's major aim was to make the child moral rather than erudite, technologically competent, socially mobile, or politically loyal made Herbart's doctrine discordant with most nineteenth-century education, as did the fact that he used materials and procedures which differed markedly from the usual educational practices of his time and which could scarcely be combined with them.

For the Herbartians, these difficulties and the resulting omissions from the pedagogical doctrine were compounded by the modifications and omissions they made in the rest of the system. With "morality" left vague by the slighting of the ethics, those portions of the pedagogy bearing directly on specific parts of Herbart's moral theory had to be omitted. Similarly, when Herbart's psychology was reduced essentially to the theory of apperception, and when that doctrine was, in turn, limited purely to cognitive thought and deprived of what Herbart had seen as its role in developing the desires and the will, the pedagogy had to be cut correspondingly.

To epitomize the account of the following pages, we shall find Herbart struggling to establish himself as a major philosopher in the golden age of German philosophy, seeking especially to develop an original metaphysical doctrine and to put psychology and pedagogy on adequate, scientific bases. Intelligent, well trained, hard working, and persistent though he was, he never achieved that eminence as a philosopher for which he strove and which he thought was his due. As an educator he had little influence on the theory or the practice of his day.

In view of that record, it is somewhat surprising that his work was ever revived. And in any strict sense it never was. The followers who attached his name to their international movement in education ignored much of his original system. They then subjected that truncated portion which they retained to corrections, modifications, and extensive additions, finding, in their opinion, sufficient warrant for these alterations either in parts of Herbart's own writings or in the changed circumstances of those other times and places in which they worked.

As a result Herbart's chief interests, his personal activity, and his doctrines all stand in very odd relations to the operations later associated with him. His name is familiar in the history of education, but that many people can associate so little with it is simply a consequence of the slight impact which Herbart's own views had, not only on the philosophy and education of his day and generation, but also on the work of those who presumably disseminated his ideas.

At the symposium of the great figures in the history of educational thought, Herbart sits like a ghost. His fame was belated and brief, and his relation to the actual ideas and practices that account in large part for his presence there is singularly unsubstantial. Inept at expressing his thought and at influencing his contemporaries, in spite of his undeniable virtues and ability, he owes his fame to later ghost-writers, notably Ziller and Rein. Skilled writers and entrepreneurs, these men found ideas in Herbart which stimulated their own thought. Doubtless they sought to transmit all that they felt was living and useful in the master's doctrine. But their purposes and their milieus were sharply different from those of Herbart, and they felt constrained neither to include those parts of his doctrine which they believed were wrong or inapplicable nor to exclude their own elaborations and contributions, even though these often had little or no relation to Herbart's theory and practice. Ultimately, many seem to have referred to him only for the sake of respectability. After all, he was a German university professor from the golden age of German philosophy who was interested in education; and education has never been a prestigeous subject.

The preceding historical sketch suggests the reasons for taking a fresh, long look at Herbart and the Herbartians. A relatively recent and vigorous educational movement has disappeared almost without a trace—a movement always connected with Herbart's name. Consequently, though Herbart actually had relatively tenuous relations with Herbartianism, we tend to view him through the distorting lenses of the activities and statements of his alleged followers. For example, no major book on Herbart has been written in English for over fifty years. This statement is equivalent to saying that the materials in English were produced during the period of English and American Herbartianism and that their accounts and assessments of him entangle him in later developments.

If we are to evaluate Herbart as a historical educator in his own right, we must look at him, his works, and his times directly, unbiased by any significance that various elements acquire simply because they were seized upon by those who in some vague sense "followed" him. This attempt to understand Herbart for himself necessarily involves us in the details of his huge, sprawling, and complicated system. This vast scheme is what Herbart believed he had to offer, and understanding his own operations and those of the Herbartians requires a fairly precise and detailed knowledge of it.

A new examination of Herbart will extricate him not merely from the biased reports of his friends, but also from those of his enemies. Many past judgments of him have been merely the products of critics who damned him because he did not agree with them, their principles, or their favored doctrine. It has been verdict first, trial later. Since modern thought is not metaphysical, his metaphysics will at least appear less outrageous to us than they did to devoted adherents of some other metaphysical system. Since the modern temper is less pious, his ethics will surely seem less repugnant to us than it did to those incensed by its neglect of the tenets of revealed religion. Certainly our familiarity with later psychological theories has rendered us much less likely to be appalled by anything "deterministic" or "mechanistic" in Herbart's view of personality or mind. In short, a less partisan approach is certain to yield different and fairer judgments.

Only after examining Herbart's own position carefully can we see the extent to which he was a "Herbartian." Herbart's own work must serve as the baseline against which the innovations of the Herbartians are plotted. Herbartianism can then be examined in turn as a movement in its own right—as a series of developments owing more to the inspiration and ingenuity of Ziller, Rein, and the other Herbartians than to its original heritage from Herbart.

In brief, the purpose of this book is to disentangle Herbart from the Herbartians and to see each element for what it actually was. If we honor Herbart merely as the alleged father of Herbartianism, then this procedure will, to a degree, lay the ghost of Herbart in the history of educational thought. But at least we will have materialized him as a philosopher and an educator into a more definite substance than that spectral figure to whom the incantations of the Herbartians are occasionally addressed. If this examination does not call him back to walk the educational world again, at least he will be better remembered.

# The Overprotected Child

The life of a professional thinker is usually lacking in those elements of power, adventure, money, or sex which are the usual stimulants to biographical interest; but an account of his life is needed to illumine the thinker's thought. Unless we choose to see all thought as the product of disembodied intellect contemplating immutable philosophic problems in the pure empyrean, experience in large part makes the man. And the man appears in his thought—not so much in personal biases or blind spots (though these may appear) as in the personal predilections apparent in the type of problem he considers important, the ends he has in view, the principles he selects as fundamental, the methods he sess as appropriate, and the other choices he necessarily makes within the domain of rational inquiry. To the bases for these decisions biography does offer some clues, even if tenuous ones.

In Herbart's case, his relations with his family, particularly with his mother, do much to explain his personality and hence, in some measure at least, his thought. Likewise, to understand his thought, we need to know something of the intellectual capital on which he could draw and the amount

of access he had to it, and to have some knowledge of the
political, social, and economic forces which beat upon him and
against which he struggled.

Although Herbart lived in troubled times and places, he
appears to have led a singularly uneventful personal life. His
biography is often reduced to the usual professorial chronicle
of positions held and books published. Certainly he took little
notice of the political, military, and social upheavals which
shook northern Europe during his adult life, and noticed little
even the repercussions of these events in his own academic
circles, although no contemporary of Napoleon in Europe
could be wholly unaffected. But if Herbart's outer life was
uneventful, certainly his inner life, intellectually and especially
emotionally, was not. To portray him as an unworldly, dis-
interested intellectual, stolidly and single-mindedly practicing
his profession of teaching philosophy while wars and revolu-
tions raged about him, does less than justice to the facts.

Herbart was born in Oldenburg, a town of Hanover a few
miles from Bremen, on 4 May 1776. American readers will be
reminded by the date that these were indeed revolutionary
times, with political revolution about to break out in France
as well. The industrial revolution had already begun in England, where Watt had invented the steam engine eleven years
earlier, though spinning by steam did not appear until Herbart
was nine years old.

Intellectually this was also an exciting time in which to be
born. David Hume died in August of that year, and Rousseau's
death followed in another two years; but both of them had
contributed much to the intellectual ferment of the age. Bee-
thoven and Hegel were mere boys of six, but Kant, Goethe,
Herder, Lessing, Schiller, and Mozart were at or were ap-
proaching the height of their mature powers. In the field of
education, Rousseau, Basedow, and Pestalozzi had long been
active and influential. To be born in 1776 was to be born near
the acme of "German" culture.

His parents were a curiously mismated pair. His father,
a judicial counselor (*Justizrath*) and administrative counselor

(*Regierungsrath*) in the town, is described by Herbart's close friend, Smidt:

> His official duties, to which he devoted himself with professional zeal, seemed to absorb his whole activity. He was seldom seen except in his study, in court, or evenings, at his club, where he got a few hours' relaxation from his heavy day's work through a little card-playing. Silent, dry, and phlegmatic, he seemed to avoid all liveliness as being destructive of his customary circle of thought, yet without any particular effort to overcome tendencies of this kind since it too would have had a similar disturbing effect. Content to do his duty in his appointed round, he strove for nothing more in the world. The entire management of household he left to his wife. So he was always described to me, and so I always found him on visits.[1]

Herbart's mother, the daughter of a physician, was quite clearly of a very different temperament. Again, Smidt's portrait is clear:

> She was born to command; she wanted to be creative and effective, to seize upon a variety of life-tasks and to accomplish them; she looked and moved on all sides. But in this masculine character, a feminine depth of feeling was not lacking. I have often seen her in such tears as could well out of only one whose spirit was moved to its inmost part. But as there is no light without shadow, so any grace, except for the lively glance of the eyes, was lacking, as was any trace of beauty. Bearing, gait, manner of speech, and gesture all lacked charm.[2]

The usual description of her as a woman of strong will and quick resolution gains concreteness from a story she herself later told Smidt about accompanying an old friend of the family on a trip toward Switzerland in a last-ditch effort to save his life. As she was measuring out the laudanum to ease

1. Smidt, *Recoll.* in K. Kehrbach and O. Flügel, *Johann Friedrich Herbart Sämtliche Werke in chronologischer Reihenfolge* 1:xxix–xxx. Hereafter cited as *SW.*
2. Smidt, *Recoll.* in *SW* 1:xxx.

his pain, the invalid asked for an overdose, pointing out that he had no one dependent on him and no hope of recovery. After a moment's consideration she complied, and the next day took his body back to Oldenburg for burial.[3]

Smidt draws the obvious conclusion concerning the union between the different personalities he sketched, "That this marriage . . . was an unfortunate one and that our friend . . . had no happy childhood under the paternal roof can easily be assumed from these relations."[4] It is a familiar fact that an unhappy childhood is often a fairly conscious motivation in the lives of those who choose to work with and for children— "I will do better for other children than adults did to me when I was a child." Smidt's own insight, without our later studies to guide him, suggested that Herbart's lifelong concern for education sprang in large measure from this source.[5]

But Herbart's relations with his parents, particularly his mother, were much more complicated than merely those of the child of an unhappy marriage, having to live through an unhappy childhood. As a very young child, Herbart fell into a kettle of very hot, almost boiling water.[6] This accident presumably led to lifelong trouble with his eyes, to an equally persistent general weakness, and to his mother's following a rather Spartan regimen with him in early childhood and keeping him from school until he reached the age of eleven. Most biographers recount the accident and its alleged consequences in flatly factual style. Because of this mishap, they do not find it strange that his mother should have sought to harden him by cold baths, light clothing, hard bed, and similar ministrations in the manner of the opening sections of Rousseau's *Emile;* that she should have had him tutored at home, supervising his

3. Smidt, *Recoll.* in *SW* 1:xl–xli.    4. Smidt, *Recoll.* in *SW* 1:xxx.
5. Smidt, *Recoll.* in *SW* 1:xxxi.
6. F. Bartholomai, "J. Friedrich Herbarts Leben," in *Joh. Friedr. Herbarts Pädagogische Schriften,* 7th ed. by E. von Sallwürk (Langensalza: Herman Beyer and Söhne), p. 4. See also A. M. Williams, *Johann Friedrich Herbart* (London: Blackie and Son, 1911), p. 8; and W. Rein in Thilo, Flügel, Rein, and Rude, *Herbart und die Herbartianer* (Langensalza: Hermann Beyer u. Söhne, 1897), p. 16.

early education even to the extent of learning Greek herself; that she should have accompanied him when years later he departed to the university and still later when he went to his tutoring job in Switzerland; and that she even picked out a girl she wanted him to marry.[7] Similarly, when Herbart, during his university years, found himself unable to work or when he apparently contemplated suicide—if indeed he really did and his statement is actual autobiography and not just a literary effort,[8] since he sent copies of it to his friend Rist [9] and probably to others—the biographers have often attributed these difficulties to that same unfortunate tumble into the kettle or to the strain engendered by deep philosophic thought.

Unprofessional diagnosis at this distance in time and space must be extremely tentative. But Smidt surely put us on the right track when he suggested Frau Herbart's motivation: having found her husband wholly unsatifactory, she attempted to produce a satisfactory son to replace him in her life.[10] As the obvious hostility of many of her actions toward Herbart will make clear, her protection was overprotection. As for Herbart's physical ills, we can at least remember that this is the "eye trouble" of a man who was for his time professionally well read in a number of different fields, who wrote (and presumably read proof on) more than a dozen major books, and who earned his living as an active university professor. As for general weakness, he was a healthy youth, a student who traveled over Germany and took riding lessons [11] and an adult who had many periods of normal health. The kettle cannot have been that traumatic nor mother's remedies that efficacious.

The choice of a tutor for Herbart, Hermann Uelzen, who later became a pastor at Langelingen near Celle, has usually been judged a happy one for a future philosopher. Trained in the Wolffian philosophy (which was based on Leibnitz and was the dominant pre-Kantian view in Germany) and in Protestant theology, Uelzen did not limit his instruction to mere transmission of doctrines but paid considerable attention to

7. Smidt, *Recoll.* in *SW* 1:xlii.    8. *SW* 1:34–35.    9. *SW* 19:83.
10. Smidt, *Recoll.* in *SW* 1:xxx.    11. *SW* 16:37.

the bases of distinctions and to grounds for doubt. Treating the questions of ethics, psychology, and metaphysics in this problematic fashion, he aroused his pupil's interest in these topics at a very early age. As a result, by the time Herbart was fourteen he was writing essays on the freedom of the will.[12] Endowed with a phenomenal memory, he could easily reproduce what he had read or heard, being able, for example, to write down almost verbatim sermons he had earlier heard at church.

In music he was both interested and gifted. He studied simultaneously violin, cello, harp, and piano. By the age of eleven he was a well-known local performer on the piano,[13] and he continued-to play this instrument throughout his life, even publishing a sonata for it.[14] It is hardly surprising, therefore, that many of the illustrations in his psychological works concern musical tones and that the rules of harmony and discord as found in classical harmonic theory influenced his psychological theories concerning the consonance and dissonance of presentations or ideas.[15] This was one mode of perception in which he was experienced and expert.[16]

At Michaelmas of 1788 he entered the second class of the Oldenburg Latin school (which was elevated to a gymnasium while he was attending it). Still extant is an outline he did, in the summer of 1789 while was still thirteen, of a proof for the existence of an eternal God.[17] In the fall of 1789, he entered the first class when he was still less than fourteen and studied, among other subjects, logic and Kant, with the *Metaphysics of Morals* making a particularly strong impression on him.[18] As might be expected of an introverted, precocious child who was three to four years younger than his classmates, he seems to have had only two close friends, Bonus and Langreuter.

The young scholar may seem to have thrived on this heavy

12. SW 16:4.    13. SW 16:4, n. 1.    14. SW 17:8, 12, 13; 19:152–53.
15. E.g., SW 17:245.
16. See Willi Kahn, "Herbart als Musiker," in *Herbart Studien*, vol. 4, ed. G. Weiss (Langensalsa, 1926).
17. SW 19:58–59.    18. SW 12:172; 13:313.

diet of metaphysics and music, but Herbart some years later gives us a glimpse of his feelings at the time. As a tutor he endorses his charge's request to be allowed to hear a series of lectures with the comment: "The most important thing is that he wishes it *now*. . . . My own sad experience makes me regret daily that so little attention was paid to such wishes when I was young." [19]

In 1793 as "first-boy" in Prima or sixth form, he delivered the congratulatory oration to graduates departing to the university, "Some Comments concerning the Increase and Decline of Morality in States"; [20] and Herr von Halem, an old friend of the family and the father-in-law of his friend, Langreuter, published it in the *Blätter vermischten Inhalts*,[21] of which he was editor. On Herbart's own graduation from the gymnasium in the spring of 1794, at the age of eighteen, his Latin oration was a comparison of Cicero's and Kant's views concerning the *summum bonum*.[22] Plainly, the philosophic interests which his tutor had engendered were still strong. And the judgment of Manso, the head teacher of the school, is a characterization of Herbart which was true of him the rest of his life: "Among the graduates, just as among all his fellow students, Herbart was always notable for his order, his fine bearing, his zeal for study and his determination, and he attempted to develop and increase his good natural endowment through tireless diligence." [23]

During this period, reports on his health show an interesting variation. At age eleven he could join friends in a hike to a cloister seven miles distant. Though he had some difficulty in making the trip back, this expedition was obviously not the undertaking of a sickly child. Likewise, when he was twenty-two he could look back and say that at fourteen dancing, shouting, and jumping were the height of his existence.[24] In the same vein and from a greater distance (1831) he could pronounce, "In my youth I could without doubt call myself comparatively healthy." [25] Possibly the comparison was not

19. *SW* 1:42.   20. *SW* 1:lxx; 16:4.   21. *Bl. verm. Inh.*, 6:60ff.
22. *SW* 16:5.   23. *SW* 16:5.   24. *SW* 16:96.   25. *SW* 9:355.

with other young people but with other more sickly periods in
his own life. At any event, the kettle of hot water does not
seem to have marred irremediably a fourteen-year-old who
can jump and dance. Yet his health was poor when he left the
gymnasium and departed for the University of Jena, though
he himself calls it "a weakness of body *and soul.*" [26] His eye
trouble returned, and he suffered from abscessed teeth and
swelling of the cheek.[27] A notable point is that he was accompanied by his mother. She was ready to leave her husband and
eager to see the world—and probably hated to see her son
escape from under the maternal thumb. A causal relation between Herbart's health and her decision to accompany him
may perhaps be seen as operating in either direction.

Although he went to Jena in the summer of 1794, he did
not matriculate until fall. He mixed little with his fellow students, presumably because of his ill health.[28] But a friend of
his at the time, Rist, speaks of his unpolished but mild character,[29] and Professor Woltmann characterized him then as a
"philosophic type" but one who had ripened too early and on
only one side—one in whom "the liveliness of youth" was completely lacking.[30] Herbart was always to have difficulties in
personal relations.

Although he was presumably going to study law, out of
deference to his father's wishes, he began by devoting himself
entirely to philosophy. Jena was at that time the scene of great
philosophic activity. The Kantian philosophy had been introduced there by Erhardt Schmid, and after 1785 Jena's *Allgemeine Litteraturzeitung* was the chief organ of the Kantian
movement. In 1788 Karl Leonhard Reinhold became professor
at Jena. His "Letters on the Kantian Philosophy," which first
appeared in Wieland's *Deutscher Merkur* in 1786, were a
powerful influence in the spread of Kantianism in Germany, as
well as a strong stimulus to public interest in philosophy gen-

26. SW 16:9, 11. Italics mine.    27. SW 16:12.
28. SW 19:62, 63. For Herbart's personal relations and details concerning his friends, see Walter Asmus, *Der "Menschliche" Herbart* (Düsseldorf: A. Henn, 1967).
29. SW 16:7.    30. SW 16:11.

erally. His interpretation of Kant became essentially the school version, particularly at Jena, and the alterations and criticisms Reinhold made in explaining and defending the doctrine probably influenced Herbart's own views of the Kantian position. But Herbart knew Kant's great work directly as well as at second hand, for in 1795 he spent an hour each day working through Kant's *Critique of Pure Reason* with his friend Rist.[31] When Reinhold departed to Kiel in 1794, he was followed at Jena by Fichte, one of the major "post-Kantians," who moved from what they felt were the difficulties or faults of the Kantian "idealism" to new varieties of their own.

Herbart was not Fichte's student merely by virtue of attending his lectures and eventually becoming recognized as his keenest student. Frau Herbart made the great man's acquaintance, became a close friend of Frau Fichte's,[32] and even argued hotly with Fichte himself about the passivity which he assigned to the female personality in one of his works.[33] And both Frau Herbart and Fichte were closely connected with two other major influences on Herbart's personal and intellectual life at this time.

The first of these was the Literary Society, a group of six or eight students who, in addition to informal gatherings, held formal meetings every two weeks at which they presented papers and held discussions on political, philosophical, and literary matters and similar topics. This group was also known as the Society of Free Men, since none of them belonged to a student fraternity, although their society did not stand in open opposition to these corps. A second and somewhat overlapping group was established by Fichte himself upon his arrival at Jena. Not impressed with the contribution made to the intellectual life by the students' societies, with their emphasis on drinking and dueling,[34] he set up, with the collaboration of Woltmann and some other colleagues, a luncheon group with whom he met regularly, for a period even in his own home. Within these groups Herbart managed to make friends, with

31. *SW* 16:8.  32. *SW* 16.58.  33. *SW* 16:42-43.
34. Rist's *Lebenserinnerungen* in *SW* 16:6.

several of whom he kept close ties over a long period. Frau Herbart seems to have thrived on these parts of student life much more than did her son. In addition to meeting Fichte, she made the acquaintance of Schiller, whom Herbart accompanied on a trip to Leipzig,[35] and became a friend of her son's friends. One of these, Steck, saw the relation between mother and son as rather idyllic—"She is he and he is she"—and wrote to his own mother wishing that she were there; [36] but we cannot be certain that Herbart saw the situation in the same light.[37]

The more closely acquainted with Fichte's views Herbart became, however, the more he found himself unable to accept them. He communicated his doubts and criticisms to Fichte on several occasions, but the response, or lack of it, on Fichte's part was always less than satisfactory.[38] Later he was to say, "Fichte taught me primarily by his errors." But as Herbart went on to acknowledge, Fichte had the virtue of striving for clarity in his investigations, and thus the points of disagreement could serve as firm bases for Herbart's own later thought.[39] As he put it in the one-paragraph Latin autobiography he prepared when taking his doctorate, "I know not how it came about that, though he tried that I should penetrate deeply into his mind, he moved me from any idealistic views whatever and led me into the exactly opposite path." [40] In short, Herbart began his own more mature philosophizing with a grounding in Wolff and Kant, the latter in a form (Reinhold's) which was somewhat critical of it, and with a definite reaction from Fichte's version of idealism.

Another probable influence on his later work came from the first publication in 1795 of the fragments of Parmenides as part of the great German drive in classical philology and an awakening interest in the history of philosophy. Rather than drastically modifying the Kantian idealism as did Fichte,

---

35. *SW* 16:10, n. 1.    36. *SW* 16:39.
37. See Walter Asmus, "Johann Friedrich Herbart als Jenenser Student," in *Erziehung als Beruf und Wissenschaft*, ed. Asmus and Ruppert (Diesterweg: Frankfurt a. M., 1961).
38. *SW* 16:9, 28, 31, 46, 102.    39. *SW* 5:107; 1:94.    40. *SW* 1:366.

Schelling, and Hegel, Herbart turned back toward the realism of the pre-Socratics: the absolute being of the Eleatics and the absolute creature or atom of Heraclitus (as well as the absolute qualities of the Platonic forms, but with those qualities seen as qualities of permanent "reals"). He was in almost daily discussion with Eschen (who was a student of the classicist, Voss) in regard to Homer, and possibly it is from these discussions that Herbart's idea of beginning foreign-language instruction with Homer grew. Though "Back to the Greeks" was never a war cry with Herbart, his philosophic and pedagogic activity involved much of it. Beginning language instruction with Homer was almost a trademark of Herbart's later pedagogical doctrines, and in the Herbartians this emphasis on the Greeks increased and developed into the doctrine of having the child move successively through the cultural epochs.

Although Herbart's activities were primarily philosophical at this time, the fact that he delivered a paper to the Literary Society on the duty of the state in regard to the education of children is some evidence of an interest in education at this period. We also know that his friend Rist, as early as 1795, saw Herbart's thought as wholly directed toward the education of youth.[41]

During the Jena period, Herbart's relations with his mother grew steadily worse. She was so active and he seemed to her so passive that she was convinced that he could never make his way in life, particularly through philosophy, which would "earn no bread." On the basis of this conviction that he was incompetent, she so tied up her estate that on her death he would receive only the interest until his fortieth birthday, when he could finally receive the principal. Yet Herbart was clearly no spendthrift, and during his student days he put by a small sum each year as insurance against falling into such financial straits that he would be forced to return home and take up the sort of legal or bureaucratic occupation which both parents would have preferred for him.[42] In the general relations between mother and son at this period we see the

41. SW 16:8.   42. Smidt *Recoll.* in SW 1:xliii.

familiar pattern of the dominating mother, who has done her best to produce a passive child but wishes him suddenly to become aggressive in early adulthood in order to win his way in the world.

In 1797 a position as tutor opened in Switzerland. Karl Friedrich von Steiger, Landvogt of Interlaken,[43] had commissioned a Swiss friend of Herbart's, Fischer, a fellow member of the literary society, to find a tutor for his children. When Herbart was consulted for suggestions, his mother immediately urged that he take the post himself. Herbart demurred, pleading that he had not yet completed his studies in Jena and would need at least six months' additional work in the library at Göttingen before he could take his degree. But his mother, worried as usual about his making a living, was insistent, and Herbart agreed. Having had her way, Frau Herbart experienced "the happiest day in her life." [44] In addition to the two boys for whose education he was originally to be responsible, there were two younger sons as well as three daughters falling in age between the third and fourth boys; a fourth daughter was born later.

His departure for Switzerland, in the company of several friends *and Mama*, took place on 25 March 1797. At Bern, Frau Herbart turned back to Oldenburg. At Zurich Herbart first met Pestalozzi, the most famous educator of the time, whose work was to serve as the starting point for Herbart's own educational doctrine.

Herbart had actually contracted to serve as tutor for two years, but he went prepared to stay for eight or ten, since he felt that the projects he was mapping out for himself would require extensive preparation. Since he was to teach geography, history, physics, mathematics, German composition, Latin, and Greek, and also wished to include music, four to six hours daily were devoted to lessons; and he also wanted to be a

43. W. Asmus points out that the family was not entitled to the "von" until 1838, but I have followed the tradition (Walter Asmus, *Johann Friedrich Herbart: cine pädagogische Biographie* [Heidelberg: Quelle & Meyer, 1968] 1:332).
44. SW 16:71–73.

companion to the boys outside the schoolroom. Yet Herbart strove to keep some time free each day, not merely for preparation but for his own work.[45] Although he felt that there were gaps in the boys' previous education, teaching materials were abundant and he was warmly welcomed into the circle of the family.[46] The contrast between life in this large and apparently happy family and his previous experience as an only child in a warring household must have been tremendous, and the virtues of being an educator were probably enhanced by the surroundings. Every two months he filed a report with Herr von Steiger, and five of the twenty-four are extant.[47] Although the details of this work need not concern us at this point,[48] his experience with the three oldest boys, each of whom possessed a very different personality and presented different problems to the tutor, shaped his later educational thought. He was afterward to see service as a private tutor as the best means for developing the "real educator." [49] These three boys, characterized in considerable detail by Herbart in his reports to their father, appear again and again as anonymous examples or evidence in his later psychological and educational writings. At this time he first tried out the idea of beginning the study of the classical languages with the reading of Homer. Characteristically, here as in his later educational theory, Herbart did not follow any of the dominant educational patterns of his day (e.g., those of the humanists, pietists, or philanthropists), but insisted on working out his own theory, though he was familiar, for example, with Basedow's writings.[50]

Early in 1798 the threat of war and mobilization arose in Switzerland when the canton of Vaux (Waadt) appealed to France in a quarrel with Bern. As usual [51] Herbart, who rarely read newspapers, paid little attention to political matters, and the von Steiger family was little affected [52] until the oldest of his charges, Ludwig, became liable for military service. Then,

45. SW 16:48–49.   46. SW 1:41; 16:60–62.   47. SW 1:37–70.
48. For the older literature on his stay in Switzerland, see SW 16:61, n. 1.
49. SW 3.80.   50. SW 19:58.   51. Smidt, *Recoll.* in SW 1:xxxii.
52. SW 16:88.

also characteristically, Herbart did not worry about the physical danger involved, believing that fighting for his native land would do more for the boy's character than any amount of learning or instruction. He was concerned about the moral dangers of life in camps and outposts.[53]

Meanwhile, he had been continuing his own philosophic work, and in late August 1798, he went to a little resort, Engistein, and there, at age twenty-two, worked out his *First Problematic Sketch of an Epistemology*,[54] which established the main lines of his thought. As Bohlendorf reported to another of Herbart's friends, "Herbart has found his system." [55]

Feeling that he now had the keys to his own philosophic future, Herbart wished he could devote more time to his own work. But, apart from the need to earn a living while developing his philosophy, he felt some obligation to the von Steigers. Although Ludwig had now returned from the army and was studying to become a forester, Herbart believed that another change in tutors would be deleterious to the education of the next two boys. A further complication was added by the fact that his parents had now found a new post for him. He was to become the companion of an Oldenburg nobleman who was setting out on a long trip through Europe; at the completion of this journey he could return to a judicial position in his native town.

Herbart took the whole matter up with Herr von Steiger and with his parents. If he could be assured by Herr von Steiger that his work had been satisfactory enough for him to be kept on for another eight to ten years, then he would remain to complete the education of the two younger boys. His only stipulation would be that he must have six weeks each year free for his own philosophic work. With this much preparation, he assured his parents, he would have no difficulty in obtaining a position in philosophy and thus providing for that future, which had always been a cause of such concern to them.[56]

53. SW 1:51–53.   54. SW 1:96–110.   55. SW 16:97.
56. SW 16:82–91.

Herr von Steiger was enthusiastic, and his parents, though not enthusiastic, were at least willing for him to follow this plan.[57] Both of them were apparently resigned to the expectation that Herbart would never return to Oldenburg to take up the kind of career they wanted for him. Despite more than twenty years of parental pressure, Herbart was still struggling to go his own way. That he still worked away on his own philosophic course in the face of the guilt he must have felt in disappointing parental hopes and despite the demands of his tutorship, which he sought to fulfill conscientiously, is a clear indication of his drive and of his devotion to that work.

Yet to break away and stay away from his parents was not easy. That same letter to his parents which set forth his plans and asked for their permission is full of phrases which reveal his inner conflict: "Thus far I have been little in accord with your wishes, and that pains me"; "I need the help of both my parents; I stand at a parting of the road; whichever direction I take, I cannot go forward with a ready and happy heart, if one of you sorrowfully turns his face from me, if the hopes of Mother and Father and my own cannot blend into one, if both of you, with one mouth and one voice, cannot wish me luck and God-speed."

Only six months after this long-term program had been worked out with all parties, Herbart left Switzerland to return home. Herbart cites a long list of grievances to justify this change of plan—having more children forced on him than he had contracted to care for, the loss of free time which had been promised him, the changed attitude and bearing of the children's parents toward him, and several more;[58] but these complaints sound more like the statements of a man offering excuses than of one giving reasons. For example, the charges against the von Steigers are hardly consonant with the warm mutual admiration and affection which quite clearly existed later between him and the family.[59]

The reasons from this list which are usually emphasized by biographers to account for this reversal of intention are

57. *SW* 16:99.   58. *SW* 16:116.   59. *SW* 16:132, 138–39.

likewise not wholly convincing: the political situation in
Switzerland, the deteriorating relations between his parents,
and an illness of his mother. As for the political situation, the
worst had already happened by the time Herbart originally
outlined his proposal to his parents in late June 1798. In
January France had already freed Vaux from Bernese rule,
and in February had declared the establishment of the Hel-
vetian republic. When Bern had unsuccessfully resisted in
March, France sacked the city and imposed an indemnity of
seventeen million francs. Of this sum Herr von Steiger had to
pay his share, and the life of the Swiss aristocracy was clearly
going to be changed by French domination; but it was certainly not a matter of total confiscation or the guillotine. Herbart was not the sort of man to concern himself with political
matters or to desert his charges unless things had reached such
a pass that the von Steigers could not continue to have a tutor.
This obviously was not true, since on his departure we find
that he was charged with the task of finding his own successor
and left his friends Eschen and Ziemssen in charge until, after
several disappointments, he finally found Segelken of Bremen
to take over the job.[60] As for any function he might have performed in mediating between his parents, his whole past experience should have shown how futile any such hopes must
be. As his friend Gries pointed out to him in the tones of a
Dutch uncle,[61] his parents were not warring, with his father
more or less mewing his mother up in a room,[62] simply because
he had left their roof; and his returning would not effect a
cure. His mother's illness, in turn, was a still less plausible
motive. Although she was ill, the sickness was not acute, particularly at the time he made the decision, and Herbart plainly
did not treat it as such. He took three months for the trip,
visiting in Jena, Göttingen, Bremen, and elsewhere on the
way.[63] Even with the necessary allowance for the winter season, the bad roads, and the general slowness and difficulty of
travel in those days, this is hardly the schedule of a man
dashing to his stricken mother's bedside.

60. SW 16:143.    61. SW 16:125–26.    62. SW 16:113; 19:115.
63. SW 16:129ff, 134–35, 139.

The causes for the change in plan must have been internal. In spite of his continual efforts to lead a life which did not conform to his parents' hopes and expectations, such revolt as this does not come easily. We need not be surprised that no sooner had he succeeded in organizing a ten-year program to free himself from his parents in both habitation and career than the ambivalence of revolt and submission led him to jettison it. As he himself said, he was "compelled," not "summoned" by his parents. Corroboration of this view can be found in the fact that when he finally did arrive in Oldenburg he offered to give up his philosophic hopes and to complete his training in law in order to follow in his father's footsteps at Oldenburg.[64] This gesture, which he himself called a "sacrifice" and which even his parents knew better than to accept, could have had no possible bearing on any of the reasons usually alleged for his return to Germany. His renunciation was simply a slightly more adult version of the peace offering of the disobedient child who finds his guilt intolerable.

In the fall of 1799, before leaving Switzerland, he had visited Pestalozzi's school at Burgdorf. His impression was fully recorded in his later essay, *On Pestalozzi's Latest Writing: "How Gertrude Teaches Her Children."* [65] Initially Pestalozzi had a profound effect on Herbart, and his other writings on Pestalozzi and his own earliest education efforts show the results of this visit.

Herbart left Switzerland on 6 January 1800, and finally arrived at Oldenburg in April. As might have been expected, his presence did nothing to narrow the constantly widening rift between his parents. Consequently, in the following year his mother went off with a Dr. Joseph Harbauer, the much-traveled personal physician of the king of the Netherlands, whose patient she had been.[66] Even Smidt, who wanted this part of his "Recollections" to be "off the record" and is hence not particularly reticent, was careful to point out that this alliance was not an affair of sex: Frau Herbart herself said that she was an "ugly old woman." She had simply found in Dr. Harbauer an active, educated, congenial man with whom

64. *SW* 16:120, 215.   65. *SW* 1:139ff.   66. *SW* 16:113, 115, 119.

she could travel and see the world after having been disappointed in both her husband and her son.[67]

She died at Paris, still with her doctor, in December 1802,[68] and Counselor Herbart died in Oldenburg in August 1809. But this visit of Herbart's in 1800 actually closes the epoch during which he was the rebellious child striving to break free from his family and his home town. Hereafter he was to be on his own.

Herbart's life up to this point clearly seems to have left its mark on him. By the constant pressure of a domineering mother who sought to control his external life, Herbart was turned toward an inner life. That he had difficulty in casual contacts with people and that he paid little attention to external events (even though these were, for a considerable proportion of his life, nothing less than the Napoleonic wars) is scarcely surprising in one who found early that his only chance to be his own man lay with his own inner thought. Nor is it astonishing that this inner life should be whole-heartedly devoted to philosophy—a pursuit which utterly precluded that career in the legal bureaucracy which both his parents desired for him and which particularly irritated his mother, inasmuch as it negated all her hopes of that life of action and influence which she hoped to lead through her son. And Herbart did more than disappoint her positive hopes; he even managed to select a career in which, she felt certain, he could not even earn a living. One can push children only so far.

In these early experiences, too, we have a probable source of that characteristic of his later thought and work—his integrity or, if you prefer, his pigheadedness. As a student of Fichte, he could not be a follower of his teacher; as Kant's successor, he could not be a Kantian. For his philosophic system and his educational theory he had to find views distinctly his own; and once he found them, he held stubbornly to them in the face of criticism, unpopularity, or other pressures. This way of doing battle—by retiring to one's inner citadel and stoutly

67. Smidt, *Recoll.* in *SW* 1:xxxviii.
68. See *SW* 16:259, n. 1, for evidence that the year is 1802 and not 1803.

defending it—was one that we have seen Herbart learning early, and we shall see him practicing it for the rest of his life.

This tactic makes it plain that Herbart did not enjoy open battle. The conflict between himself and his parents and between his mother and father was not of his choosing. As was suggested earlier, therefore, it is probably not coincidental that harmony and the avoidance of strife play such important roles in his system. After a youth marked by constant discord, Herbart must have seen these principles of peaceful relations as even more self-evidently desirable than have others in the history of thought who have also adopted them.

But physically, at least, he could now break free and open a new chapter in his life.

# 3

# Going His Own Way

Since Herbart's continued presence at Oldenburg was useless as far as his parents were concerned [1] and was not conducive to his own studies, he betook himself to Bremen, where he lived for about the next two years at the home and the country estate of his friend Smidt.[2] Smidt had known him only briefly at Jena, where Herbart, as a newcomer in addition to being the opposite of gregarious,[3] conducted himself very quietly.[4] But they became better acquainted in the course of a month-long excursion they made with some other friends just before Smidt left Jena. Herbart asked Smidt to intercede with his parents to allow him to continue his philosophic studies, and Smidt visited Oldenburg for this purpose.[5] Herbart's mother took a strong liking to Smidt,[6] and he served regularly as intermediary and general friend of the family. As the interchange of letters shows, the friendship between the two men ripened over the years, and Herbart felt free to move in with Smidt.

1. SW 16:213, 215.   2. SW 16:194.   3. SW 16:34–35.
4. Smidt, *Recoll.* in SW 1:xxviii, xxix.
5. Smidt, *Recoll.* in SW 1:xxix; see also 16:12, 13.   6. SW 16:22, 24.

After some despondency,[7] a natural consequence of his quarrel with his parents, this period was a particularly pleasant time in Herbart's life. Smidt and his friends, busy with their own careers, left Herbart undisturbed at his philosophical and especially mathematical study;[8] and Frau Smidt, her three sisters, Smidt's sister, and some of their married friends played a significant role in his life during this period. As Smidt later noted, these young women, interested in the development and education of children, were flattered that a male intellectual in nineteenth-century Germany would be interested in their concerns and would talk to them without condescension.[9] Emotionally Herbart found in this group of "safe" women a warmth and a respect which he had never before received from any female—particularly not from his masculine, dominating mother. Intellectually they offered him the opportunity to think over and reorganize his own educational ideas, which he had developed from his experience as a tutor and from his observation of Pestalozzi and reading of his works. It was quite fitting, therefore, that the "three women" to whom in 1802 he dedicated his essay *On Pestalozzi's Latest Writing: "How Gertrude Teaches Her Children"* [10] should be Frau Smidt, her sister, and her sister-in-law.[11] At this same time he was regularly tutoring a young man for university entrance [12] and was also teaching mathematics at the Domschule. The natural consequence of all this pedagogical activity was a series of papers and books on education: *General Thoughts for a Pedagogical Plan of Instruction for the Higher Studies* (1801); *Pestalozzi's Idea of an ABC of Sense Perception; On Pestalozzi's Latest Writing: "How Gertrude Teaches Her Children"* (1802). As the appearance of Pestalozzi's name in two of the titles indicates, Herbart was very close to the Swiss educator at this stage in his own thought.

His philosophic products in this period are much less

7. SW 16:180–81.    8. SW 16:150.
9. Smidt, *Recoll.* in SW 1:xxxiii–xxxvi.    10. SW 1:137ff.
11. Smidt, *Recoll.* in SW 1:xxxvi.    12. SW 16:187–88; 29:125.

extensive: a lecture at the Bremen museum entitled "On the Necessity of Ethics and Religion in Their Relation to Philosophy," and two essays.

His departure from Smidt's home in Bremen to go to the University of Göttingen in May 1802 fell at a very difficult point in two areas of Herbart's life which were always delicate—finances and health. Apart from the savings of his student days, his salary in Switzerland, and probably some slight returns from later tutoring, Herbart had been without income except for an allowance from his parents; he had been living and would continue to live at Göttingen for a while, on the generosity of Smidt and other friends.[13] As his mother had feared, philosophy had not yet "earned bread." But fortunately his friends were well situated financially, and both they and he had so much confidence in his star that this dependency seems to have caused little conscious difficulty on either side.

Yet Herbart's health again began to concern him, and in the winter of his first year at Göttingen he felt he was about to die.[14] For explanation we cannot resort to that oft-cited fall into the kettle of hot water, particularly after his own remarks about his later youthful health and his general well-being in Switzerland. As Bartholomäi suggested, without stating it bluntly,[15] this was a period of extreme stress for Herbart; and this fact is probably not unrelated to his bodily and physical ills. His relations with his parents, always tempestuous, had now been broken off forever. Yet at twenty-six he had not yet even started on a career; in fact he was not yet even self-supporting. Then too, he was returning to the competition of university life and to his final examinations for the doctorate. In such a situation he was neither the first nor the last student to develop psychosomatic symptoms.

Herbart took his doctorate at Göttingen on 22 October 1802 and began lecturing there as privatdozent in the winter

13. *SW* 17:33.   14. *SW* 17:33–34.
15. Bartholomäi, "J. F. Herbart's Leben" in *Joh. Friedr. Herbarts Pädagogische Schriften,* 1:56.

of 1802–03. The second set of Latin theses which he publicly defended in taking his doctorate [16] were highly characteristic of his own thought and personality as well as prophetic of his future professional career. Notably, the last three of them concern education. The first of these (10) has been the battle cry of all those who have urged the scientific study of education: "The art of teaching does not depend on experience alone." The next (11), "Poetry and mathematics are a great force in the education of children" has become, thanks in part to Herbart and his followers, more of a commonplace now than the challenge it was then. The last of these educational theses (12) is typically Herbart's: "The education of children ought to begin with instruction in Greek, specifically with Homer's *Odyssey*, with no prose at all and minimal use of the dictionary."

In the philosophic area, it is worth noting that one thesis (5) flings down the gauntlet to the Kantian forms of time and space and another (7) asserts the contradiction inherent in Fichte's concept of the ego. The remaining theses in religion, philosophy, and political science are scarcely less controversial. Herbart was going to fight under his own flag even if he was the only one to rally to the standard. As he was later to say, "I am especially grieved that I cannot agree with the nation's foremost thinkers." [17]

Realizing that his philosophic views would find favor with neither the Kantian nor the Fichtean school,[18] he prudently chose pedagogy as his subject, and his *Two Lectures on Pedagogy* are part of this academic debut.[19] Pedagogy led him to ethics, on which he first lectured in the summer semester of 1803.

His lectures were popular, and he felt that he concentrated nearly all the philosophic activity of Göttingen in his auditorium.[20] Herbart was now gaining academic visibility. Because of his local popularity as a lecturer and because of his publications, in 1805 he received a call to Heidelberg as *pro-*

16. SW 1:278.    17. SW 17:23.    18. SW 16:254.    19. SW 1:279ff.
20. SW 16:279. Such seems to have been his reputation, see SW 14:3–4.

*fessor ordinarius* or regular full professor.[21] Although the "lordly setting" of Heidelberg attracted him, he refused this call as he refused, six months later, a similar invitation to Landshut.[22] He felt that in many respects the situation at Göttingen afforded him exactly what he needed at this stage in his career.[23] Remaining at Göttingen, he was made *professor extraordinarius*—professor not in the regular academic "line" of voting and control, and hence a position somewhat less attractive than that of *ordinarius*. Of some interest is the fact that the Latin oration, "Commentary on the Basis of Plato's System," with which he read himself into this post, was unfavorably reviewed by Böckh, then a young classical scholar at Heidelberg, in the Jena *Allgemeine Litteraturzeitung* [24]— the first of many adverse and even hostile reviews his works were to receive over the years. Yet characteristically, although Herbart published a reply, he told Smidt that Böckh's review was the only one worthy of the name.[25]

Herbart was now writing copiously. In 1806 he published his *General Pedagogy, Chief Points of Metaphysics,* and *Chief Points of Logic.* In 1807, he completed three more publications, including his *General Practical* (i.e., ethical) *Philosophy,* which he had thought in 1805 was almost ready for the press.[26]

By this time (1807) Herbart had published at least in outline the main parts of his system, except for his psychology. But his works found the philosophic spotlight fairly well preempted. Kant had died in 1804, but his thought still formed the starting point for German philosophy. Herbart's old teacher, Fichte, was the preeminent figure, with major works already in print, such as *The Foundation of the Complete Theory of Science,* the *Basis of Natural Right,* and the *System of Ethics,* as well as his more popular books, *The Closed Commercial State* and the *Vocation of Man.* The precocious Schelling was already at the height of his prowess and fame, having

21. *SW* 16:268–75. See also von Sallwürk, "Herbart's Berufung nach Heidelberg," *Deutsche Blätter für erziehenden Unterricht* (1888), no. 10. 22. *SW* 16:279–81; 19:144–45.   23. *SW* 16:275.   24. *SW* 1:311ff. 25. *SW* 17:29.   26. *SW* 16:271.

published his *Ideas concerning a Philosophy of Nature, On the World Soul,* and his *System of Transcendental Idealism.* Hegel had belatedly entered the lists, having finally succeeded in getting onto paper his first book, *The Phenomenology of the Spirit.* Herbart was trying to play ball in a big league, and, quite apart from the severity of the competition, he would not use the popular technique of idealism.

When, in October 1808, Königsberg invited him to Kant's former chair in philosophy, now rendered vacant by Krug's departure to Leipzig, Herbart was extremely receptive. Göttingen had become much less attractive,[27] because the Napoleonic wars were reducing student attedance and the students who did come were less interested and less competent in philosophy.[28] Herbart's customary lack of concern with political events and his general disengagement from them (though the French had exacted a contribution of 1,500 francs from him, which he had had to borrow from Smidt)[29] were not likely to make him popular with either colleagues or students, who were much involved in the happenings of the times. As he said of himself, he was no "world-improver" (*Weltverbesserer*).[30] Königsberg, on its side, had much to offer: a post as *ordinarius* rather than *extraordinarius* in what Herbart considered "the most renowned chair in philosophy"; four times the salary (1,200 talers instead of 300); and the fact that Prussia, after being thoroughly trounced by France in 1805 and 1806, was undertaking a sweeping program of reforms and innovations, including educational ones.[31] In the words of King Friedrich Wilhelm, "The state must replace with spiritual power what it has lost in physical."

Probably not the least of the advantages of the Königsberg offer was the leverage it gave him in improving his financial condition, quite apart from the larger salary it offered.[32] As was indicated earlier, his mother had put her estate in trust for him until he should reach age forty. His call to Königsberg, as *ordinarius* in a famous chair, made it evident that both now

27. SW 17:6, 30.   28. SW 17:28–29.   29. SW 17:3, 6.   30. SW 18:13.
31. SW 17:28.   32. SW 17:29.

and in later years he would not need protection from his own prodigality or incompetence. With the help of his and his family's old friend Herr von Halem,[33] he took legal action in Oldenburg to have his mother's will set aside, and in December 1808 he got control of the principal, about 12,000 talers (an amount ten times the annual salary offered at Königsberg) after paying off his indebtedness of 600 talers to Smidt and other friends.[34]

Before accepting the call to Königsberg, however, Herbart did ask for certain changes in his prescribed duties. Of chief interest here was his request to include pedagogy among the subjects on which he would lecture, and "since it is not merely learned, but shown and practiced," to have for advanced students a seminar (though it was not entitled that officially until 1833) in which both demonstration and practice teaching could take place.[35] Since the king of Prussia officially approved all the requests, at Easter of 1809 Herbart left Göttingen for Königsberg, where he was to spend the next twenty-four years of his life.

The outstanding feature of his personal life during this period was his marriage to an English girl, Mary Jane Drake. According to Smidt, while Herbart was still a student at Jena he very seriously expressed the opinion that anyone who wished to devote himself to scholarship dare not think about marrying until he was forty, but that then he had a duty to do so, for otherwise he had no prospect of being able to supervise his children's education till their maturity. Smidt then adds a sentence which will strike some as non sequitur; others as an insight: "It did not therefore surprise me that his own marriage was childless." [36] But with several major publications behind him and a secure position at Königsberg, Herbart obviously felt he did not need to wait quite so long. He made the acquaintance of this young lady at the first house in which he lived in Königsberg. Her father had been a merchant at Memel, but, ruined by the Napoleonic wars, he had returned

33. *SW* 17:10–11.   34. *SW* 17:33, 26.   35. *SW* 19:150–52.
36. Smidt, *Recoll.* in *SW* 1:xxxv.

to England, leaving his daughter in Königsberg. Why he left
her there, or with whom, and what she was doing are all
questions not very clear from the record. She had no relatives
there [37] and was merely living *en pension* at the home of
Consistorial-Räthin Hesse.[38] But however she arrived there,
she was always fond of the town, was homesick for it after
the Herbarts moved to Göttingen,[39] and returned to it after
Herbart's death.

One evening (so a lady who was present told Bartholomäi
later),[40] Miss Drake and Herbart were at a party where parlor
games were played, and Herbart's name was given out as a
riddle. The first player gave the first syllable as "man" (*Herr*);
the second player hinted the second syllable as "an adornment
of a man" (*Bart*, "beard"). It was then Miss Drake's turn to
"do the whole word," and her contribution was "the adornment
of the university" ("Herbart"). This was pretty heady stuff to
feed a professor of thirty-four who had seemingly had little or
nothing to do with women except his masculine mother and
his friends' wives. It is no cause for surprise, then, that after
knowing her for six weeks he decided to marry this insightful
eighteen-year-old. After prolonged negotiations with her local
guardian in Memel and her father in England, they were
married on 13 January 1811.[41]

Since none of our informants claims beauty for her, we can
be fairly sure that she was not handsome. Physically her only
claim to distinction seems to have been that "the glance of her
soulful brown eyes was unforgettable." [42] It is possibly worth
recalling the earlier quotation from Smidt to the effect that
Herbart's mother's sole claim to beauty had been similar. But
there the resemblance stopped. The wife was warm and sympathetic, not only to others but also to Herbart, even supporting such of his educational activities as spilled over into their
home.[43] (She later put her capital into a house large enough to
accommodate boarding pupils as guinea pigs for Herbart's

37. *SW* 17:104.    38. *SW* 19:181.    39. *SW* 18:22.
40. Bartholomäi, "J. F. Herbart Leben," p. 78.    41. *SW* 17:93.
42. Bartholomäi, "J. F. Herbarts Leben," p. 78.    43. *SW* 17:132.

pedagogical seminar, caring for as many as thirteen of these young children, and pitching in to help with their teaching in various emergencies.[44]) As the quotation from Smidt has indicated, the marriage was childless, but the scanty record suggests that the twenty-nine years of marriage were happy for both parties. Herbart, who can scarcely be said to have made his choice on the basis of great experience with women, was fortunate. The wife, who was about half her husband's age at their marriage, lived to be eighty and to attend the celebration of the one-hundredth anniversary of her husband's birth. She died on 2 December 1876 at Königsberg.

Much less satisfactory were Herbart's relations with the intellectual "establishment" of Prussia, with which his move to Königsberg brought him into personal contact. During his first summer there he became acquainted with Wilhelm von Humboldt, the Prussian minister of the interior for education and a prime mover in the founding of the University of Berlin, which was to become the model for the German university of the nineteenth century. Von Humboldt was a force to be reckoned with in the learned and political world, and he was not impressed:

> It is hard to decide about him [Herbart] for sure. In general, my first impression remains: I do not rate him high. Yet from time to time some things occur which make me doubtful again. If I did not have so little leisure for exact reading, I could easily decide for certain.[45]

Goethe, too, evidently did not get around to reading Herbart, for he said, "He pleases me more close at hand than he did at a distance from the reviews of his books." Needless to say, a favorable impression on these influential personages (even if based on superficial acquaintance or inadequate knowledge) would have given a powerful forward thrust to Herbart's reputation and career. The kind of assessment recorded above was to follow him throughout his academic life, and his later

44. *SW* 17:104; 15:122; 14:170, 180–81.
45. Humboldt's letter to F. A. Wolf, 30 June 1809, quoted by Bartholomäi, "J. F. Herbarts Leben," pp. 73–74.

disappointment in failing to secure the chair at the University of Berlin when Hegel died was probably in large part due to this impression he regularly made on the powerful.

Having begun as a child the struggle to be his own man, Herbart continued it throughout his life. Starting as a student of Fichte's, he was not content to remain a follower but immediately moved away from Fichte's position. He could not be just another Kantian but could only be "a Kantian of 1828." [46] And not to be a "real Kantian" while at Königsberg, whose chief claim to fame up to that time was that Kant had taught there, was to commit the unforgivable sin in the eyes of all Kantians then and thereafter. Likewise, Schelling's views seemed to him at first to offer something, at least the most acceptable version of idealism; [47] but he later came to regard that school as a disaster.[48] And in his later years he could find little in common with the absolute idealism of Hegel which swept through Germany. As the title of one of his rejoinders makes clear,[49] his entire life was a struggle against the popular philosophic schools. As a result, he was a member of no clique which would review his books with loud hosannas or send counterblasts against unfriendly reviewers from other cliques. He was a "loner," an outsider. Just as we must be surprised and pleased that he managed to break free from maternal domination and to achieve a career of his own choosing and a happy marriage, we must feel the same emotions at seeing the scholarly eminence he managed to attain almost single-handed. In his own way he was "busy and useful," as even von Humboldt said of him; and a popular lecturer who had also published tome after tome was a hard man to ignore completely.

But apart from this failure to achieve membership in the establishment, the consequences of which became apparent only gradually, his life at Königsberg was pleasant. He was frequently invited to the court, though he did not enjoy the society there—it would be hard to envisage a personality less likely to succeed in the role of courtier.[50] His lectures were so

46. *SW* 7:13.   47. *SW* 16:42.   48. *SW* 4:8.   49. *SW* 3:317–51.
50. *SW* 17:62–63, 157.

crowded that students had difficulty even finding a place to sit, to say nothing of one in which they could take notes.[51] He served on educational commissions and boards, both public and private.[52]

Most important for a professor, his scholarly output continued. A major field of this activity was psychology, an area which he had long regarded as of paramount importance but one in which he had not worked out his views in detail. He published, in addition to several minor treatises, two major works: the *Textbook of Psychology* (1816) and *Psychology as a Science* (1824–25). He had fully developed his psychological doctrine by about 1814, but the political situation of Napoleon's defeat, the Congress of Vienna and other major events made the time seem impropitious for publication.[53] As a result, he published the simpler, more practical *Textbook* after only a brief delay but postponed the more pretentious treatment for a full ten years. The *Letters on the Application of Psychology to Education* (1831) also fall within this field. As will be evident later, Herbart, by denying the doctrine of mental faculties, by using mechanical and mathematical models, and by generally trying to make psychology an exact science, was breaking new psychological ground.

In the philosophic area, his major publication while he was at Königsberg was the two volumes of his *General Metaphysics* (1828–29). This doctrine too had been worked out much earlier and had been published in rather abbreviated form in the *High Points of Metaphysics* in 1806. This later full exposition of his views, set against a detailed historical background, was postponed for twenty years. But his *Textbook for the Introduction to Philosophy* (1812), written during Napoleon's Russian campaign while French troops occupied Königsberg, is both important and interesting, for it is probably Herbart's best effort at showing in relatively brief compass what he thought the tasks and problems of philosophy were, and how, by attempting to answer the questions involved, one

51. *SW* 4:15.   52. *SW* 14:140, 142–43; 15:11; 17:56, 62.
53. *SW* 17:111, 113.

would necessarily arrive at his own philosophical position. This text went through four editions, and Herbart also regarded it as one of his best, though unpretentious.[54] The much later *Encyclopedia of Philosophy* (1831) was intended in part to perform a similar function of epitomizing Herbart's views. A variety of minor papers, including several on education, are also products of his stay at Königsberg.

The fourth facet of Herbart's activities at Königsberg which merits notice is the practical course in pedagogics, to supplement his lectures, which he had made one of his conditions for accepting the position. Herbart's proposal for this seminar,[55] though the actual class was not conducted along precisely the lines specified,[56] was approved by von Humboldt, and Herbart was empowered to hire an assistant for it. The course appeared in the official announcement for the summer of 1810: "Teaching exercises (*Didaktische Übungen*) carried on by ten to twelve competent students under my direction and with my collaboration." [57] As has been the case with nearly every laboratory school thereafter, the procedures used gave rise to some controversy, with the parents of the children who formed the demonstration class establishing the familiar pattern of worrying about what was being done to their offspring. The seminar ended with Herbart's departure from Königsberg and was in many respects the least successful of all his activities.[58] He looked back upon his hope of improving education by this means as merely a youthful dream, but he was glad that he had made the attempt. But this undertaking had consequences for Herbartianism, if not for Herbart. Brzoska, who was the assistant for this seminar, later became a professor at Jena and in 1836 wrote a book entitled *The Necessity for Pedagogical Seminars at the University*, which he dedicated to Herbart; [59] and Brzoska's successor at Jena, Stoy, who had

54. SW 18:253.    55. SW 17:14.
56. See Herbart's annual reports, SW 14.
57. Bartholomäi, "J. H. Herbart's Leben," p. 78, n. 1.
58. SW 18:214.
59. H. G. Brzoska, *Die Notwendigkeit pädagogischer Seminare auf der Universität*, 2d ed. by W. Rein (Leipzig, 1887), p. viii. See also Brzoska's letter to Herbart, SW 18:241–42.

also been a student of Herbart's, founded a pedagogical society there in 1843, from which developed the seminar and practice school that, particularly later under Wilhelm Rein, became the hub of Herbartianism.

But Herbart was already beginning to see his probable future in Prussia. Students were few in number and ill prepared.[60] Also, his alienation from the dominant philosophic sects, particularly from Hegelianism, which had been developing into the quasi-official Prussian philosophy,[61] and his unpopularity with people of power and influence now began to have clear consequences. When Hegel's death in 1831 rendered vacant his chair at the now prestigious University of Berlin, Herbart discovered that he had no chance at the post. The Minister of Education, von Altenstein, was probably disappointed in Herbart by this time, and Johann Schulze, who was very influential with the ministry, was a thoroughgoing Hegelian. After all, in 1821 Herbart had expressed quite bluntly to von Altenstein his opinion of German idealism: "It is the unfortunate character of contemporary philosophy to postulate rather than prove, to be enthusiastic about figments of the imagination in which, when seen in the light, there is neither sense nor reason and in which the true needs of human life and spirit are ignored."[62] As a result, a relatively unknown follower of Hegel was selected for the chair at Berlin.[63]

In the face of this rebuff Herbart submitted his resignation at Königsberg on 22 April 1833 and returned to Göttingen, where a chair had become vacant with G. E. Schulze's death.[64] When he originally left Göttingen for Königsberg, he thought he would be welcome to return, and this now proved true.

Not surprisingly, he suffered poor health again during the period from 1829 to 1832. For example, in 1831 he recalled his youthful good health only to add, "And now—but silence about that."[65] For these were the days of disillusionment with his general popularity and reputation. With the completion of the

60. *SW* 17:21.    61. *SW* 4:5–6; 17:124–25.    62. *SW* 14:189.
63. *SW* 17:260–61.
64. *SW* 18:4. His heart was warmed by the farewell tendered him by students and faculty (*SW* 18:25–29).
65. *SW* 9:353; 17:201, 203. 309.

second volume of his *General Metaphysics* in 1829, Herbart felt that he had made his main contribution: "My work is done, and what is still left to be said will cost me but little trouble." [66] But then came the clear realization that not only was he unpopular with the politicians, academic and otherwise, but also he had made little impression on the philosophers. After a lifetime spent in showing that the followers of Kant, Fichte, Schelling, and Hegel all were wrong, he should hardly have been surprised that there were persons left in Germany who could be right; that is, who could be Herbartians. He was, as one of his friends said, "A voice crying the wilderness." [67] As early as 1808, he had realized that he was cast as a rebel against the dominant philosophic movements of his time; but having devoted his entire life to philosophic thought from the time he was twelve, and having spared no efforts in these labors, he felt he had no choice but to state the convictions he had arrived at. The floodtide of German idealism simply submerged his isolated realism. Aside from Drobisch and Strümpell he had almost no followers within the profession, and he feared lest within ten years he would have no philosophic audience at all. In the 1830s he even seems to have developed that mild paranoia typical of those who feel they have been unjustly passed over, for he became temporarily estranged even from Drobisch and Strümpell on the grounds that they were distorting his doctrine, were trying to rival him, or were not giving him credit for what they had learned from him.[68]

Although his unpopularity was primarily the inevitable consequence of his warfare with the dominant philosophic trends of his day, he believed that at least a partial cause of his failure to recruit more followers was his never having published an exposition of his total thought, particularly a "popular" exposition of it. That even intellectuals like von Humboldt and Goethe would not undertake the labor of plowing through his technical treatises had long been evident; and he was even

66. SW 17:201.    67. SW 17:163.
68. SW 17:23, 219, 311; for Strümpell, see SW 18:161–65, 167–68, 179; for Drobisch, SW 19:18–24, 28.

more aware of the misunderstandings and confusions which had stemmed from his publishing his total doctrine in parts, with the related pieces separated by rather long intervals. Consequently, in 1831 he wrote his *Encyclopedia of Philosophy*, partly to remedy this lack. In the field of pedagogy Herbart felt a similar need for a single, coherent, comprehensive statement of his views. The *Outlines of Pedagogical Lectures* (1835) was intended to fill this gap, and its second edition of 1841 was designed to be still more complete. Although he published a number of papers in this period, the two volumes just mentioned and his *Psychological Investigations* were his book-length productions.

Upon Herbart's return to Göttingen his auditorium was as thronged with hearers as it had been in previous years, and he seems to have spent much time preparing his lectures.[69] Even the messages sent through the student grapevine that Herbart's lectures were difficult, and warnings from a theological colleague about the religious errors in his doctrines, failed to keep serious students away.

His popularity was, however, dimmed by a political episode which, as such matters always had, found Herbart at less than his best. At the death of William IV of England in 1837, because the Salic Law precluding female succession prevented Victoria from becoming queen of Hanover as well as England, the reign passed to her uncle, the Duke of Cumberland, who became Earnest August. As his first step toward establishing an absolute (and reactionary) monarchy, he set aside the liberal constitution of 1833 and demanded from all state functionaries, including professors, a new oath of allegiance to him. Seven of Herbart's liberal colleagues refused to sign, claiming they were still bound by their former oath to support the constitution, and ultimately three of them were banished from Hanover. Herbart, as dean of the philosophic faculty, had urged compliance with the royal wish. With his habitual disinterest in politics, where "going his own way" seems to have meant for him ignoring political events rather than revolting

69. *SW* 18:40, 140.

against authority (as he did with his parents, his teacher, and his fellow philosophers), Herbart saw this struggle about the oath as disturbing that peace and quiet so necessary for a university and as setting a dangerous precedent.[70]

(To anticipate some points which will concern us later, clearly it is not wholly coincidental that several of Herbart's "basic ethical ideas" and their social extensions rest on the principle of avoiding strife. Likewise his fundamental metaphysics involves a continual struggle between basic entities, but a struggle which does not really amount to anything because each act of destruction on the part of one entity calls forth an equally effective act of self-preservation on the part of the other and both go on as before. Perhaps Herbart simply had had too much strife early in his life.)

He recorded his side of this university controversy in *A Memorial on the Göttingen Catastrophe of 1837*, which was published only in 1842, posthumously and for private circulation. Whatever the rights or wrongs of the matter, Herbart's position was seen by many as a weak knuckling under, and this judgment produced considerable coldness toward him among both students and colleagues. For a time at least this episode cast something of a pall over his last years at Göttingen.

On the morning of 11 August 1841 he lectured as usual. That evening he suffered a stroke, and on the 14th he died, in his sixty-fifth year. The students paid him what was then at Göttingen the unusual honor of conducting him to his grave with a torchlight procession.

70. SW 19:6.

# 4

# Why Fame Did Not Knock Then

At the time of Herbart's death, few would probably have thought that much more would ever be heard about him. He had, to be sure, held some fairly distinguished university positions; he had written rather voluminously from a distinctively personal point of view and set of principles; his lectures had always been well attended. This was evidently the career of more than a run-of-the-mill university professor, but he scarcely seemed destined for the worldwide fame which eventually became his.

His publications, by and large, had not been favorably received. He had few major followers. A particularly insightful mourner at the funeral might possibly have predicted for all his work the fate which has attended his philosophic writings—continuing citation as extended statements of a distinctive point of view, but as a position merely theoretically conceivable and perhaps historically interesting, not as one subsequently fruitful or currently viable.

Herbart's later revival was, of course, an educational revival, and any renewed interest in his philosophical and psychological work grew mostly out of reawakened interest in his pedagogical doctrine. But even in the field of education Herbart had at his death relatively little claim to lasting fame. Despite the efforts of Hess [1] and some others to run schools on Herbartian principles, these undertakings had not been particularly influential. His educational writings had not been popular, and he had few, if any, more pedagogical disciples than he had philosophic ones. His educational views were not the sacred dogma of any large group of teachers or institutions in the German states or elsewhere. He had given up his program for training teachers when he left Königsberg, and he had thereafter served on fewer public and private boards and commissions.

The brief account of Herbart's life and times in the preceding chapters does, however, strongly suggest some possible reasons why his work and writings failed to have much impact during his lifetime. These points merit more detailed inspection.

First, his prose style was unfortunate. Complaints about style are easy to make, of course, and disagreements are commonplace. What one critic judges clear and incisive, another sees as pedestrian; what strikes one reviewer as exciting and beautiful strikes another as overblown and pretentious. So here, Herbart's style has been praised by some readers and students as "lapidary." [2] But no one seems to have praised it for its readability, and many have seen it as a major reason for Herbart's lack of popularity. [3]

A case in most apposite point is that of Drobisch, whom

1. *SW* 18:120–22. (The literature on Hess's school is also cited in the note there.)
2. E.g., Jean Paul Richter, *Levana*, anon. Engl. trans. (London, 1901), p. 81; F. Bartolomäi, "Johann Friedrich Herbarts Leben" in *Joh. Friedr. Herbarts Padagogische Schriften*, 1:116.
3. E.g., K. Richter, *Die Herbart-Zillerschen formalen Stufen des Unterrichts* (Leipzig, 1888), p. 6; G. Ediliam, *Kritik der Zillerschen formal Stufentheorie* (Leipzig, 1909), p. 24; B. C. Mulliner, *Herbart's The Application of Psychology to the Science of Education* (New York, 1898), p. xxvii; H. M. Felkin and E. Felkin, *An Introduction to Herbart's Science and Practice of Education* (Boston, 1895), p. 1; O. Browning, "Preface" to F. M. Felkin and E. Felkin, *Herbart's Letters and Lectures on Education* (London, 1898), pp. x–xi.

Herbart regarded as his closest and most competent disciple, especially in psychology and the metaphysics related to it. In the early 1830s Drobisch carried on a prolonged and highly technical correspondence with the master, pointing out his difficulties in understanding sections of Herbart's books and raising problems and objections. Although he was always ultimately satisfied by Herbart's detailed replies, he eventually felt free to chide Herbart for always putting everything "in the nutshell" [4] and to lament how much there was in the letters which was not in the books.[5] If Drobisch, whose ability, interest, and good will are beyond question, found the going hard, the reactions of those less able and less devoted are certainly understandable.

Simply too many of us, friends and critics, native speakers of German and foreigners, have complained about the style for these charges to be dismissed lightly. In my personal opinion, Kant, Fichte, and Hegel appear as veritable Hemingways of the philosophic German of the period when compared with Herbart. Undoubtedly, at least part of his potential audience found his books hard to read and still harder to understand even after making the effort to plow through them. The difficulty is not that he writes the tortuous periodic sentence so beloved by the German academic philosophers, although he occasionally produces these compound-complex mazes. Usually he writes a relatively short sentence. But he begins with one syntactic structure only to abandon it; parallel concepts are often not expressed in parallel form, and parallel forms house nonparallel thoughts; modifiers are awkwardly placed, and literal and figurative expressions of an idea are stirred together. The same obscurity and fuzziness which marks the sentences also characterizes larger units like paragraphs and sections. He seems an unlikely candidate to be a popular author, widely read and well understood.

4. *SW* 18:189.
5. *SW* 17:193. Earlier, Dissen, whom Herbart himself had chosen as his successor at Göttingen, had reported his troubles with the *Chief Points of Metaphysics* (*SW* 18:48); and Brandeis, another close associate, had troubles with the psychology (*SW* 18:264).

But in view of Herbart's documented popularity as a university lecturer, these strictures on his prose style seem to indicate that his writing was different from his talking. Some possible evidence that this was so can be found. In his *Encyclopedia,* which, because of its particular purpose and audience, Herbart felt should be written "in a more flowing style" [6] we find occasional passages which sound like the well-grooved lecturer in his classroom; for example, a meticulous step-by-step progression by a series of rhetorical questions, each specifically answered.[7] These passages are some of the simplest and clearest in all Herbart's works; but they are rare. As the letters to Drobisch show, Herbart could write clear exposition; he merely chose, it seems, not to do so most of the time. When Herbart sat down to write a monograph, his idea of academic propriety seems to have complicated his style.

Jachmann asserts in his review of the *General Pedagogy* that "The language intentionally seeks out obscure and incomprehensible expressions and turns of phrase and often produces the appearance of new and profound philosophic discoveries where the reader finds, after useless effort, only the most commonplace and trivial thoughts." [8] Insofar as one subscribes to this judgment, one anticipates the possibility that competent rewriting could make the doctrine intelligible to a wider audience.

Second, even had Herbart possessed an eminently readable and lucid prose style, he would have had difficulty in expounding his views because of the sweep of his system, which did little to make things easy for his contemporaries or favorable to himself. As we have seen, even before 1800, while he was still serving as a tutor in Switzerland, he had developed the general structure of his thought and thereafter wrote with this plan clearly in mind. But since his readers never had this comprehensive view, many of his statements and arguments seem to hang in the air.

This difficulty most obviously beset his major educational work, the *General Pedagogy.* He wished to publish it while his

6. SW 4:24.    7. E.g., SW 9:61–62.    8. In SW 2:146.

practical experience in Switzerland and Bremen, his visits to Pestalozzi and his work on the Swiss's writings, and his educational thinking and discussion in Bremen all were still fresh in his mind—especially before they were pushed into the background by the pressure of his current philosophical work. But he had not yet published the ethical, metaphysical, and psychological studies which were necessary to make his educational doctrines comprehensible to any except those friends and students who had heard him present these other speculations orally. "My pedagogy was nothing without my view on metaphysics and practical philosophy." [9] As a result, as he himself says:

> The outline was only imperfectly clothed, with some parts left standing almost naked and puzzling while other parts were more completely worked out, depending upon whether there was greater or less hope that it could be clear to a public which could not know my philosophic foundations. Today it would be easy for me to give that skeleton completely different flesh; but how that would have been possible nine years ago . . . I cannot say.[10]

In the face of protests or misunderstandings, Herbart was likely to say:

> Patience, my good man. You do not have the key to the book; hence your very natural complaints. But wait a bit; I have gone to fetch the key.[11]

But this sort of promise was not likely to make the spirit of the reviewers more friendly or the task of his readers more bearable.

The situation which occurred with Herbart's publication

9. SW 2:163.
10. SW 2:168–69. A later statement is equally explicit: "But to prevent anyone's imagining that the book would be completely comprehensible in itself, the exposition of the main concepts was intentionally kept brief and aphoristic so that its inadequacy would be evident to everyone" (SW 3:153). In the book itself he hints at this same point (SW 2:26–27, 89).
11. SW 2:164.

of his *General Practical Philosophy* in 1808 is equally illuminating and suggestive, for it demonstrates the difficulties
Herbart's system caused him even after he had worked out
and published major sections of it. After an introduction
(which does not really introduce the book, being devoted
primarily to a discussion of the distinction between "judgment"
and "desire"), Herbart blankly presents the core of his ethical
theory, without background, without context, without supporting arguments. The reviewer in the *Hallische Allgemeine
Litteratur-Zeitung* [12] was not hostile, but he was puzzled by
this bleak presentation of the bare bones of an ethical theory
by a man claiming to be a systematic thinker. In a desperate
effort to tell the public what the book contained, the reviewer
was eventually reduced to listing the chapter titles. He con-
cluded this reprise of the table of contents with the judgment,
"One finds under these individual rubrics many striking ideas
which bear witness to the author's acumen as well as his ethical
sensitivity (or should I say "taste"); but they are those of an
observing and reflecting mind rather than a scientific, profound, or organizing one." [13]

Herbart, in his reply,[14] defends himself against the impli-
cation that he had hastily gotten the book published before it
was written by pointing out how long ago he had developed
his total system. As for justification and context for the ethical
theory, he contents himself with pointing out that the reviewer
could have found what he needed by consulting the appropriate passages in the *General Pedagogy,* the *Chief Points of
Logic,* and the *Chief Points of Metaphysics,* which were, so to
speak, "on sale at all bookstores."

Here a judge, even one as generally favorable and partial
as I am, must side with the reviewer. Herbart has miserably
failed to produce a comprehensive, intelligible single volume
on the subject he wanted to treat, even though ethics is relatively isolated in his system and he did not have to deal
simultaneously with the complications of related fields of philosophy. The man who was noted as a lecturer and was des-

12. In SW 2:506–13.    13. In SW 2:512.    14. SW 2:512–15.

tined to become famous later for his analysis of the necessary steps in instruction proved himself singularly incompetent at straightforward exposition. (This inadequacy of the *General Practical Philosophy* as a self-contained treatise may be at least a partial explanation of the fact that this treatment of this major part of Herbart's system was never translated into English, despite the later spread of Herbartianism in English-speaking territory.)

Similar difficulty (this time resulting from the system) besets the psychological works. As Josiah Royce was to say years later, reviewing the English translation of the *Textbook of Psychology*, "The work is, on the whole, so dependent upon the author's metaphysical presuppositions, and upon the considerations which he developed at length in his *Psychologie als Wissenschaft* . . . that, as it lies before me, the present text can hardly be of much service to students whose only acquaintance with Herbart is to be derived from its pages." [15]

As far as a summary of his total system is concerned, we have already seen that he made two attempts, the *Introduction to Philosophy* and the *Encyclopedia*. But Herbart was quite clear about the limitations which he imposed on each. The mass of material was so large and so complex that Herbart himself seems always to have felt that he had to cut corners in some fashion to reduce this vast bulk to a single volume or to bring it within the interests or capacities of a single audience.[16] The *Introduction* was intended quite literally to introduce students to the study of philosophy—the purpose for which he used the book in his own courses and for which he had written and published it. As such a general introduction to philosophic activity, it stressed the necessary fundamentals and the problems toward which the student's own later philosophizing would be directed. But the *Encyclopedia*, as Herbart saw it, was intended for a more mature audience which had already studied philosophy and wished merely to brush up on old knowledge or to revive old interests. For them he thought it appropriate to skip over the fundamentals and to

15. *Educational Review* 4 (1892), p. 185.    16. SW 9:24.

dodge the more complex and abstruse problems; the emphasis should be on the results of philosophic investigation, with the author feeling free to select topics on the basis of their general interest rather than their pivotal position in philosophy and philosophizing. For those who wished to pursue various topics further, Herbart included references to his earlier monographs; but he makes no attempt to epitomize these matters or to render the *Encyclopedia* a summary of his total position.[17]

In short, Herbart never produced a comprehensive synoptic view of his own system, a single volume which the reader could master and then feel that he had the word. Even as late as the second and third editions of the *Introduction* he was still suggesting an extended (and rather vague) course of readings for any would-be disciples:

> Those who wish to learn the system must, of course, start with the *Introduction*. But then the path leads to my *General Practical Philosophy* (and they must get some help from my *Dialogues concerning Evil*) and to the *Textbook of Psychology* (with some help from the *Chief Points of Metaphysics* and the treatise, *De attractione elementorum*).[18]

Yet he did not hold any Platonic view that systematization of his thought was impossible; on the contrary, he expressly felt, as we have seen, that parts of his thought were always very directly related to other parts and that he could only be understood all in a piece.

The situation in regard to his educational thought is much the same. As we have seen, the *General Pedagogy* was, by his own assessment, uneven, puzzling, and full of lacunae. His letters on the *Application of Psychology to Education* (though the title is not Herbart's) must likewise have been a disappointment to many teachers and to many students of Herbart. Granted that the work is unfinished and that the connections between psychology and education are much more apparent in the last five letters than in the first thirty, nevertheless the

17. SW 4:24; 9:19.  18. SW 4:17.

work scarcely constitutes that sort of bridge between the two fields which one would expect from a man who had so ceaselessly asserted the dependence of education upon psychology.

Any doubts aroused by the preceding work are likely to be confirmed by the *Outlines of Pedagogical Lectures.* Herbart's best-known pedagogical works, *The ABC of Sense Perception,* the *Aesthetic Idea of the Universe,* and the *General Pedagogy,* stand very early in the sequence of his published works, all preceding the publication of his major studies on metaphysics, ethics, and psychology. But one might expect the *Outlines,* written toward the end of his career (1835), with its second edition coming at its very close (1841), to be not merely the most mature and comprehensive, but also the most broadly "systematic" of his educational works. And so, in some respects, it is. For example, the relation of the fundamental "moral ideas" to education, and hence what is specifically involved in asserting the ethical aim of education, receive much greater development and clearer delineation. But although the connections of education to ethics are thus clarified, its connections to metaphysics and psychology are not. The relations of the world of moral action to the world of reality, events, and appearances are not mentioned. Similarly, his theory concerning the nature and origin of our "presentations" or ideas, despite their fundamental importance for his educational doctrine, is never put into its metaphysical frame; and the psychological arguments and examples are drawn for the most part from the pedagogical folklore of the experienced teacher rather than related to Herbart's own psychological laws of the "statics and mechanics of mind." This last situation may be merely the consequence of a rhetorical concern, the anticipation of an audience composed primarily of pedagogues. But whatever the reasons, in this very late work Herbart is scarcely systematic in relating education to those other philosophic fields with which he always insisted it was closely associated.

The chapter "The Art of Education" in the *Encyclopedia* is also illustrative.[19] In some respects it does summarize briefly

19. *SW* 9:137–51.

Herbart's educational position, as Ulich has suggested.[20] But it is far from comprehensive and would probably not seem adequate to a reader less able than Ulich to supplement it unconsciously from his knowledge of the rest of Herbart's work. To epitomize the 139 pages of the *General Pedagogy* and still give it the necessary supplementation in the 14 pages taken up by the "Art" would be difficult, and Herbart makes no real attempt to do so. The "Art" does have considerable value and importance, since Herbart felt free to include here, presumably as "topics of general interest," matters which he passed over or touched only lightly in his other works; but it is scarcely a summary.

In short, for a man who felt he could be understood only in terms of his total work and who was seeking readers and followers, Herbart did very little to put the necessary vade mecums in their hands. To ask that a reader possess his major works and collate them properly while trying to read any given one was patently to ask too much. Reviewers who complained of loose ends or who failed to understand Herbart's intentions or arguments were not necessarily guilty of ignorance, incompetence, or malice.

A third factor restricting the spread of Herbart's views during his own lifetime was his isolation from the mainstream of German philosophy and even his opposition to it. This isolation had several consequences for his educational as well as philosophic influence. Originally, before his own philosophical (and psychological) works were published, he was liable to be misunderstood because his readers sought to interpret and supplement publications like the *General Pedagogy* by employing the doctrine then current in Germany. The confusions and absurdities occasioned by this procedure were obvious to him, but, as the remarks quoted earlier in this chapter show, he saw no way of avoiding this difficulty. But even after his views had been published in full, they were never easily accessible, and they were never popular with those who managed to become acquainted with them.

20. Robert Ulich, *History of Educational Thought* (New York: American Book Co., 1950), p. 281.

More often than most books, his works received unfriendly reviews. The first paragraph of a very long (and belated) review of the *General Pedagogy* by Jachmann in the influential *Jenaische Allgemeine Litteratur-Zeitung* gives the flavor:

> Rarely has the reviewer been so deceived by a book as by the present one; he has found almost nothing in it—he will not say, of what he justly expected, but—of what, according to the title, he was warranted in expecting. The book proclaims itself a general pedagogy derived from the aim of education and thus as a general theory of educational science derived from a principle which embodies the aim of education and which binds its theorems into a system. But in the entire book no principle is presented. That morality is the highest aim of education is introduced only casually and through reference to an earlier treatise by the author and is contradicted by other assertions of the author. Of a deduction of the science of education from this principle so casually introduced, no trace can be found, and consequently the book contains only an aggregation of all sorts of psychological, anthropological, ethical, and pedagogical comments and admonitions, without any internal organization into a systematic doctrine. The organization of even this aggregation is illogical. Scarcely a single concept is defined, properly developed, and worked out. Finally, the language intentionally seeks out incomprehensible expressions and turns of phrase and often produces the appearance of new and profound philosophic discoveries where the reader, after useless effort, finds only the most commonplace and trivial thoughts. The reviewer will now put the reader in a position to convince himself of the truth of this judgment from the book itself.[21]

This was hardly the kind of review calculated to make the reader dash out to buy the book or to adopt it as his pedagogical guide. Although Herbart often replied to reviews (as he did to this one) and usually felt they were unfair, he ultimately became somewhat resigned to this treatment. As he wrote to Drobisch about a review of his *Psychology as a*

21. In *SW* 2,512.

*Science,* "From it you can see how little hope I have of ever reading a rational word about my work." [22] We are, of course, more familiar with the unfavorable reviews than the favorable ones, since it was to the negative reviews that Herbart replied, and they must therefore be included in the *Complete Works* if his rejoinders are to be intelligible. In any case, these adverse reviews are numerous and rather damning.

Certainly the reputations of Kant, Hegel, Fichte, and Schelling shone brighter, their doctrines were more favorably received, and their works were more widely read and discussed. Herbart, listening to his own drummer, was grossly out of step in the philosophic parade. His failure to gain the original appointment at the University of Berlin and his even more obvious repudiation when that chair was open again at Hegel's death were both evidence of his past isolation and unpopularity and a cause for more of the same in the future.

The educational equivalent of this philosophic isolation, which is even more relevant to our concerns here, can best be seen in connection with the pedagogical seminar which Herbart conducted during his years at Königsberg.[23] True, during this period pedagogical activity was something of a side issue for him, as both he and others recognized,[24] but the seminar and his *General Pedagogy* were his most probable means of influencing the education of his time. We have already seen the problems inherent in the *General Pedagogy* and the kind of reception it inevitably got. The seminar met with no greater success.

The seminar's existence was precarious throughout its entire history. Herbart's annual reports are clearly the accounts of a man who feels he is struggling against almost insurmountable difficulties; the university has too few students, especially too few who are interested and capable in pedagogy; too few parents are willing to supply pupils as experimental subjects

22. *SW* 17:16.
23. Herbart summarizes his procedures, which he felt were finally the best within his power, in his report to the ministry for 1821–23 (*SW* 14:200–203).
24. *SW* 15:36, 115.

for his practice teaching; requests to the ministry for staff, building, and equipment are met very slowly or on an ad hoc or temporary basis rather than by the permanent arrangements which Herbart sought. Often he seems to be filing a complaint rather than a report. But from the other side, we can imagine von Altenstein, the Prussian minister concerned, looking at this same record and finding in it, with some justice, plain evidence of the ministry's continual support for Herbart's project. By and large, these are the familiar difficulties in trying to build an institution within a bureaucracy which has limited funds. Each side was, in its own way, right. The real difficulties lay deeper.

The ministry was primarily interested not just in subsidizing Herbart's interests, but in improving the quantity and quality of the teachers available to the Prussian schools. But in this effort, it did not, as Herbart himself acknowledges,[25] keep a tight rein on him, or demand that he run a narrow training program fitted to the immediate needs of the existing schools. Although the king apparently felt he was acquiring in Herbart merely a devoted follower of Pestalozzi,[26] von Altenstein knew what he was doing. He was quite clear in his own mind and in his written instructions that what he wanted was an experimental trial of Herbart's ideas, in the hope, of course, that they could ultimately be used to improve the whole Prussian school system, particularly the gymnasiums. Herbart did not, however, regard the operation in quite the same perspective. He saw the seminar as an opportunity to instruct students in the proper educational ideas and methods— his own, of course. He realized at the outset that teachers trained by him would find no favor with the "modern mystics," and the "educational revolutionaries," or with "schoolmasters who oppose anything new." [27] Nonetheless, Herbart had some hope that he would manage to improve, even reform, educational procedures.[28] But not only was Prussian education non-Herbartian, there were some obvious reasons why exerting influence was difficult and why the two points of view could not easily be made to mesh.

25. *SW* 14:206; 15:38; 17:104.   26. In *SW* 14:67.   27. *SW* 14:67.
28. *SW* 14:203, 205.

German university students at that time were interested primarily in such traditional specialties as theology, philology, and law, not in pedagogy. (Herbart suggests that a partial cause of this lack of interest may well have been that most lectures on pedagogy—not his own, of course—were really not very interesting because they merely stayed on the empirical surface of the subject, "which everybody knows about anyway.") [29] To be sure, many of these students would eventually land in teaching posts for life; but then we encounter that hardy perennial of educational controversy, the debate on whether the well-trained classicist, for example, needs to know anything about the art or science of teaching in order to teach boys Latin and Greek. Certainly many people in important positions thought not; and the students, if left to their own devices, without the external pressures of examinations or licences, tended to pursue only their immediate specialties— partly in the belief that they were more likely to be hired as sound classicists than as skilled teachers.[30] Herbart himself states another aspect of the same problem:

> Pedagogy, considered as a science which should be taught and learned, has to contend with a special difficulty of which only long experience has gradually made me aware. Specifically, all its major concepts lie within the circle of common talk and likewise in the well-worn rut of what everyone thinks he knows. Consequently the precise scientific investigations on the establishment of which the direction of pedagogical procedures really rests are blurred and spoiled with unbelievable ease.[31]

As a result, even Herbart, whose pedagogical lectures were apparently much more profound and attractive than most, sometimes found difficulty in getting an audience and then in finding among these few auditors enough competent candidates to man his practice seminar. Thus in two years (1818 and 1819) he had only three takers for his pedagogical lectures; [32] but even in 1830, when he had "at least forty diligent

29. *SW* 15:35.    30. Castell in *SW* 15:116.    31. *SW* 14:225.
32. *SW* 14:160. B 1820, however, this number had risen to twenty (*SW* 14:179).

auditors" for the lectures, only four presented themselves for the examination.[33] In consequence he was often forced to accept into the seminar students whom he considered less than qualified or even desirable, even candidates who had not yet attended the basic pedagogical lectures.[34] It was to overcome these difficulties that Herbart was continually asking the state to impose additional formal requirements and to appoint him to the Provincial School Board. Sooner or later most of these requests were granted.

Yet the seminar had more profound difficulties than merely not flourishing and suffering from the usual disparagement of education as a field of study. Herbart's general theory as incorporated in the seminar and certain practices regularly followed in it were totally alien to the education of the day and almost unassimilable with it.

For example, Herbart's theory demanded individualization of instruction: the teacher must deal with the student as he is, both in his particular natural endowment and in his specific fund of past experience. Individualization of instruction naturally leads to the instruction of individuals as the ultimate point in the scale of individualization. For the seminar Herbart's doctrine always was "more teachers [i.e., students doing practice teaching] than pupils." [35] As a result, during the year that he had thirteen pupils living in his house, he felt this group was too large in proportion to the number of students in the seminar, placing an undue burden on them. In Herbart's opinion, when a teacher has to deal with a throng of students, his natural response is to develop a bureaucratic routine, which is contrary to true education. Although Herbart believed that there were certain parts and forms of instruction which were best carried on in large schools and classes, he felt that such instruction could be performed only by teachers who were already fully trained; for the early stages of training, he regarded the intimate relation between individual teacher and individual pupil as indispensable. Consequently students in

33. *SW* 15:35. In 1824 about the same attendance at the lectures had produced twelve examinees (*SW* 14:234); in 1827, five (*SW* 14:257).
34. E.g., *SW* 14:135–36, 161.   35. *SW* 15:108, 122.

the seminar did their practice teaching mostly with individual pupils or with a group of three or four at the most.[36]

The question always remained, therefore, just how much of what the student learned in this extremely atypical situation could be relevant or applicable when he found himself teaching the necessarily larger classes of twenty to thirty pupils in a public school. As Castell, who served for a time as first teacher in the seminar and as tutor for the children living in Herbart's house, declared, "The seminar did not teach how to handle a class."[37] Discipline, lesson-planning, and all the rest in the public-school situation would quite clearly be on a very different scale and, very probably, of quite a different kind. Understandably enough the ministry was always asking Herbart to show that he had in fact prepared teachers for the Prussian schools rather than just skilled tutors for upper-class children[38] and to structure his operation by developing a set of rules and principles as a supplement to his annual reports, which were essentially a series of case studies recounting the increasing skill of the individual students and the continuing progress of their individual pupils. Herbart kept stalling, giving a variety of excuses.[39] But each year during the 1820s the ministry raised with increasing urgency the question whether the seminar should continue on its customary course or whether it should take a new tack less peculiar to the ideas and personality of its director.

The stress on individualized instruction was indeed a major point in Herbart's general theory, a direct consequence, as we shall see, of his psychological theory. There were, however, certain other practices (which were standard procedures in the seminar and which loomed large in Herbart's own writings) which were equally at odds with the method of the contempo-

---

36. *SW* 15:32; 14:25–26, 89.   37. *SW* 15:122.
38. See especially the comments of Castell (in *SW* 15:117–18) and of the Provincial School Board (in *SW* 15:129).
39. E.g., *SW* 14:233 where he lists the pressure of other duties, the desire to utilize his psychological investigations which were still incomplete, and the necessity that educational experience be protracted if it is to be sound.

rary school. Whether these procedures too are necessary deriv-
atives from Herbart's total "system" or whether they merely
reflect Herbart's personal predilections and habits is an issue
which can be decided only on the basis of the total system.
For present purposes it suffices that they are less obviously
entailed by the principles of the system than are such matters
as individualization. Castell (after Herbart's death), in his
1842 review of the work of the seminar, considered them
merely practical details unrelated to Herbart's principles and
felt free to omit them in conducting his own "Herbartian"
private school.[40]

The most obvious example of these practices is Herbart's
insistence on beginning the study of the classical languages
with Greek (rather than Latin) and in Greek, on beginning
with the *Odyssey* and then starting Latin with the *Aeneid*. As
we have seen, he hit upon the idea of beginning with Greek
and the *Odyssey* when he first served as a tutor in Switzerland,
and it was the regular procedure in the seminar. But the student of classical philology who went through Herbart's seminar and then became a teacher in a gymnasium would immediately find himself teaching Latin first, not Greek, teaching the
authors within each language in a very different sequence, and
even to some extent teaching a very different set of authors
from those he had practiced in the seminar. It is scarcely
surprising that there was some doubt how useful the training
in the seminar was for future teachers in the Prussian gymnasiums.[41]

Finally in 1831 a decision was reached, the fruit of a long
report by Herbart [42] and a very lengthy and precise statement
of Herbartian principles and procedures [43] by Dr. Taute, a
privatdozent at the university who was then serving as Herbart's long-requested assistant. (Taute's statement impressed
von Altenstein as being "profoundly written and extremely
noteworthy.") [44] Taute was to continue on the permanent pay-

40. In *SW* 15:118–19.
41. *SW* 2:14; 1:39, 61; 9:37, 143–44, 151; 14:200–201.
42. *SW* 15:31–38.    43. In *SW* 15:39–63.    44. In *SW* 15:67–68.

roll, and the seminar was to continue to run in its existing form during Herbart's lifetime or as long as he chose to conduct it. But this decree (which still contains the usual plea for the preparation of a complete set of rules and regulations for the seminar) was primarily a tribute to Taute's persuasiveness and an acknowledgment that Herbart did have an intelligible theory which he was putting into practice. The decision did not alter the fact that Herbart's ideas and practices so deviated from current educational procedure that they could have little influence on it at all. The university's abandonment of the seminar immediately after Herbart's departure to Göttingen, despite Taute's plea to be allowed to continue it, seems a natural and inevitable happening.[45] Herbart, despite his "eloquence, erudition, adroitness, and activity," [46] had done little to influence Prussian education through the seminar because his ideas and practices were so patently alien to the educational enterprise of the time.

Partly as a consequence, no doubt, of the preceding factor, the fourth influence came to be Herbart's lack of a coterie of devoted adherents and admiring students. Despite his popularity as a teacher, few of the students who thronged his lecture hall became *his* students, to spread his fame and doctrines during his lifetime. He kept close touch with the band of friends from his university days, but none of them was ever so situated as to aid substantially the propagation of his reputation or his ideas. Herbart did not make new friends or even acquaintances easily. He gave the impression of coldness and austerity; only the few who ever penetrated this barrier found the lonely heart which sought and extravagantly admired friendship. In any case, Herbart's very devotion to the independent pursuit of truth (the result both of personality and of intellectual conviction) would have prevented his acquiring

45. Reusch's survey of the situation at this time seems an objective one (*SW* 15:91–94). See also the later (1859) report by the Provincial School Board (in *SW* 15:129–31).
46. Castell in *SW* 15:116.

a throng of intellectual satellites, handy though they would have been for the sake of fame and influence.

These four causes (difficult style, extended and complex system, professional isolation, and lack of influential devotees) seem sufficient, particularly in combination, to explain Herbart's lack of impact upon the educational thought and action of his time. Other reasons can be and have been adduced, but the preceding set seems to include enough major factors; besides, some of the other suggestions appear unconvincing. An example of this is the hypothesis that the *General Pedagogy* was neglected because it appeared in the same year as several other major works on education.[47] This view implies that, like the Boston ladies who did not want to go to New York to buy hats because they already owned hats, the man who has bought or read one book on education has no interest in another very soon. The practice of the book trade over the centuries seems to deny this suggestion. The publication of one book on a topic is almost certain to coincide with that of several others. The multiplicity of titles is usually seen as reflecting great current interest in the topic and even as generating additional interest by bringing the general topic more forcibly to the attention of the reading public. A book may be judged inferior to its competitors—as the *General Pedagogy* probably was for the reasons Herbart himself recognized. In this case the busy man will select only those books which reviews, rumors, or guesswork suggest as superior; but mere simultaneity of publication is not in itself fatal.

The four reasons advanced here are, to be sure, all superficial or irrelevant in the sense that they have little or nothing to do with the merits or demerits of Herbart's doctrines in themselves. Yet these factors clearly seem sufficient to explain why Herbart's views, however profound, insightful, and true

47. E.g., W. Rein, "Herbart als Pädagog," in Thilo, Flügel, Rein, and Rude, *Herbart und die Herbartianer* (Langensalza: Hermann Bayer & Söhne, 1897), p. 32; F. Bartholomäi, "Johann Friedrich Herbarts Leben," p. 64.

they may have been, had attained so little influence at the time of his death. At any rate, as we shall see later, when Herbart's educational thought ultimately gained popularity many of these difficulties either had been surmounted or had of themselves ceased to exist. Then popularity was possible at least in part because these hinderances were no longer operative.

# 5

## "Herbart Has Found His System"

There have already been many passing references to Herbart's "system": [1] how he evolved it while still a university student, how he spent the rest of his life expatiating upon it (making astonishingly little change in it over forty years), and how he and others had difficulty in coping with it. As the quotations already cited in other connections have made clear, Herbart himself believed that he had a complete and articulated conceptual scheme and that he always thought and worked within it.[2] If, then, we are to understand and judge Herbart as he presumably would have wished, we must grasp at least the general outline of this total structure and the mutual relations of its elements. Although the preceding chapters have probably suggested some parts of this scheme, a more exact sketch of it and some filling in of detail are now necessary.

Herbart was a philosopher, and he sought to organize in his system the whole of what he considered the field of philosophy.[3] Sciences are often characterized by the subject matter

1. Chapter title is from SW 16:97.  2. SW 2:163; 4:17.
3. This exposition follows very closely Herbart's own statement in his *Introduction to Philosophy*, SW 4:42–49.

with which each deals: botany studies plant life; astronomy the heavenly bodies, and so on. But the field of philosophy cannot be marked off in this fashion, says Herbart, for its subject matter is concepts, and concepts are in some sense common to all the sciences. Philosophy must be characterized, therefore, not by its subject matter but by its way of working with that subject matter. Philosophizing takes place in experience when we fix our attention on a given object, collect the thoughts that arise in this process, and—most important and most complicated—try to unify these thoughts. Herbart calls this whole process the reworking (*Bearbeitung*) or development of concepts. This way of working with concepts, this elaboration of them, is the distinguishing mark of philosophy in contrast to all the other sciences, and the three major kinds of such elaboration give rise to the three corresponding major fields of philosophy.

The first consequence of directing our attention toward our concepts is that they become "clear" and "distinct." Herbart means by these terms what they denoted in the traditional philosophical language of his day. A concept becomes "clear" by being distinguished from other concepts; for example, "man" is not "pig." A concept becomes "distinct" by having its attributes or elements distinguished within it—"animal" includes "man." Distinct concepts can be organized into "judgments," that is, propositions which assert some predicate of a logical subject—"All men are animals" or "All men are mortal." Judgments, in turn, can be organized into "inferences," such as the familiar syllogism ("All men are mortal; Socrates is a man; therefore, Socrates is mortal"). These processes of clarifying, distinguishing, and ordering concepts constitute the domain of logic, the first of the three major fields of philosophy. Believing with Kant that Aristotle had all but perfected logic, Herbart attempted no original contribution in this field, and his *Chief Points of Logic* is only a summary for student use. Logic is, however, important for Herbart. Most of his metaphysics is based on logical considerations: his psychology considers how these logical processes arise and are carried on; in education, assisting the pupil to clarify, distinguish, and order his concepts is an important task. However, the student of Herbart needs to know no special "Herbartian logic," but only the traditional variety.

But our perceptions of the external world and of ourselves give rise to many concepts which, as they become clear, reveal themselves as contradictory. That is to say, the chief task of metaphysics is to help us understand our experience correctly. In thinking about this experience we use concepts like "change," "cause," "substance," and "self"; but as we examine them, we see that they involve contradiction. Yet for Herbart, as for Kant, the very basis of rationality is the so-called law of identity or noncontraction; *A* must always be *A* and never *not-A*. A rose is a rose is a rose and not sometimes a peony. Hence, if we are to understand our experience aright, we must think about it in noncontradictory concepts; and our concepts must undergo, consequently, a process of "enlargement" (*Ergänzung*) to purge them of their contradictions. "Enlargement" is thus a second major way of working with concepts and gives us the second major field of philosophy, metaphysics.

Within "general" metaphysics, Herbart distinguishes four subdivisions, though they are closely interrelated. The first, methodology, deals with general principles of proper method and proper order of procedure. Ontology, the second, deals with what is real. The third part Herbart calls synechology, the study of those forms of experience which have continuity as their essential characteristic (e.g., space, time, and motion). The fourth subdivision, eidology, examines the possibility of knowledge, a problem which interested Herbart greatly because of the doubts and restrictions which had been placed on human knowing by the work of his immediate predecessors— the Humean skepticism, the Kantian critique, and the extreme idealism of Fichte.

In addition to "general" metaphysics, Herbart sees three

varieties of "applied" metaphysics, distinguished by the kind of object toward which metaphysics is directed: when it is applied to the external world, natural philosophy or cosmology results; when applied to the internal world or life of the mind, psychology; when applied to the supernatural world or the divine, natural theology. Moreover, because the principal concepts with which metaphysics deals are so general, they apply to all human knowledge. As a result, progress in any given field tends to depend on the adequacy (or noncontradictory nature) of those concepts which metaphysics can supply for those other inquiries. As a result, some acquaintance with metaphysics is necessary if any inquiry is to be carried on with the proper concepts. For students of Herbart, that statement has an important corollary: since Herbart has a particular view of metaphysics, some understanding of his metaphysical views is presumably necessary for understanding any Herbartian inquiry.

There is a third class of concepts which requires treatment in still a different way and thus generates the third major field of philosophy. These concepts are like the metaphysical ones in that they are not adequately dealt with at the level of mere clarity and distinctness, as are the logical ones. But whereas the metaphysical concepts require only change through "enlargement," this third class of concepts requires, in addition, a judgment of approval or disapproval. This third group of concepts defines Herbart's third major field of philosophy, aesthetics.

Like the metaphysical concepts, the aesthetic concepts divide into "general" and "particular" or "applied." The general aesthetic concepts have another point of difference from those of general metaphysics. The latter must be derived from what is given in experience and proceed from the knowledge of it; they cannot be arbitrarily devised, imagined, or postulated, for the function of metaphysics is to help us understand our experience as it is in fact given to us. That is, common thought has developed concepts like "change" in order to describe and think about what is a common and obvious phenomenon in everyday human experience. If, as we try to clarify it, "change" proves contradictory, then metaphysics must undertake to "enlarge" this concept until it loses its contradictory character; but that ultimate metaphysical concept, whatever it may be, must still be applicable to experience and help us understand what we commonly call "change."

The general aesthetic concepts do not suffer these limitations. Once such a concept has been taken from experience, it can be considered from the standpoint of approval or disapproval, without any regard for what is actually given in experience. That is, the concept of "beauty," once taken from general experience, can be developed even though nothing corresponding to the final form of that "beauty" may actually occur in our experience (though an artist may then attempt to create it in some medium). Similarly, we may take from experience the idea of a "good man" and develop it into a concept of which we aesthetically approve, even though such a "good man" does not (and perhaps even cannot) appear in our daily experience.

If these general aesthetic concepts are directed toward what is given in experience, this application of aesthetics engenders a whole series of "practical sciences" or "doctrines of art." These doctrines state how anyone who undertakes to busy himself with a certain object of experience ought to handle it if he is to win the fundamental aesthetic judgment of approval rather than disapproval. The precepts or maxims of these doctrines are, for the most part, merely hypothetical or conditional: that is, *if* one chooses to concern himself with this art or this object, *then* he must operate in this way rather than otherwise in order to win approval. If we wish to compose music, then the "doctrine of art" for music (e.g., its rules for harmony, counterpoint, form) tells us how we must go about it in order to produce an aesthetically pleasing composition. But we need not all be musicians; or, having tried our hands, we may give up.[4] In these latter cases, the hypothetical precepts of that particular art are not binding upon us.

4. *SW* 1:264.

But one of these practical sciences involves an object with which we are necessarily continuously concerned—ourselves. Inevitably our actions are liable to judgments of approval or disapproval from ourselves or others, which Herbart believes are ultimately aesthetic in nature. Therefore, in this one "practical science" par excellence, "practical philosophy" or "ethics," the maxims are categorical, not hypothetical or conditional. One has no choice. One *must* behave in *this* way.

To summarize, Herbart divides philosophy into three main fields: logic, metaphysics, and aesthetics. Logic is not further subdivided, though the procedures of clarifying and distinguishing concepts, asserting judgments, and making inferences are distinguished. General metaphysics contains four parts (methodology, ontology, synechology, and eidolology) and three fields of application (natural philosophy, psychology, and natural theology). General aesthetics is undifferentiated, but applied aesthetics includes numerous practical sciences, among which practical philosophy, or ethics, is major.

Where is education in all this? Everywhere; or, more exactly, all these fields bear on education. Herbart sees pedagogy as primarily a joint application of ethics and psychology.[5] But, as is evident from the preceding outline, ethics itself is an applied branch of aesthetics and hence involves the relevant principles of general aesthetics. Likewise, psychology as an applied field of metaphysics similarly involves the relevant principles of general metaphysics. Moreover, metaphysics would enter in any case insofar as it furnishes the proper conceptual tools for all inquiries. Finally, logic, as the fundamental instrument of all the sciences, is necessarily relevant at every turn.

In short, if we take Herbart's claims to a system seriously, to talk about education properly is to talk about it within the context of his total philosophic system. Although the field of philosophy is divided, these are not independent parts, but are interlocking and interacting. It is small wonder then that he despaired of clothing and clarifying that "outline" which he presumably had in mind when he wrote the *General Pedagogy*

5. *SW* 9:304.

and that he was able to do little to improve the situation in subsequent attempts. Since, however, we can be less concerned than he was with specific admonitions and details, this general structure within which his pedagogical thought presumably rests can be sketched fairly briefly in the following chapters.

# 6

## "Morality: The Sole and Total Task of Education"

Since education is to find its end in ethics [1] and its means and hindrances in psychology,[2] Herbart's ethical doctrine is the natural and even necessary starting point for any attempt to examine his educational thought as "systematic." That the determination of the ends of education falls within the domain of ethics (taken as including politics) is a proposition which would win the assent of almost any philosopher. Statements concerning the ends of education are not logical, descriptive, or predictive; they are normative statements concerning desired or ideal states or activities for man or concerning the ends of human action. As such they fall within the philosophic field traditionally concerned with such states, actions, and ends.

In asserting, however, that education must derive its end from ethics, Herbart means something much more narrow and precise than the mere assertion that such statements are normative in general. Education is not merely to make man "better" in some sense; it is to make him "morally good." Instruction for other purposes, say vocational or nationalistic

1. Chapter title is from SW 1:259 and 3:343.    2. SW 10:69; 9:342.

ones, may be necessary, useful, and even desirable for man; but it is not what Herbart calls "educative instruction" (*erziehendes Unterricht*), that is, instruction designed to educate man in this strict sense, to make him a moral being. This is the only kind of education in which Herbart is interested, and it is to this end that his whole pedagogical apparatus is devoted.[3] To neglect or ignore this is to distort Herbart's intention.

As was indicated by the preceding chapter's sketch of Herbart's organization of the total domain of philosophy, he sees ethics as a subdivision of aesthetics. His motives in making this assignment seem fairly clear. Like Kant before him, Herbart was worried about the contingent nature ascribed to ethics by many ethical theories. Too much was left to circumstances and chance, too much to individual judgments and tastes. The good man may be powerless to act and hence to produce the good he intends; his well-intentioned actions may in fact produce unforeseen evil results; one man's calculation of the good or evil consequences likely to result from a given action often differs from that of his fellows. Both Kant and Herbart, therefore, sought to find for ethics a foundation so firm that its general laws, at least, would be as necessary as those of the physical science of their time. The moral life was to be no more "iffy" than the motions of the heavenly bodies.

To find this firm and necessary basis for ethics, Kant had turned to logic. To him it seemed that because few additions had been made to this field since it was originally developed by Aristotle, it was, first of all, an established science. More important, syllogistic demonstration *demands* assent; once the premises have been established, the conclusion necessarily follows.

Seeking similar universality, necessity, and subsequent consensus for ethical judgments, Kant felt that this could be achieved in two steps. First, the very heart of logic or of human rationality was the law of identity or noncontradiction. A must always be A and never *not-A*. This principle of non-

3. *SW* 2:10, 27–28; 9:140; 10:140.

contradiction could be applied to ethics through the "maxim" (or principle or proposition) which "determines" (i.e., guides or directs) the will in any given action. Kant's categorical imperative asserts that our ethical test is whether this maxim can be generalized into a universal law without falling into *logical* contradiction in some fashion. The test of our new universal law is not whether the proposition is repugnant to our moral sense, whether it leads to evil consequences, or, indeed, whether it leads to any consequences at all; the question is simply whether the universal proposition destroys itself logically by falling into internal contradiction.

Herbart sought the same universality, necessity, and consensus for ethics, and in several essential respects he adopted Kant's general position. First, Kant had sought to find for morals its proper and separate sphere: "Such a metaphysics of morals ought to be isolated and not be mixed up with any anthropology, theology, physics, hyperphysics and, still less, with any occult qualities (which we can call hypophysics)." [4] Herbart praises Kant for this stand, especially for keeping his metaphysics of nature separate from his metaphysics of morals and not mixing up the problem of "Ought" with the problem of "Being" as had some of Herbart's contemporaries.[5]

Second, Kant had found the supreme good in the good will itself, as the familiar opening of the *Fundamental Principles of the Metaphysics of Morals* announces:

> Nothing can possibly be conceived in the world, or even out of it, which can be called good without qualification except a *good will*. Intelligence, wit, judgment, and the other mental talents . . . or courage, resolution, perseverance . . . are undeniably good and desirable in many respects, but these gifts of nature may also become extremely evil and mischievous if the will which is to use them . . . is not good. It is the same with gifts of fortune. . . .

4. Kant, *Grundlegung zur Metaphysik der Sitten,* 3d ed. by K. Vorländer, "Der philosophischen Bibliothek, no. 41 (Hamburg, 1962), p. 30.
5. *SW* 4:108–9. See also *SW* 2:87, 94; 9:266.

A good will is not good because of what it does or brings about . . . but simply by virtue of its willing.[6]

Herbart adopts the same position.[7]

Third, Kant had felt that nothing new or abstruse was required as the basis for ethics: "In order to know what I have to do for my will to be good, I have no need of ingenuity drawing a longbow." [8] Likewise, Herbart points out that there is actually nothing new about his "five fundamental ethical ideas." Their very familiarity over the centuries is a partial warrant for their correctness. And since Herbart believes that to make a startlingly new discovery in ethics would in itself be somewhat suspicious, he is happy to find his fundamental ideas prefigured in the thought of Plato, Cicero, Adam Smith, Kant, and a number of others. He sees his own contribution as that of clearly showing their basis, ordering them in the proper sequence, and showing that the set is complete and exhaustive.[9]

At this point Herbart parts company with Kant. Kant proceeded by finding that will "good" whose maxims were at least in accord with the moral law (as tested by the categorical imperative) rather than the inclinations. But Kant, in getting to the categorical imperative, seems to Herbart to have moved too fast, since Herbart believes that the categorical imperative combines and masks certain prior and more fundamental judgments which are aesthetic in character.[10] As a result, although Herbart too seeks a firm foundation for the will's being good in itself, he turns to aesthetics rather than to logic to find this base.

In Herbart's aesthetics, music, with the classical harmony and counterpoint of his day, serves as the model. As was evident in chapter 2, Herbart was a trained and devoted performer of music throughout his life. It is not surprising then that music suggests itself as the basic model for his aesthetics and that, in turn, he sees in aesthetics the means of doing for ethics what Kant had sought to accomplish through logic.

---

6. Kant, *Grundlegung zur Metaphysik*, p. 11.
7. E.g., *SW* 1:259–60.
8. Kant, *Grundlegung zur Metaphysik*, p. 22.
9. *SW* 9:78–79.    10. *SW* 1:262–63; 2:95; 3:236–37.

For Herbart, aesthetic judgments call forth feelings of pleasure or displeasure. The paradigm here is the simultaneous striking of two musical notes. The tonic together with the third or the fifth produces a harmony which is pleasurable; the combination of the tonic and the second or the sixth produces a disharmony which is displeasing. Important consequences for aesthetics in general and ethics in particular follow from this model, which Herbart regarded as embodying a fundamental and incontrovertible musical fact.

These aesthetic judgments are necessary and they arise in us involuntarily immediately upon the full presentation of their proper object.[11] That is, the harmonies are heard as concords and are immediately pleasing, without our will's being involved; discord is similarly heard as displeasing. These judgments arise as soon as the notes are heard, and there are no reasons, arguments, or proofs which can be given or need to be given. "If, however, the teacher of counterpoint were asked for proofs, he would only laugh, or pity the deaf ear which had not already perceived them." [12] Yet these judgments demand our assent (though of a very different kind) [13] just as does logical demonstration.

Another important consequence of this musical model is that aesthetic (and hence ethical) judgments concern not single elements but relations between elements.[14] A single note, say middle C, is not in and by itself harmonious or inharmonious and hence pleasing or displeasing; it becomes so only in relation to another note struck simultaneously. It is the resultant chord which embodies concord or discord and calls forth the judgment "pleasing" or "displeasing."

Yet these fundamental aesthetic relations about which there can be no dispute are *simple* relations. Differences in taste and conflicting opinions about works of art ("artistic" judgments) grow out of the fact that total works of art (pictures, musical compositions, statues) combine large numbers of these simple relations and their corresponding "aesthetic" judgments into very complex wholes. Such general "artistic"

11. SW 2:45.    12. SW 1:264.    13. SW 9:204–5.
14. SW 4:113–14; 2:344.

judgments are extremely complex and equally fallible. As a result the best general aesthetics is that which most clearly connects these complex wholes (constituted by the work of art and judgments upon it as a whole) to the underlying simple relations and the infallible judgments evoked by them. Here again music furnishes the paradigm:

> But he [the observer] must take apart the series of perceptions which the work of art has woven together and must study them, partly individually, partly in their relations, until he finds the elements of beauty and their conditions. Clearly no other art does this as easily as music, where one needs only to read the score in order to have soprano, alto, tenor, and bass individually before him. Thus the artistic, loud-storming fugue is analyzed before one's eyes down to its last constituent. . . .[15]

Herbart's admiration for "classical" art (frequently expressed in his educational works) rests on the same foundation: "But there are works of art which we call classic, that is, works which through their precision work decisively so that they unite the judgments in a definite fashion. Such works create a generality through which the particulars are elevated to the state of a general reason." [16]

If this doctrine seems a rather naive theory of intuitive judgments, it is because much of its sophistication is masked under the phrase which declares that such judgments can occur only "under the *complete* presentation of their object." [17] The term "complete" covers a variety of objective and subjective conditions which must be met. For example, on the objective side, the work of art may be so complex in structure or so extensive in space or time that those fundamental relations which are the proper "objects" of the aesthetic judgment may be hard to discover and, when found, hard to relate to the larger judgments. On the subjective side there are also conditions for the "complete" presentation. For example, the observer must not only have the requisite capacities and

15. SW 9:112.   16. SW 9:105.   17. SW 1:264; 2:45, 344ff.

knowledge, he must be in a properly equitable and judicious frame of mind. (Herbart was as worried as Kant that the "dear self" would bias the judgment through its prejudices, interests, and inclinations.) [18] In short these judgments, on the infallibility of which Herbart relies, are not just the snap judgments of anyone at any time or place.

Within the narrower field of ethics, then, Herbart sees these aesthetic judgments as directed toward five proper objects or relations, the basic relations within which the will can stand. The proper or harmonious relation in each case specifies a fundamental moral "idea" or principle. The will standing in this proper relation calls forth the involuntary ethical response of "approval": the will in the improper relation evokes "disapproval," the ethical counterpart of the aesthetic judgment of displeasure evoked by the musical discord.

To anticipate briefly, the educational consequences of this view will be that the aim of education becomes the production of a will which stands in the proper relation in each of these five instances, and each part or element of education is to be judged by its contribution to this general end. To educate is to produce a will of this sort.

1. The first relation [19] in which the will can stand is one internal to it, the relation between what Herbart sees as the two parts or aspects of the will in regard to any single volition of any given individual. On the one hand there is what he calls the "objective" or "obeying" will. This is the will arising from the inclinations, the desires, and the passions. On the other hand there is what he calls the "subjective" or "commanding" will, the will based on the intuitive ethical judgments of approval or disapproval. Confronted with any given volition of the objective will, the subjective will immediately passes judgment upon it. Harmony between these two "sides" of the will is the first mark of the "good" will and it is as absolutely pleasing as a musical concord. This harmonious relation is the first ethical idea, the idea of *inner freedom* (*innere Freiheit*).

That it is so named is part of Herbart's legacy from Kant.

18. *SW* 2:92.   19. *SW* 2:90–91, 355–57; 4:118–19; 10:71.

Kant too had seen the maxim which determines the will as derived from two possible sources, the inclinations or the moral law. As he saw it, moral action in the strictest sense had to be undertaken "out of respect for the law itself," [20] completely without regard to the inclinations of the actor. But Kant despaired of ever finding an absolutely clear empirical case where "the dear self" could be completely ruled out, and hence he was content if the maxim, even if somewhat infected by the inclinations, was shown by the test of the categorical imperative to be at least in accordance with the moral law. Thus, ultimately Kant's concord between the will and the law is not too different from Herbart's.

"Freedom" arises in a similar fashion. Kant's introduction of logical necessity through the categorical imperative might seem to threaten the distinction he wished to preserve between the "necessity" at the base of the metaphysics of nature and the "freedom" he wished to preserve for the metaphysics of morals. How can man be free if the moral law is imposed upon him? Kant's answer, in briefest compass, was that man is still free because he imposes the law upon himself; his will remains autonomous because it gives the law to itself rather than becoming "heteronomous" by having it imposed from without. Similarly, for Herbart there is freedom here because the moral judgments are self-imposed,[21] the subjective will imposing them on the objective; and that will is most free whose volitions are most approved by these judgments.

2. The second ethical idea also concerns the volitions of a single willing being, but it treats the varied strivings of this single will rather than each individual striving. In this examination of the strivings of a will, Herbart wishes to leave out of account the material content (the specific objects toward which these strivings are directed) and to consider only the relative size or strength of these efforts. In the purely formal and quantitative consideration of these strivings simply as strivings, Herbart sees three quantitative criteria as applicable.

20. Kant, *Grundlegung zur Metaphysik,* pp. 19–20.
21. *SW* 9:57–59; 1:262; 2:94.

First is the *intensity* of each striving. The strong will in the sense of intense striving always calls forth our admiration, irrespective of the object or end toward which it is directed. The will strong in overcoming obstacles always, so Herbart feels, wins our admiration and approval.

The second quantitative criterion Herbart calls *extension,* the diversity of the various acts of striving of a single will, the total range of objects toward which the will is directed, even though these objects themselves are left out of account and only the number of vectors of the will, so to speak, is considered. Once again, Herbart feels that we always approve more highly of a will which is active in many directions than of one whose strivings are pointed toward only a few of the innumerable possible objects. (This particular criterion of this second basic "idea" is destined to have great influence on education, for it is the basis for Herbart's emphasis on that many-sidedness of interest toward which much instruction is directed.)

The third quantitative criterion is *concentration,* the unification of this manifold of strivings, a new and more comprehensive intensity arising out of extension. Through concentration the will is capable not merely of intense effort within a limited range of objects or of relatively less effort dissipated over a wide range of objects, but of new intense acts of willing which, though diverse, are unified.

This second ethical idea Herbart calls *perfection (Vollkommenheit),* taking the term in its etymological sense from *perficere,* to work out or work through, to achieve, to complete. This idea describes the will with drive. Not only is this idea formal, since the objectives of the striving are disregarded, it is comparative or relative because there is no absolute standard for applying the criteria. But when two wills are compared, Herbart feels we always admire the stronger, more efficient, more concentrated of them more than we do the weaker. As far as the goodness of the will is concerned, since we have excluded from consideration the objects toward which the will is directed, the "perfected" will may strive for evil as well as good objects; yet Herbart feels that we necessarily admire a wide-ranging, powerful will even though it moves toward evil objects. As he says, Alexander, Caesar, mountain ranges, and volcanoes are all admired for their sheer power. Obviously, however, this second basic idea by itself will not produce a *good* will, and this fact is one of the major reasons Herbart frequently repeats that the five moral ideas cannot be considered or pursued in isolation but must limit and modify each other. Yet Herbart also explicitly warns us against taking this idea of perfection as merely an intensification of some other virtue; rather, it is the necessary condition of virtue. As Kant would say, a will which does not posses this drive, this push, falls into self-contradiction, in that a will is not really a will unless it wills forcefully. Partly because of the very obviousness of this characteristic of the will as will, Herbart believes that the idea of perfection is the most accessible of the moral ideas; even children and savages recognize it and approve the will which stands in this relation.[22]

3. The third ethical relation in which the will can stand is that of *benevolence* (*Wohlwollen*). It arises when the will of one individual recognizes and comes to terms with the will of a second being. But though this idea involves the will of a second individual, the relation is still internal to the first will since the second will is taken merely as an object of the first will and not as an element in a mutual relation between two wills. Only the idea or representation of this second will is necessary, as is evident from the fact that the relation still stands even though the first will's idea of that second will is erroneous. The first will is simply well disposed toward the strivings of another will. There is no question of actually producing the well-being of that second individual, and benevolence is not to be confused with nepotism or sympathy. The idea is not pure when it is motivated by the joy of doing good to others; the relation stands in itself. Yet this, Herbart feels, is that one among the moral ideas which most demonstrates the value or disvalue of character, and exhibitions of benev-

22. SW 2:358–60; 4:119–20; 9:210, 83, 78–79; 10:72–73, 143.

olence please us unconditionally just as manifestations of its opposite evoke our immediate disapproval.[23]

4. In the relation of the fourth basic idea,[24] *right* or *law* (*Recht*), two wills are directed toward an object which only one of them may have. In this situation, the second will (or will of another) is no longer merely considered as an object or idea by the first one, but is taken as a will in its own right. Because both wills are focused on the object rather than on each other, there is no question of intention; both wills strive for the same thing. This clash of wills threatens to produce strife, a type of discord which is immediately displeasing to the aesthetic judgment. Effort to prevent this strife leads to right or law, which allows one will to obtain the object and prevents the other will from doing so. The sanctity and the validity of law, therefore, ultimately rest on the fact that the strife which law prevents would be absolutely displeasing to the aesthetic judgment.

5. The fifth basic moral idea,[25] *requital* (*Billigkeit*), also involves two wills and is also negative in the sense that it arises out of ethical disapproval rather than out of approval, as did the first three ideas. With "law" there was no question of intention, since the two wills were regarded as directed toward some object rather than toward each other. Here both violation of the law and the question of evil intent enter. Such acts, if unrequited, produce an imbalance of good and evil between the two wills, and this imbalance is a lack of harmony which calls forth our disapproval, whereas requital in the shape of reward and punishment restores the balance and gains our approval.

Herbart feels that of all the five moral ideas this last has most often been neglected or even lost sight of. In Cicero's *De officiis*, for example, he has no difficulty in finding precise equivalents for the first four ideas (though he thinks Cicero had them in the wrong order), but extracting the fifth is a more

23. SW 2:361–64; 4:120; 9:209–10.    24. SW 2:364–69; 4:120.
25. SW 2:369–75; 4:121–22.

difficult process.[26] Herbart's justification for this idea of requital lies in the criminal law, which, he insists, cannot rest
on the idea of right. Right is concerned only that each should
have his own and, when confronted with violations, right
knows only restitution or indemnity, not punishment. The
approval which we feel upon seeing someone "get his just
deserts" involves more than mere right; and the difference in
the criminal law between manslaughter and murder points to
the fundamental ethical importance of intention.

These five ideas, the first three internal to one will and
the last two involving relations between two wills, cover the
possible relations in which the will can stand. Strictly speaking, of course, it is no more possible to prove that this list
constitutes a theoretical exhaustion of the possibilities, says
Herbart, than to prove the fundamental approval or disapproval attendant upon these relations or the fact that a chord
in a major triad is harmonious and pleasing. But Herbart suggests that we can gain some reassurance by running various
tests on the list. If, for example, we try to extend the list by
taking more than two wills into account, we find that we are
getting mere multiplication or complication of the original
five, but no new idea based on a new relation. Or suppose we
move in the other direction and try to find an idea lying
beyond "inner freedom"; we find that that idea of an accord
between the will and its own moral insight is itself the basis
of morality and hence nothing more basic can be found:

> If man did not perceive his own will, if he did not see the
> image of his own will, or if he regarded it with indiffer-
> ence, without praise or blame, then there would be abso-
> lutely no idea and no doctrine of ethics—just as little as
> there is among the nonrational animals. Now the idea of
> inner freedom does not merely *rest* on this basic relation
> between the will and its intuitive insight, but it is itself
> its most complete conception and judgment. Consequently,
> the effort to get behind this, any effort to put something
> in front of this first point in this whole line of reasoning—

26. *SW* 9:79, 82–83; see also 2:133–34.

whoever would seriously try this must have understood nothing about anything.[27]

Thus, for all intents and purposes the list—inner freedom, perfection, benevolence, right, and requital—stands. And though Herbart was not particularly interested in religion and did not develop his ethics on a religious base, he obviously feels that their fundamental nature is equally obvious there:

> One utters words without sense if one talks about God without at the same instant thinking of Him as the holy one, whose will corresponds with His insight [inner freedom], as the exalted whose might is revealed in the starry heavens and the worm [perfection], as the charitable one whom Christianity depicts [benevolence], as the righteous one who was already recognized in the Mosaic laws [right], and as the avenger whom the sinner fears as long as grace is not made known to him [requital].[28]

Although the ideas are discovered and discussed separately, Herbart is always careful to point out that they must not be so considered and that exclusive concentration on any one (or any few) of them in either thought or action is wrong:

> There can be no greater error than to isolate a single one of the practical ideas in order to demand ordinances developed for its sake alone. Nay rather, only all of them combined can give direction to life; otherwise one runs the gravest danger of sacrificing the rest to that one; and thereby a life, which from one side is very rational, becomes on other additional sides irrational. This warning is so much the more necessary, not merely because the so-called natural law is handled separately, but also because, apart from all scientific distortion, each man usually has his own moral one-sidedness. . . . The one strives simply for culture (*perfection*); another knows only love (*benevolence*) and has no regard for equity or law; a third would make the state a mere pressure-machine in the name of right, without regard for justice or for benevolent and educative arrangements.[29]

27. SW 9:212.    28. SW 9:266–67.    29. SW 4:123; see also 9:267.

Although these five relations seem to Herbart to cover all the possible relations in which the will can stand in regard to itself or to another will, he sees one situation in which an extension of these original five is possible—a society cohesive enough that the will of its members could be treated as if it were the will of a single being. This social will could then stand in the same five relations as does that of a single willing being, and five "derived," "social" ideas would arise.[30] Herbart feels that even the emerging nations of the Europe of his day show how this is possible. He undertakes, consequently, to derive these five corresponding social ideas from the five fundamental ones. But the order of their development is not the same. Because they are social ideas they most naturally develop first from the more "social" of the basic ideas, those that involve two wills, that is, right and requital. The progression then runs backward through the list with the social equivalent of inner freedom coming last because it presupposes the highest degree of internal coherence and unity.

Living together, members of such a society would seek to avoid strife or to repress it if it breaks out. Thus a *system of law* (*Rechtsgesellschaft*), derived from the idea of right, concerning actions and the use of property arises. Here there is a social contract in that each member agrees that all the others shall keep what they have and that he himself will be secure in his own possessions.

But transgressions are likely to occur, and the disapproval aroused by these unrequited doings and sufferings leads to a *system of requital* (*Lohnsystem*), of rewards and punishments to redress the imbalance. To remain in the society each member agrees to abide by the law and to accept the rewards and punishments thus entailed. Just as the basic ideas of law and requital were negative in that they arose from efforts to avoid and suppress strife and hence to escape the attendant disapproval, so the systems of law and of requital are negative in this same sense.

But the benevolent spectator would see more to societal

30. SW 2:385–405.

life than this negative avoidance of social discord, and would seek beneficent social action which would win positive approval. Out of benevolence, therefore, develops a *system of administration* (*Verwaltungssystem*) aimed at the greatest possible well-being for all the members of the society through a rational distribution of the available goods; and the original benevolence of the individual spectator evolves into the mutual benevolence of all the members.

This system of administration is concerned chiefly with economic goods; but there are also spiritual goods, so to speak, and the basic idea of perfection (with its criteria of intensity, extension, and concentration) has its social parallel in the *system of culture* (*Cultursystem*). This system contributes toward "intensity" through social arrangements which support and develop the relatively feeble strivings of some individuals until all become equally resolute. It seeks to develop "extension" by making all members sensitive to the actions and achievements of all the others. "Centration" is then attained through the specialization of each individual member. As Herbart formulates this extension and concentration for members of the society, "Each is to be a connoisseur of everything; each is to be a virtuoso in one specialty." [31]

The counterpart of inner freedom (harmony between the objective will based on the inclinations and the subjective will based on moral insights) obviously demands the highest degree of integration in a society.[32] It demands universal obedience to the dictates of a mutually shared set of moral insights. Each individual is activated by a spirit which he does not feel is merely his own, but which he cannot feel is foreign to him. "The gap between the One and the Others, each of whom follows merely his own judgment and wishes to be left to his own knowledge, this dead and empty contradiction, disappears." [33] This situation does indeed require the name of a *perfected society* or, as the German literally puts it, an "ensouled" one (*eine beseelte Gesellschaft*).

This, in briefest compass, is Herbart's theory of morality,

31. *SW* 2:28.   32. *SW* 2.405–8.   33. *SW* 2:387.

the end toward which education is to be directed. His educational theory will then presumably show how the good will, as defined by these ethical ideas, is to be achieved, and how each of the various elements of education contributes toward this end. But at this point it is appropriate to anticipate a bit of the educational doctrine by indicating how Herbart believes the very nature of the various ideas determines the order and manner of their development by education.

In Herbart's opinion, most of the five ideas have little meaning for a child at the age when education begins. The exception is the idea of perfection which, as was noted earlier, is comprehensible even to children and savages, who admire the strong will. But the idea of perfection is threefold, involving intension, extension, and concentration, and not all three aspects are equally feasible as objects of educational concern at the outset. Intension, the quantitative strength of the will's thrust, seems to Herbart to be largely a matter of natural endowment. For constitutional reasons some children have stronger wills than others, and education can only take its pupils as they come. Concentration in its turn seems to Herbart to be possible for children only at a later age and, since logically it presupposes both intension and extension (because a wide diversity of individually strong strivings is to be brought into a new intensity by concentration), concentration cannot serve as a starting point for education. These eliminations leave only extension, and it meets all the criteria which Herbart applies. Since he sees the child as an active being with powers and capabilities, even though these are as yet undeveloped and undirected, the requisite natural capacity is at hand for education to work on. The further condition that education should have some effect is also met: by presenting a wide variety of objects, education can stimulate the child and set him in motion toward this array of diverse objects; in this way the child's strivings, whatever their natural intensity, can be extended to a wide range of objects. To present these objects is to instruct. As a result, the ethical doctrine that the better will is ideally the one directed toward the wider range of objects passes over into the pedagogical doctrine that the early, and always major, task of education is to develop many-sidedness of interest through instruction. Because of this direct efficacy of instruction in producing many-sidedness of interest, with its counterpart of "perfecting" the will through extension, instruction will be that part of education which is initially prominent and perennially important.

The next ideas to emerge are those of right and requital, which develop out of the children's association with each other. In fact, provided proper limits are imposed by the discipline of the school and the influence of the teacher,

> the moral perceptions which belong thereto would be among the first and most natural if children were allowed to accommodate themselves to each other and associate with each other in their own way and could judiciously be left to themselves. For where human beings—big or little—rub against each other, the relations with which these moral perceptions are connected develop spontaneously in abundance.[34]

By elimination it is obvious that the ideas of benevolence and inner freedom are late to appear and difficult to attain,[35] and consequently all discussion of their development is best postponed until the requisite educational apparatus is available in chapter 9.

34. *SW* 2:134, 138; 10:72–73, 192.   35. *SW* 10:71–72.

# 7

# "To Distinguish between That Which Is and Has No Becoming and That Which Always Becomes but Never Is"

Once ethics has determined the general aim of education (morality, the development of a will which stands in the relations specified by the fundamental ethical ideas), then psychology, which is to reveal those psychic mechanisms which education must use or combat in developing a will of this sort, might seem the next topic for consideration.[1] As chapter 5 showed, however, the progression cannot be so simple and direct. In the terms of Herbart's views concerning the relations between the sciences, psychology is one of the fields of "applied metaphysics," and the attempt to apply any science presupposes knowledge of that science. Or to make the same point in non-Herbartian terms, psychology deals with the functioning of mind; but what that "mind" is which functions and what the larger contexts are within which it functions are not for Herbart psychological questions, since "mind," "self," "the external world," and similar concepts are not to be defined as mere parts or sums of psychic functioning. On several counts the status of these concepts is that of metaphysical problems, and hence they must initially be given adequate

1. Chapter title is from SW 9:216, quoting Plato, *Timeus* 27D.

metaphysical treatment. Furthermore, Herbart believes that psychological inquiries, like all others, depend on metaphysics to secure a proper set of general concepts.

At least a very cursory consideration of Herbart's general metaphysical position seems therefore an indispensable preliminary. (Insofar as that statement proves true, it is interesting to note that despite Herbart's influence on education in the English-speaking world, his metaphysical works have never been translated into English.) But much of his metaphysics is not essential to our present interests. Herbart as a professional philosopher intends his metaphysical works to be full-scale treatments of the problems of the field, not mere propaedeutics to psychology or education. Many time-honored problems and many major elements in Herbart's metaphysics, therefore, can (and must) be ignored by the following survey, focused on only those parts of the doctrine bearing most directly on his psychological and educational theory.

The neat fashion in which the five fundamental ethical ideas constitute a limited yet complete set of principles for practical philosophy is likely to lead one to hope for a similar set of principles for metaphysics. Herbart considers this hope vain. At best, he believes, we can discover certain "pivots" on which metaphysical thought has always turned.[2] These are the outstanding examples of those concepts through which we try to understand our experience but which prove upon scrutiny to be crammed with those contradictions which make metaphysics necessary. Although, consequently, these concepts are foci of metaphysical thought through the ages, these topics or commonplaces form a mere list, not a logical unit.[3]

---

2. It is interesting to note that A. E. Taylor, writing on metaphysics almost a century later (1903) suggests "four problems of great generality and considerable difficulty: substance, quality, relation and causality." He too points out that it is difficult to talk about *substance* apart from its *qualities* and their *relations* to it and that the question of causality can be raised in such a way as to include the other three. A. E. Taylor, *Elements of Metaphysics* (London: Methuen; New York: Barnes & Noble, 1961), pp. 122–23.

3. SW 9:213–223, 252–53; 8:72–87, 210; 4:176.

Because metaphysics is for this reason a relatively unstructured field, it can be treated equally well in several different fashions. For example, in his *Encyclopedia,* on the one hand, Herbart lists four of these pivotal concepts: inherence or substance, change, matter, and the ego or self. There he suggests that the logical way of working with them is probably to move from the general to the particular; and the most general seems to him to be "inherence"—that is, the inherence of multiple characteristics in a single object which is taken as real and called a "substance"—although this same topic appears in more particular form in connection with each of the other three topics. On the other hand, in his *Introduction to Philosophy* he lists only three such pivots (the thing with multiple characteristics, change, and the self) and there suggests that the long history of discussion about "change" possibly entitles it to priority. These differences merely reflect and reemphasize the point already made—Herbart's view of metaphysics as an unstructured field. These topics are not separate, or even separable, but are inextricably intertwined; and as a result the number of pivots selected and the catchwords used to denote them can be relatively arbitrary choices. Discussions of one inevitably lead to discussions of the others, as Herbart himself exemplifies by his increasing use of footnotes, cross-references and insertions in successive editions of the two books just mentioned. Yet these pivots cannot, in Herbart's opinion, be reduced to a single problem or principle, as he thinks was demonstrated by the unsuccessful efforts of Fichte to rest everything on the "ego."

If the task of philosophy is to explain experience, what is the "given" in experience which it attempts to explain? Common sense replies, "Things"—people, mountains, houses, pencils. What do we know about things? Their many qualities or characteristics. Snow is white and cold and damp and light. Iron is black and cold and dry and heavy. And certainly these qualities are in some sense "given" us in experience since we cannot by some effort of will perceive snow with the qualities of iron or vice versa. But what do we know about snow and iron in themselves? Apparently nothing, since our experience, coming through the senses, gives us only these lists of qualities and imparts no knowledge whatever about the "thing" with which we thought we started. The thing has turned into a mere congeries of qualities. As a result, human thought has hypothesized a "substance" or substrate as the basis or ground in which these qualities are thought to inhere at least temporarily. Whatever it is that is white and cold and wet and the rest we will say is a substance we call "snow." But we know nothing about snow as a substance; we use the word merely to fill the subject position in the series of judgments or propositions: ". . . is white," ". . . is wet," and so on. But A is never A (snow is never known to us as snow), but A is always only a and b and c and d . . . (white, wet, cold, . . .).

The same is true of the "self" or the "ego." What do I know of myself? (And this shift to another pivot, the "self," in a discussion of "substance" merely illustrates the constant mutual implications of the topics.) I know my feelings, perceptions, states of mind, and the like: I feel sad, I see blue. But what do I know about me other than this sort of list? Nothing. "I," like "snow," merely fills the subject position in series like, ". . . is warm," ". . . is happy," ". . . is awake," and once more A is not A, but "self" is merely an alleged habitation and name for aggregations of perceptions, feelings, and the like. In short, in attempting to explain "thing" or "self" through "substance," we have fallen into contradiction and have proved to ourselves only that we can never actually know anything about such "things," but only about long lists of characteristics, none of which is the thing.

Not only do things have various multiple qualities, these qualities change. The water was hot but now it is cold; I was happy but now I am sad. (And here once more the discussion of "substance" slides toward a different pivot, "change.") Yet "a thing which at the next moment is no longer the same things as it formerly was strikes even the common reason as something contradictory."

On one occasion [4] when he deals with the problem of

4. SW 4:162–75; compare 8:87–98.

change, Herbart elects to set up a trilemma which seems to him logically exhaustive of the ways in which change can be conceived as real—that is, as being a true predicate or characterization of something that truly is. Briefly stated, the trilemma runs: either change has no cause, or it has a cause; if it has one, the cause is either internal or external. Thus the three possibilities are: no cause, internal cause, or external cause. The view which sees change as having no cause Herbart calls "absolute becoming": nothing *is* anything, but everything is in a state of becoming something else. The second position Herbart labels "self-determination," since the cause of change is in the object itself. The third possibility, where the cause of change is thought to be external, Herbart says can be called "mechanism in the broadest sense of the term."

We can also, like Herbart, look at the ultimate significance of this argument before we even begin to follow it, especially since we will not concern ourselves with all the details. For Herbart these three possibilities are an exhaustive list of the ways in which the problem of "change" can be handled. If it can be shown that *all three* are inconceivable (because they involve contradiction, deny us the possibility of knowledge, contradict experience as it is given to us, or otherwise place us in an untenable intellectual position), then we will know that change is not real—that it is not a characteristic of reality or of any real thing. To be sure, since change is given to us in experience, it will have to be accounted for in some other way; for Herbart's present purposes, however, it will be sufficient merely to demonstrate that change is not characteristic of reality. Herbart proceeds to demolish the three possibilities one by one.

Beginning with the view that cause is external, he points out that we do not experience things as permanently dichotomized into causes on the one hand and effects on the other. Rather, experience presents us with causal sequences: *A* causes *B*, which in turn causes *C*, which in turn . . . . This view leads to several difficulties. First, any one of these events in such a sequence is contradictory in its nature because it is both active *and* passive: for example, *B* is passive as the effect of *A* but is active as the cause of *C*. Second, such sequences lead inevitably to the problem of the infinite regress: if we ask what causes *A* in the preceding series, we simply push the series infinitely backward: *A* is caused by *z*, which in turn was caused by *y*, which in turn . . . .

The situation is no better for self-determination because parallel difficulties exist. The changing thing would be active as a cause acting on itself but passive as an effect of itself as cause; it would therefore be active-passive or contradictory. Likewise the abyss of the infinite regress would open before us. That is, why did the self decide to change itself? Because of a decision, which was because of a decision, because of a decision . . . .

The third possibility, that of absolute becoming, Herbart saves till the end because, although it is not common in popular thought, it has been adopted in many different guises and disguises by philosophers over the centuries. Now change, if it occurred without rule or reason, could represent absolute becoming. But it would still be contradictory in that something which has been of one sort exchanges, at a bound, that characteristic for some other; and hence persistence and change would be at odds in the same thing. In fact, if the concept of absolute becoming is strictly interpreted, change of this kind should proceed uniformly and continuously, without beginning, pause, interruption, or end. Unfortunately for this view, our experience does not give us such uniform and continuous change, but rather change which is intermittent and which, when it does occur, takes place at varying rates. Although attempts may be made to explain away this difficulty by alleging that the uniform and continuous change of absolute becoming is facilitated or retarded by other forces, they only reintroduce in new form the contradictions and difficulties of internal or external causation. Another effort to explain change as absolute becoming asserts that change is only an "appearance" of some ground of true being which itself does not change and which does not itself appear in its appearances, but only gives rise to them. But if this ground of being were truly simple, it would just remain what it is and give rise to nothing. In sum, the negative results of the trilemma are established, and "change" is shown to be as dubious a concept as substance, inherence, and self.

The preceding sketch is certainly far from a complete résumé of Herbart's arguments in treating these pivots, even in that section of his *Introduction to Philosophy* which has been chiefly followed here. These problems and suggested solutions run back to the very dawn of speculation among the Greeks, and Herbart has a professional interest in marshaling the whole host; for example, the entire first volume of his *Metaphysics* is a historical account of these controversies. The outline here is intended only to illustrate Herbart's general manner of working and to show the main avenues which lead to the central starting points of his metaphysical thought.

He postulates that the law of identity or noncontradiction must be the ultimate criterion: *A* must always be *A* and not sometimes *B*. He further postulates that "being" or "reality" in the strict sense must meet this criterion; otherwise philosophy, as the rational attempt to understand the reality which is or which underlies our experience, must end in incoherence and contradiction. His examination of the historical tradition has revealed a wealth of problems but no solution which he can regard as wholly adequate.

His way out of these difficulties is to postulate at the outset a world of reality which meets his criterion: a world in which *A* is always *A* and nothing else; where *B* is always *B* and never enters into relations, causal or otherwise, with *A, C,* or anything else. This is Herbart's world of "reals" ( *Realen* )— absolutely simple beings, each one always unchangingly that simple quality which it is, possessing no parts, no size, no degrees, unaffected in its essential nature by any other real.[5]

This device allows him to start with a noncontradictory concept, "real," and hence to hope that a further noncontradictory explanation or description can be developed from it, since those unsatisfactory concepts like substance, cause, and

5. *SW* 8:62–67; 4:180–84; 2:190.

change do not apply to it. The real is not a substance with various and varying qualities which inhere in it; it is not caused or causing. It is only that simple quality which it is; and that is that.

These initial steps at solution have, of course, no fewer historical roots than the problems which give rise to them. Herbart is manipulating past solutions as well as traditional problems. His predecessor at Königsberg, Immanuel Kant, had been "aroused from his dogmatic slumbers," as he himself said, by the writings of the English philosopher David Hume, whose skeptical position grew out of his attempt to test the soundness of human knowledge by tracing it back to its sources. Ultimately, Hume asserted, our knowledge comes from "simple ideas" or direct sense impressions, though these raw materials can be greatly elaborated and modified by imagination, reason, and other mental capacities. There are no innate ideas; no direct flashes of insight or intuitions into the nature of things. The test of any item of alleged knowledge is to analyze it to its simple ideas and see whether the elements are reducible to those simple ideas which are the basis of our true knowledge. Hume then pointed out that, as we have just seen, through the senses we learn nothing about substance or cause. We have no sense impressions of substance, but only of aggregations of many and changing qualities. We do not see, hear, or smell causes. Thus such ideas cannot be accepted as part of our fundamental knowledge, but must be secondary developments of some kind, through habit or some other mechanism. For example, when event *A* is regularly followed by event *B*, we come to expect *B* whenever *A* appears and to say that *A* "causes" *B*. But "cause" applies to our expectation, not to what we know about *A* and *B*.

Kant began by admitting the validity of Hume's argument. If our knowledge comes *solely* from experience, from the senses, (as admittedly much of it does), then it is contingent (not universal and necessary) and subject to all the limitations and illusions of the senses. Yet Kant was as suspicious as Hume concerning claims made at the other extreme, that reason alone (unaided at all by the senses) could achieve knowledge. Yet if universal and necessary (rather than empirical) knowledge was to be possible at all, and if concepts like "cause" and "substance" were to retain any efficacy as applied to the nature of things rather than just to our habits or states of mind, then some way out of this impasse had to be found. Kant undertook to find it in his *Critique of Pure Reason*, which he wrote "to define for reason its proper province." As we have seen, Herbart worked through this book himself and was acquainted with Kant's thought at first hand as well as through the Kantians.

As Kant saw it, if Hume was right in saying that our knowledge is solely empirical and our perceptions and conceptions must correspond to things, then universal and necessary knowledge would be impossible. But what if we work a "Copernican revolution" by suggesting, on the contrary, that our knowledge of things must conform to our perceptual and conceptual mechanisms? What we know, then, are phenomena—things as they appear to us or as we can conceive them, not as they are in themselves. Because all men perceive the world through what Kant called the "forms of sensibility," human beings inevitably perceive phenomena as being in these forms; that is, as being in time and space, though things-in-themselves are not in time or space. Our perceptual mechanism casts phenomena into these forms as it perceives them. Similarly, because all men use their understanding in thinking about the world, we inevitably think through what Kant called the "categories of the understanding" (cause, substance, and the rest). Things-in-themselves are not, for example, substances in causal relations, though phenomena do appear to us to be so because, if we are to think at all, we impose these structures of our conceptual mechanism and thus experience phenomena as so organized.[6]

6. Herbart's comment is incisive: "Kant in the preface to the Critique of Reason rightly recalls Copernicus. But he wrongly adds, 'If intuition must conform to the nature of objects, I cannot see how anything can be known about them a priori; but if the object (as an object of sense)

By his "revolution" Kant gained certain ends which he sought, among which was the preservation of the possibility of a priori (necessary, nonempirical) knowledge, finding the basis for this sort of knowledge in the universal structure of the human perceptual and conceptual machinery. As a result Kant's interests turned toward mind and away from things-in-themselves. Of these latter he was prepared to assert only that although we may know *that* they are, we are forever debarred from knowing *what* they are, for our perceptive and cognitive structures unavoidably infect our knowledge of them.

Herbart's reals have some similarities to the Kantian things-in-themselves. For example, both incorporate the true nature of things, but both remain fundamentally unknowable by us because our experience is of something else. But whereas Kant tended to turn from the world of phenomena to that part of them contributed or affected by mind, Herbart is more loath to leave his reals. He thinks that something more can be said about them than that they are, provided we follow cautiously the clues which experience gives us. Just as Kant, beginning necessarily with experience, made inferences which allowed him to demonstrate from other sources certain things about mind, so Herbart feels that the train of inference may be made to run in the other direction, toward enlarging, at least within narrow limits, our knowledge of underlying reality. Typical of this attitude is his belief that Kant had restricted human knowledge too severely at several points. For example, Herbart asks whether when one thinks *about* the categories one also thinks *through* the categories; [7] or was Kant himself employing a mode of thought which he was claiming was impossible and hence failed to investigate? Since Kant could know little or nothing about things-in-themselves and since

conforms to the nature of our intuitive faculty, then I can easily conceive this possibility.' This opinion is similar to what would be if one were to seek the error in the appearances in the rising and setting of the sun in the structure of the human eye. The eyes are as little guilty as the sun. The untruth of appearance lies in the *place of the observer* in relation to what he has to observe." (SW 4:179, emphasis in original.)
7. SW 4:7.

"cause" was a category of the understanding, Kant could do little with the relation between things-in-themselves and phenomena, in contrast to the relation between mind and phenomena. But how being can give rise to appearance seems to Herbart an appropriate metaphysical question, whose investigation should shed some light on what it is that appears:

> No one will believe that nothing is, for it is clear that then nothing would appear. What it is must be sought from the given in appearance, in much the same way in metaphysics as it is in astronomy from the apparent motions of the heavenly bodies.[8]

In moving beyond Kant's doctrine and in developing his world of reals, Herbart drew on many sources of suggestion. Leibnitz, whose doctrines were familiar to both Kant and Herbart, particularly through the Wolffian version in which they had both been trained, had already developed a metaphysical world of "windowless monads," isolated beings which seemed to interact and develop only because of a harmony throughout the universe preestablished by the great monad, God. Herbart gained much, too, from Plato, whose invariant forms were seen as constituting true reality in which the things and qualities of our world of experience participate to varying degrees. Most important for Herbart were the ideas of the Eleatic philosophers,[9] particularly Parmenides, of the late sixth and early fifth century B.C., the fragments of whose works had been published during Herbart's student days. Herbart be-

---

8. *SW* 4:178. "As much as there is appearance, so much is there pointing toward Being" (*SW* 8:53).

9. E.g., "The Eleatics can be regarded as the discoverers of the most important metaphysical premise: the quality of being is completely simple and may in no wise by determined by internal contradictions" (*SW* 4:181). See also *SW* 8:105. Note, for example, Parmenides' statement about Being: "For on this path there are many signs: that being has no coming into being or passing away, for it is a perfect whole, without motion and without end." See G. S. Kirk and S. E. Raven, *The Presocratic Philosophers* (Cambridge: Cambridge University Press, 1960), pp. 272–76; or K. Freeman, *Ancilla to the Pre-Socratic Philosophers* (Oxford: Basil Blackwell, 1948), pp. 41–45.

lieved that their thought would have influenced Kant also had it been accessible during his formative period.[10] To varying degrees all these, as well as other, thinkers played some part in bringing Herbart to his postulation of a world as simple, invariant, isolated entities as the starting point for metaphysical thought. These predecessors will also contribute as Herbart develops his system. It is this tendency to look back to pre-Kantian philosophy rather than to the more stylish idealisms of his own day that made Herbart appear out of fashion and even old fashioned to his contemporaries.

These initial steps in Herbart's metaphysics are clearly made at some cost. The aim of philosophy is to help us understand our experience, but certainly experience does not give us this world of single, unchanging, unrelated, simple beings. On the contrary, as the very persistence of the metaphysical pivots makes manifest, we seem to find our *selves* in a world of *substances, changes,* and *causal* sequences. Metaphysics, having performed one of its tasks by "enlarging" our concepts and so freeing us from contradictions, must now move in the other direction. Herbart's problems at this point are to show how, if the world of true being is as he hypothesizes it, the very different world of our experience comes to be, and also to indicate how his account of simple, unchanging being does in fact help us understand the quite dissimilar world given us in experience.[11] These are no simple matters, but Herbart sets about these tasks with the help of more metaphysics and some psychology.

Obviously if all that one can say about true being is that these isolated, unchanging, simple beings *are*, nothing is going to happen, since change and cause-and-effect are excluded. Human experience need not—in fact, cannot—be explained, because it is never going to arise. Yet human experience offers the data with which we start and on which we must rest. Without falling into contradiction, Herbart must introduce action of some kind into the static, placid existence of the reals; otherwise he will have painted himself into a metaphysical corner.

10. *SW* 9:216.   11. *SW* 8:98–99.

At this point Herbart does four important things. First he takes a leaf from Kant's book, who had made each human soul a thing-in-itself, a *noumenon* or rational being, in contrast to a phenomenon, that which appears in experience. Herbart endows some of his reals with souls or mind, and here the rampant ambiguity of the German word, *Geist,* glosses over some of the difficulties. To make some reals be souls has the very evident advantage of obviating religious controversy (such as that concerning the soul's immortality), for by being made a real the soul is permanently removed from time and space and from the scope of all direct human knowledge. But difficulties, preeminently the threat of contradiction, also arise. Despite the puns, the point must be made that a real cannot be just half-souled or part-minded. A given real must be all and only mind or soul; otherwise its being is no longer simple, since it consists of soul or mind *and* something else. The questions also arise whether "having mind" or "being endowed with soul" is the kind of quality which can characterize a real and also whether a mind or soul simple enough to meet the criterion for simple being can still be complex enough to transact its necessary business. For the moment, however, we can simply accept Herbart's postulate that some reals are minds or are endowed with mind ("mind" being a better English word than "soul" with which to move from metaphysics toward psychology and education). Herbart believes we are immediately driven to this postulate by the need to have some setting for that experience we call "ours," as the ubiquity of the metaphysical pivot, "self" suggests.[12]

Second, Herbart enlivens the world of the reals, perhaps by borrowing from the Greeks like Heraclitus and Empedocles (rather than the Eleatics) whose elements or atoms drew together and moved apart. Herbart now introduces the notion of the "comings and goings of the reals," as well as their consequent "togetherness" and "separation." All these terms are, as Herbart keeps reminding us, figurative language, which he employs merely to avoid inventing arbitrary technical terms. Since for the reals "space and time are obviously nothing," [13]

12. SW 4:217.   13. SW 8:113.

these comings and goings obviously do not take place in a spatiotemporal matrix. The words are intended to suggest merely the beginnings and endings of some "external relation," or "connection." But these interactions (or whatever other inappropriate word we use—and they are all wrong) must always be such as to leave completely unaffected the simple invariant nature of the reals involved.[14]

Herbart's third hypothesis attempts to deal directly with this problem of what can happen without violating the earlier postulates of simple being; this is his doctrine of "perturbations" (*Störungen*) and "self-preservations" (*Selbserhaltungen*). Still within that spatiotemporal language which is not so meant, an actual coming together of reals would involve their complete interpenetration, and hence the mutual annihilation of their original natures. But since by the definition of the nature of a real this catastrophe cannot occur, this threat to destroy on the part of one real is only a "perturbation," and an equal act of "self-preservation" occurs on the part of the other real.

With this third step Herbart seems at first glance to violate his previous definition. For to have a real, whose nature is permanently to be simply what it is, suddenly generate acts of perturbation and self-preservation seems a flagrant contradiction of all that has been said before. Herbart, at least, does not think so, and his reasons for so believing introduce another major model he adopts in his thought. In his aesthetics and ethics he takes as the model for his immediate judgments of taste and approval the analogs offered by music in harmony and counterpoint; in metaphysics and psychology he draws upon the statics and mechanics of physics, arguing by the analogy of "forces." So he does in regard to the point at issue here. If two equal weights are placed in the opposite scalepans of a balance, the beam remains motionless; in this sense nothing happens, though the two weights are "together" in the balance and each weight continues to exert the same gravitational force it otherwise would, unaffected by the exactly

14. SW 4:215–16.

equal counterforce of the other weight. Thus togetherness alters nothing and does not change the natures of the two forces, even though they are exerted against each other. In this connection two points should be noted. First, Herbart insists that this analogy is only an analogy. Reals are *not* forces, though it is sometimes illuminating to regard them as if they were. Second, the variety of these "whatever-they-are" forces mutually exerted (so to speak) by this immense variety of qualities which are the reals is exactly what is going to make for the variety of our mental life in its turn, as we shall now see.

Herbart's fourth postulate is that mind records the self-preservations as "presentations" (*Vorstellungen*) or ideas. Thus the origin of mental life lies in the approaches and withdrawals of other reals in relation to that real which is minded. Mind is thus a sort of seismograph which records the self-preservations which arise in the course of the adventures of a minded real amid other reals.[15]

These four additional postulates move the doctrine ahead a long way. The second and fourth are the foundations for Herbart's psychology, the second establishing mind and the fourth indicating how the mind becomes furnished with ideas. He thereby has something to which phenomena, the things which appear, can appear, and also the grounds for their appearing. Herbart's psychology will be concerned with the further history of those ideas which arise in this way in a mind of this kind, and further scrutiny of the difficulties and consequences of these two postulates is best postponed for consideration within the context of his psychological theory.

The first and third of these additional postulates are, however, more narrowly metaphysical. The first, that there is a coming and going of the reals, does stir up that "action" which is essential if anything at all is to happen—especially if something like human experience is to occur. The third, by postulating the counterpoised acts of perturbation and self-preservation, attempts to specify this activity in such a way

15. *SW* 8:211–12.

as not to violate the earlier hypotheses about simple being and yet to afford some clues which can be followed toward the things, changes, and causes in experience as it is given to us. This postulate seems to him the only way of escaping from the contradictions revealed by examining the dilemma of either external or internal principles of change.[16]

If one asks why and how the reals come together, there can be no answer. Herbart is still maintaining the Kantian doctrine of the fundamental unknowability of the things-in-themselves, which is, of course, what the reals are. Kant looked at the phenomena of experience and inferred the existence of the forms and the categories, the nature of which he was then able to demonstrate (to his own satisfaction, at least) from other sources (e.g., his deduction of the categories of the understanding from the forms of judgments). Herbart too is proceeding by inference, asking himself what is required if he is to get from his postulated world of simple being (a necessary starting point, he feels, if contradiction is to be avoided) to the world of human experience. Moving from simple, non-temporal, invariant elements to the complex temporal world of change is always a difficult matter, as Plato's doctrine of "participation" in his forms and Whitehead's theory of the "ingression" of his eternal objects bear witness. Bridges of some kind must be built between these two worlds. Herbart knows *something* must happen; he cannot know directly what it is. He can only infer what might not violate the principles of his real world and yet might account for the happenings in the world of experience.

Herbart took his simple beings out of space and time because these are the locales of the traditional paradoxes and contradictions of speculative thought. Yet experience, as it is given to us, appears within time and space. They must, consequently, be reintroduced. For space, Herbart's mechanism is his "intelligible space" (*Intelligibles Raum*) [17] a halfway house between the spacelessness of the world of true being and the "sensible space" of our perceptions. In this intelligible

16. SW 3:165.    17. SW 2:197–201; 8:119ff; 2:172–78.

space occurs "what actually happens" or "actual events" (*das wirkliche Geschehen*), in its turn a midpoint between the pure being (*Sein*) of the reals and the appearance (*Erscheinung*) or sensible phenomena of our experience. It is within this intelligible space that the reals come and go, not within the spacelessness of true being. The construction of intelligible space and the manner in which actual events take place within it are extremely complicated; but the function performed by intelligible space and the concepts related to it are so crucial for Herbart's doctrine that one must do some grappling with these complexities if one is to have any grasp of the system.

The most important fact about intelligible space is that it is a conceptual artifact (*Gedankending*). Unlike the Kantian "form" of space, it is not imposed by mind on things or phenomena; it is simply a conceptual tool devised by mind as an aid to its own thought, a vitally necessary aid if mind is to be able to conceive as "together" reals, which in their state of true being are isolated. Space, whether intelligible or sensible, has no reality; it is merely an *image* (*Bild*) *in mind*. This point entails that "what actually happens" and the acts of perturbation and self-preservation which underlie these "actual events" also are *in mind*, inasmuch as they take place in intelligible space. "For Being there is absolutely no change" and what actually happens is therefore as good as never happening for the truly being.[18] A marked shift has now occurred. To make the point in terms of the traditional labels, Herbart's status as a "pluralistic realist" (based on his postulation of a multitude of simple, real things) is now altering to that of a "phenomenalist" as he leaves things as real to move toward things as they appear to mind. Perhaps this is an attempt at that synthesis between idealism and realism for which he felt a need very early in his career.[19]

In generating intelligible space, Herbart seeks to ignore sensible space and to work geometrically. He suggests we begin with two reals, *A* and *B*. They can be either together or apart. If they are apart, we can nevertheless *conceive* of *A*'s

18. SW 4:216.   19. SW 1:11.

being with $B$. Thus *in thought* $B$ can furnish a place for $A$ and $A$ for $B$; and space is thus the possibility in the mind for one real to be conceived as with another. Since, however, space does not exist in reality, $A$ and $B$, even when separated, have nothing (i.e., no space) between them and are consequently juxtaposed (*aneinander*).[20] Thus by putting $A$ in the place of $B$ and $B$ in the place of $A$ and continuing in this same way to produce new points, we can generate a line infinite in both directions. A three-dimensional space can then be produced by repeating this same process in the other "directions." The lines thus generated are, of course, "fixed" (*starre*) lines constituted by a determinate number of points rather than continuous (*stetige*) ones with mutual interpenetration of their parts; but the psychic mechanism, by interpolation, then conceives of these fixed lines as being continuous. As thus generated, intelligible space is infinite in three dimensions and corresponds to the sensible space of our experience. As such, intelligible space also shares all the contradictions and difficulties of sensible space. But now these contradictions need not trouble us, Herbart thinks, since they concern only our conceptual tool, intelligible space, and are not predicated of true being.

Once intelligible space within which the reals can come and go has been provided (though this is a coming and going of images in mental space), Herbart feels he is ready to solve a number of traditional metaphysical problems. In fact, we have already had a sample in the preceding sketch of the generation of intelligible space. The concept of "continuity" as combining separation with unity or unity with separation is for Herbart contradictory, and hence, as involved in space and time, has been a notorious source of paradoxes and puzzles for metaphysics. As chapter 5 indicated, he even assigns a special part of metaphysics, synechology, to deal with these questions of continuity. A typical mode of procedure is the one we have just seen used, explanation through the psychological mechanisms. His geometrical maneuvering of the

20. See SW 7:111–12 for Herbart's detailed explanation of this term.

reals to generate intelligible space produces lines which are series of points, not continuums. But, says Herbart, between any two given points of space (or time), it is always possible to conceive of interpolating additional points; and it is this functioning of the psychic mechanisms in interpolating which makes "fixed" lines appear continuous and causes space (and time) to seem to flow uninterruptedly.

Intelligible space also enables Herbart to explain those contradictory "pivots"—substance, self, and matter. Experience gives us a world of things with multiple qualities which change at different rates. To escape the difficulties which become apparent as we reflect on these phenomena, philosophers developed the concept of a substance or underlying substrate within which these qualities could inhere even though we never experience this substance, but only the qualities. But this concept proved contradictory. Now Herbart is prepared to offer his true explanation—that in those situations in which we habitually speak of "substance," we confront in intelligible space several reals which are in conjunction with each other, united around one central member of the group. The conjunction around that central real explains the unity or oneness which we feel in regard to things or substances, though the true nature or simple quality of that central real is unknown to us. The other reals associated with the central one account for the varied characteristics we customarily associate with the things, and the comings and goings of these subsidiary reals explain the changes we experience in the qualities of things.[21] It is not, however, a simple matter of red reals replacing green reals when an apple turns ripe. The unvarying essential quality which is the being of each real does not correspond to the quality which we experience; that essential nature *as it truly is* remains forever unknowable to us. In other terms, we have merely formal knowledge of the situation, not material knowledge. We may infer changes in the relations among the reals but not the material content of those relations—what is actually so related. In short, the unchanging reals, the essential

21. *SW* 8:83–84.

natures of which we cannot know, by their varying associations in intelligible space cause us to experience what we know as things with multiple and changing characteristics.

The unity yet diversity of the "self" is explained by Herbart in the same fashion: more or less enduring, but nevertheless changing, groupings of reals about one central real. His explanation of "matter" is more complicated.[22] Herbart suggests that we begin by asking what situation the reals could occupy in intelligible space in order to account for matter. Of four possibilities he discards three, and his answer is: incomplete union or partial interpenetration. This suggestion is clearly a fiction, a postulation concerning the images of reals in mind, since reals as reals have no parts. In this realm of postulates and fictions, Herbart adds that we should also postulate that these images are in the form of two equal spheres. If, then, these two equal spheres partially interpenetrate, perturbation and self-preservation would go on within the joined parts; but to say that they occur only in the joined parts would be to take the fiction of the parts too seriously. Hence these activities must be thought to go on throughout the spheres, though to a greater degree in the joined parts. But these activities cannot exist as partial, and the force of attraction moves the spheres toward total connection or togetherness.

The foregoing account would certainly seem to Herbart superficial as well as woefully incomplete. And he would be right, for many major elements of Herbart's metaphysics (for example, his "method of relations" and his doctrine of "incidental viewpoints," to name only two) have been completely ignored. But since our concerns are not primarily metaphysical, this fragmentary sample is intended merely to portray Herbart's general mode of procedure and to sketch that part of his metaphysics "without which my pedagogy was nothing"—the sort of principle he adopted, the kinds of advantages he gained, and yet (one must say it) the failures he encountered. More important, it gives us some picture of the

22. SW 8:157–68.

kind of world, the kind of human being, and the kind of mind
with which the educator must concern himself.

It is only fair to let Herbart have the last word in sum-
marizing the point to which his metaphysics brings us:

> The content of knowledge in the metaphysical sense is
> what one knows. This is completely different from the
> material of knowledge in the psychological sense. . . .
> Sensations are the material but absolutely not the content
> of knowledge, for they are merely states within us, with-
> out any similarity, any copying, or any recognition of
> what produces them being capable of being sought within
> them. . . .
>
> . . . . . . . . . . . . . . . . . . . . . . . . . . . . . . . . . . . . . . . . . . . . . . . . . . . . . .
>
> . . . We know, at the same time, that something is
> there and that it is many and varied and that, moreover,
> *among its qualities* (which we cannot know) *relations
> occur: and determining these properly,* according to the
> hints of experience, *affords the sole possibility of our theo-
> retical knowledge. . . .*
>
> . . . Then what does it actually contain? Nothing more
> than objective appearance which is valid for every ob-
> server but offers no predicates of things themselves. How
> much have the astronomers made out of such appearance
> by combined skill and force! The average man gains from
> it his courage for life, the satisfactions of his desires, the
> healing of his pains. *We live amid relations and we need
> nothing more.*[23]

23. *SW* 8:237–39 (emphasis added).

# 8

## "Psychology Makes Mind from Series of Presentations"

Within metaphysics Herbart establishes the soul as a real.[1] "The soul is a simple being (*Wesen*), not merely without parts but also without any multiplicity whatsoever in its quality."[2] As a real it is not in time or space; it has no natural endowments or faculties, no forms, no categories, no anything except that single simple quality which it is. Like the other reals, it is involved in perturbations and self-preservations, but apart from these proceedings, the soul is merely what it is.

Although this treatment of the soul has certain metaphysical and theological advantages, such a beginning hardly seems auspicious for a science of psychology. If psychology is to study this kind of soul, psychological knowledge will be short and simple, capable of being completely expressed in some statement like, "Souls are always just what they are, and we do not and cannot know what that is." Or, as Herbart states it, "The simple *what* of the soul is completely unknown and remains so forever. It is as little a subject of study for philosophic speculation as it is for empirical psychology."[3] Obviously then, psychology is not going to study that simple quality

1. Chapter title is from SW 5:180.   2. SW 4:363.   3. SW 4:364.

that the soul is, that is, the soul *as a real*, but rather something we can call "mind." But this shift does not avoid the problems. What precisely can Herbart mean by calling soul "the substance of mind" (*die Substanz des Geistes*) [4] or by asserting that "The soul is called mind [*Geist*] insofar as it has presentations, disposition [*Gemüth*] insofar as it has feelings and desires"? [5] How can he move from a simple, unchanging real (the soul) to something that has the multiple, varied, and changing characteristics of "mind" as we know it in experience?

But if we leave metaphysics aside for the moment (as Herbart himself does for simplicity at the beginning of his *Textbook of Psychology*),[6] we encounter within the traditional domain of psychology fundamental preliminary problems concerning its proper methods and subject matter. Like many another philosopher and behavioral scientist before and after him, Herbart looks to "real science" to find a model he can use in his effort to make psychology a science, and by so doing he discovers what he considers several useful clues.

First, he notes a contrast between psychology and the other sciences in their modes of procedure. Most science begins with a "natural history," the collecting of particular objects or the recording of specific observations. Only when the science has a mass of these items does it attempt to move to abstract generalities like "species" or "genus" or "law," and then everyone realizes that these are in fact abstractions and not the "hard data" of the science. In contrast, traditional psychology, he feels, has always begun with "faculties" or "capacities" or "categories"—extremely abstract concepts—and in so doing psychology has gotten the cart before the horse. Herbart believes that a truly scientific psychology must reverse the field and begin with concrete particulars; [7] otherwise it necessarily degenerates into a mere mythology which no one can take seriously. Unfortunately—and this is a crucial point—there are no obvious concrete particulars which can serve as material for a natural-history stage for psychology in the way that the collection of rocks and minerals can serve as a starting point for mineralogy.

4. *SW* 4:301.  5. *SW* 4:380.  6. *SW* 4:301.  7. *SW* 4:320–23.

Herbart is also struck by certain other features of the usual scientific procedure, and the points he enumerates in the following brief paragraph can hardly be overstressed in any attempt to understand his psychological method.

> Empirical physics, unacquainted with the real forces of nature, has attained certain laws to which phenomena conform. By leading back to the latter it brings unity to the manifold of phenomena. Experiments by means of clever apparatus and calculation—these are the great aids to its discoveries.[8]

According to Herbart's views, then, even the physicist does not know the *real* forces of nature; for, in terms of his metaphysics, the secret of these real forces lies locked up in the natures of the reals and in the causes of their comings and goings, with the resultant perturbations and self-preservations. Other philosophers, such as Kant, also agree that the real forces are unknown. Yet despite this fundamental ignorance, the physicist has managed to evolve laws to which phenomena conform. Since these laws do not concern real forces (which are unknown and unknowable), they are what Herbart calls "fictions," merely something dreamed up as an aid to thought. And this aid lies in the fact that these fictions, when applied or "brought back" to phenomena, do order them. This success of physics in working with and through fictions suggests to Herbart that psychology, which also cannot know real forces, would profit from an analogous set of *fictions*, which could give rise to equally fictitious laws, which in turn would serve to organize those phenomena with which psychology deals.

Herbart also notes the use physics has made of experimental apparatus. But "psychology may not experiment with men, and there is no apparatus for this purpose." Undeniably, Herbart as an innovator would have won a more respected place in the histories of psychology had he turned to empirical work with experimental subjects. As the quotation indicates, however, he refused to do so, though his reasons are, in my opinion, often misunderstood. His "may not" does not reflect

8. *SW* 4:304. See also his prefatory statement 5:185.

a moral judgment based on some concept of human dignity or on the belief that the possibility of harm to the experimental subject was not to be entertained.[9] Surely in this case he would not have said in the next breath, "and there is no apparatus for this purpose." Herbart was not the sort of man to urge morality merely because the means to its contrary were not available. Nor yet is it, as sometimes seems to be implied by the historians,[10] that he was just not clever enough to conceive how psychology could become an experimental science equipped with hardware.

The real point is that Herbart believes that psychology *can not be* experimental. He might have turned to experiments had he believed that mind was a bundle of faculties, capacities, traits, primary abilities or any of the rest—entities which can be isolated and measured or otherwise manipulated. Or if he had thought that mind had some given structure or nature like the solar system or electricity, he might well have made use of observation, experiment, and apparatus somewhat in the modern mode in order to understand its workings. But in his view mind is not an existing natural object with a given structure or with standard components, something that can be taken apart or experimented with. On the contrary, mind is *built up,* for the most part out of the individual's experience, particularly his social experience; and its structure is the specific organization arising out of the mutual relations of the single elements in a given mind at a particular time and place. It is therefore foolish to attempt to observe or experiment with the capacities, nature, or structure of *mind in general,* since there is none. Organization is given a particular, individual mind by *its* specific components.

Since the real problem, as he sees it, is to explain how mind builds itself up out of the mutual relations of components entering it through experience, he is in a sense close to the British associationists, though apparently he became acquainted

9. E.g., T. Ziller, *Allgemeine Pädagogik,* 3d ed. by K. Just (Leipzig: Heinrich Matthes, 1892), p. 53.
10. E.g., E. G. Boring, *A History of Empirical Psychology* (New York and London: D. Appleton-Century Co., 1929), p. 243.

with their work only after the outlines of his own thought were clear. But by and large he tends to regard their "laws of association" as another example of the empiricist trying to look at mind "from the outside." [11] But always his harshest words are reserved for those empiricists who study mind but disregard the social context:

> To plant reason and rationality side by side in the simple human soul is not the work of the Creator but the masterpiece of the psychologists. . . . For what do these psychologists think of the barbarians and semibarbarians, of Bushmen and the inhabitants of New Hollandia? To prove in an empirical fashion that all these men possess so-called reason—that they cannot! They would likewise come to realize that only in the case of a very small fraction of mankind does one observe what they call reason. They would have to conclude that this small part possesses an inherited culture which has grown slowly and gradually.[12]

It was Herbart's emphasis on the cultural dependence of mind which enabled him in 1813 to make the point which we have managed to rediscover and claim as a new insight in working with the "culturally deprived"—"the children of the lower social classes whom one can call really 'speechless' and to whom one must teach the words and expressions at the same time they ought to be learning how to use them." [13]

In short, since "there are no general facts—the true psychological facts lie in the momentary states of individuals," [14] observation and experiment that require the existence of such general facts are impossible for the new science of psychology.

From the paradigm of inquiry in physics, however, Herbart does believe that psychology can adopt the use of mathematics, particularly the calculus, and he sets forth his arguments at some length in his treatise, *On the Possibility and Necessity of Applying Mathematics to Psychology.*[15]

In sum, then, even though psychology cannot be experimental, it can to a considerable extent follow the lead of the

11. *SW* 5:180–81.   12. *SW* 4:244.   13. *SW* 14:73.
14. *SW* 4:310.   15. *SW* 5:93–122.

other sciences, notably physics, in most of the other respects of procedure. It can start with concrete elements rather than vague abstractions. Since such concrete elements "do not lie obviously at hand," they must be searched for or thought up. Once they are obtained, then just as the physicist formulates his laws concerning fictitious forces, so these psychological elements can be treated *as if* they were forces. Psychological laws (however fictitious) can then be formulated through mathematical descriptions of the interplay of these "forces," in the expectation that these equations will serve to describe psychological phenomena just as the fictitious laws of physics give unity and structure to the manifold of natural phenomena. In short, Herbart intends to follow very closely the model he finds in physics—even to developing a "statics and mechanics of mind" comparable to those branches of physics.

The "fictitious" nature of this whole undertaking must not be forgotten, lest Herbart's psychology be completely misunderstood. He got to "reality" and to "real predicates" freed from contradiction when through metaphysics he arrived at the realm of the reals. With that base firm, he can tolerate lack of reality (i.e., fictions) and contradictions at less fundamental levels. Since he sees science and mathematics using fictions without harm—in fact, with great benefit—he believes psychology can do the same. As a result there is an "as if" quality about Herbart's psychology which leads to misunderstanding if his new science is construed as an attempt to assert empirical laws about real psychic forces or real psychic entities.

Herbart's adoption of this general position is, of course, part and parcel of his regarding psychology as a branch of metaphysics, a view to which he believes he is led by the nature of the subject matter involved. Psychology, like all other sciences, must start at the only possible point—experience, particularly "inner" experience; but almost immediately it is confronted by contradictory notions such as the ego or self. It must therefore follow the procedure of metaphysics and enlarge its concepts by discerning the effects in experience of beings and forces which lie beyond and behind experience, though psychology, like metaphysics, can only postulate their existence and not know it. Herbart's whole psychology, therefore, is simply a network of hypotheses designed to explain experience without falling into contradiction. Its aim is to produce general laws, for the human mind is to exhibit a regularity equal to that of Kant's "starry heavens above"; apparent aberrations are, like the wanderings of the planets, to be explicable in terms of some greater, underlying regularities.[16] But these laws are fictions about fictions. It is easy for the reader (and possibly even for Herbart) to forget this when confronted by statements like "At its very beginning the rising conforms to the square of the time if the new perception comes suddenly, but according to the cube of the time if the latter (as is usually the case) develops in a gradual and slow apprehension." [17] Visions of tachistoscopes may dance in the modern reader's head, but such experimental operations are definitely not what is involved here.

Even to conceive of a psychology of this sort is probably difficult for most of us, to say nothing about accepting it. As a result, for our present purposes understanding the bases of Herbart's psychology is far more important than grasping the details, especially the page after page of mathematical calculations which constitute the bulk of his psychological monographs.

Having taken this general procedural model, Herbart then begins to follow it, and his first step is to find the fundamental building blocks, even though they do not "lie obviously at hand." His search brings him to the quotation which furnishes the title for this chapter: "Just as physiology builds the body out of fibres, so psychology builds mind out of series of presentations [*Vorstellungen*]."

Here we must pause to note a linguistic complication. "Presentation" is perhaps the most common English translation for Herbart's term *Vorstellung*, and for that reason I use it throughout this book, despite a certain awkwardness. None of the English possibilities is really good. At the time of Locke, "idea" was a fairly appropriate rendering, but since his day "idea" has been limited rather narrowly to concepts, whereas

16. SW 4:331, 373; 5:202.    17. SW 4:376.

Herbart's term has a much wider range. In modern English to say, "I have an idea of red" is not the same thing as to say "I perceive red" or "I have a sensation of redness." Herbart's term includes percepts as well as concepts, with his "simple presentations" being fairly close (though not exactly equivalent) to what we would call "simple sense impressions" (to which we would not usually refer by "idea").

If one asks, "What are presentations?" Herbart's answer is that "they are the self-preservations of the soul as a real." [18] Thus we are back in metaphysics again at the point we left it at the beginning of this chapter and we face the question, "How does the soul come to have presentations?" Herbart's verbatim answer will (I trust) be clearer in the light of the preceding chapter.

> Between several different simple beings there exists a relation which, with the help of an analogy from the physical world, can be called "press" and "counter-press" [*Druck und Gegendruck*]. Since, to be precise, press is halted movement [*eine aufgehaltene Bewegung*], this relation consists in that something *would be* changed in the simple quality of each being *except that* each one resists and preserves itself in its own quality against the disturbance. These self-preservations are the only thing which really happens [*wahrhaft geschieht*] in nature, and this is the junction of Happening with Being [*die Verbindung des Geschehens mit dem Seyn*].
>
> The self-preservations of the soul are (in part at least and so far as we know them) *presentations* and, what is more, *simple presentations* because the act of self-preservation is simple just as is the being which preserves itself. At the same time there is an unlimited manifold of many such acts which are different precisely as the perturbations are. In view of this, the multiplicity of presentations and the endlessly varied combinations of them present no difficulty. [19]

18. SW 5:387.
19. SW 4:364. The emphasis in the translation reflects that of the original.

In other words, the soul, like the other reals, engages in self-preservation when perturbed by the approach of other reals. But, oddly enough the "ensouled" real also has presentations which either are these acts of self-preservation or are the consequences of them and which vary with the sort of "perturbation" evoking them. These presentations are for Herbart the basic elements which go into the making of mind.

This set of postulates for psychology does, however, raise problems. We have already noted the difficulty involved in having a simple being which only *is* some quality also perform acts of self-preservation (which are certainly not that quality), and we have seen how Herbart does not feel that this assumption violates his fundamental postulates concerning simple being. Now he seems to be pushing our credulity one step further by having some of these simple beings experience presentations as side-effects, so to speak, of their own self-preservations. And what is more, of these presentations there is a "multiplicity" in "endlessly varied combinations," all in some sort of relation to this simple being, the soul.

It certainly seems on the basis of Herbart's statements that the soul is what has presentations. For example, there are the quotations cited at the beginning of this chapter to the effect that soul is the substance of mind and that the soul is called mind when it is spoken of as having presentations. And many more similar passages can be adduced; for example,

> The subject which has presentations is a simple substance and rightly bears the name soul. The presentations contain nothing taken from the outer world; nevertheless they do not arise of themselves but are produced under external conditions and are determined in their quality just as much by those conditions as by the nature of the soul itself. Accordingly the soul itself is not a power which has presentations, but it becomes one under certain conditions.[20]

All such statements seem to assert that the soul has presentations and some commentators have adopted this view despite

20. SW 5:253–54.

its obvious difficulties. But this view seems rather simple-minded, if not impossible, and Herbart is usually more complex, if not more profound.

Others who have worked with Herbart have attempted to avoid the difficulty by pointing out that psychology does not work with pure soul but with "embodied" or "immattered" soul, and they often seem to feel that merely stating this fact solves the problem. Their fact is true enough for Herbart; but as a solution, in itself it is scarcely adequate. For one thing, this is not the course Herbart himself follows when he discusses soul-body relations. As "A Glance at the Relations between Soul and Body" shows,[21] he considers other problems in this context and contemplates only very general relations. He takes up those situations where "pressure" (*Druck*) exists because bodily conditions prevent the recall of an idea (as in sleep), or where there is "resonance" (*Resonanz*) when the recall is facilitated by intoxication or passion, or finally where synergistic states exist. Or else in this context he emphasizes the mutual relations between the soul and the brain in language which makes the soul the site of presentations:

> Now between the soul and the body there is the same mutuality of causal relation as there is mutually between the brain and the nervous system. Thus all the presentations, desires and feelings, *though collected in the simple being of the soul, nevertheless cannot* conform merely to the inner laws of their own mutual influences, but their change and relations are the result of all states in all individual elements of the brain and nervous system.[22]

In short, merely noting that the soul is now linked with the matter of the body does not solve the question of how the presentation can be in the soul or, if they are not there, where they are.[23]

21. SW 4:384–86.
22. SW 6:298. The emphasis in the translation reflects that of the original.
23. H. Ströhle, *Herbarts Psychologie in Verhältnis zu seinem Erziehungsideal,* (Stuttgart: C. Belser, 1903) summarizes the problem, citing the earlier work of Quäbecker, Osterman, and Hartenstein (pp. 16–18).

We get closer to what appears to be Herbart's own way of attempting to solve the problem if we are careful to note the point he makes explicitly—that to talk about the location of the soul in the body is to employ a fiction, since the soul, as one of the reals for which "time and space are nothing," really isn't anywhere. With this realization that we are now in the realm of fictions and images, we can then turn to a passage which, though far from pellucid, probably puts us on the right track to the real problem if not to an adequate solution:

> The contrast between *soul* and *matter* is not a contrast in the what of the beings but a contrast in our manner of apprehending [*Auffassung*]. Matter, represented [*vorgestellt*] as a spatial real with spatial power (as we are accustomed to thinking of it) belongs neither to the realm of being nor to that of true happening [*wirkliches Geschehen*] but is a mere appearance. This same matter is real, however, as a sum of simple beings, *and in these beings something truly happens which has as a consequence the appearance of spatial existence.*
>
> The explanation of matter rests simply and solely in this, that one shows how, to the inner states of being (the self-preservations) certain spatial determinations belong as necessary means of apprehension by observers, which spatial determinations, because they are nothing real, must correspond to those inner states so that an appearance of attraction and repulsion arises. The equilibrium of these last two determines for matter its degree of density, likewise its elasticity, its crystaline form in free condensation—in a word, its essential properties which, as such, are based in the qualities of the simple beings.[24]

To a considerable extent, Herbart is simply repeating here the doctrine of his metaphysics. The reals are just what each is. But because they come and go in intelligible space, they give rise to "true events" or "what really happens." These events are "true" and something "really" happens, however, because these events reflect directly the *formal relations* involved in the perturbations and self-preservations of reals in

24. SW 4:365.

the realm of true being, though they are not indicative of the *material content*—that is, the true natures or simple qualities of the reals involved. This was Herbart's metaphysical doctrine from the standpoint of epistemology—How can we gain any knowledge of true being, which, strictly speaking, we cannot know? His answer is that our knowledge of true events gives us, within limits, some knowledge, since the formal relations of true events do correspond with the actual relations between real beings.

But now we need to remind ourselves where this intelligible space is within which these true events occur, within which the reals "come and go." Herbart's answer that true events are "images in mind" made it possible for him to move, more or less plausibly, from the simple, unchanging world of the reals to the changing, complicated, and contradictory world of experience. But having made that difficult transition by the aid of images in mind, Herbart seems in some difficulty in explaining these images. Presentations seem to end up as a "middle ground" between noumena and phenomena; that is, they are not reals or true predicates of reals, nor yet are they phenomena, since they are the medium through which phenomena appear. They are a bridge or halfway house between the objective and subjective worlds.[25] As such, they have rather odd metaphysical status, and are plainly tinctured with the dye of "fiction." As a result, they are hard to talk about, and it is no wonder that Herbart falls back on language which suggests that the "ensouled" reals "have" presentations even though they do not. But since, as we have seen, all psychology is for Herbart a fictional or postulational system (regardless of how he sounds), we should perhaps not worry too much about the actual status and location of the presentations. Nevertheless, the point has been worth some laboring, since once it is past the rest of Herbart's system follows fairly easily.

If these and some other difficulties are disregarded, Her-

25. *SW* 6:272. Compare B. Petronievics, "Über Herbarts Lehre vom intelligiblem Raume," *Archiv für Geschichte der Philosophie* 27; new series 20 (1914); 157–60.

bart has succeeded in finding in the presentation that simple element he was seeking. His next problem is to suggest how these presentations interact to produce psychic phenomena, and in this part of the inquiry too he continues to follow his physical model. Using his fiction that the presentations may be treated *as if* they were forces (even though they are not), and starting with the simplest possible situation within which two such forces could interact, he attempts to develop increasingly complex situations until he has developed a set of laws which he believes can organize all the diverse phenomena of mind. It is the presentations working in collaboration or in opposition to each other which determine psychic phenomena and so build mind, not "faculties" or the "structure" of mind a priori.

The simplest situation is that in which a mind containing a single simple presentation encounters a second simple presentation. (This situation is, of course, as fictitiously simple as that of Newton's first law, which portrays a universe containing only one body in uniform, rectilinear motion, with no second body existing anywhere to affect the speed and direction of the first one.) By and large, says Herbart, these two presentations will tend to "arrest" (*hemmen*) or mutually inhibit each other. This is what colliding forces do. There is also a metaphysical basis for assuming mutual arrest in that the presentations are part of the efforts at perturbation and self-preservation of reals coming together, and hence the presentations may well exhibit similar tendencies toward mutual destruction. Finally, there is a psychological argument in favor of asserting that the presentations will tend to inhibit each other: if there were no such mutual resistance, all presentations would merge into one, and the content of consciousness would be a unity rather than that manifold of varied elements with which experience presents us.[26]

Yet it also seems plausible that the clash between presen-

26. SW 4:374. "Arrest" has been used as the translation merely because it is the traditional choice of most English translation. "Inhibition" would be closer to modern usage.

tations will not be equally severe in all instances—that some pairs of presentations may tend to blend with little or no reciprocal resistance into a fairly harmonious whole of some sort, whereas the opposition between other pairs will prevent anything more than an uneasy amalgamation. Herbart sees as the causative factor here the degree of similarity or difference between the two presentations involved. Presentations of different kinds usually would not oppose each other but would blend together into "complexions" (*Complexionen*). For example, colors would not oppose sounds, and hence black and a noise may become elements in a complexion which is ultimately called "dog." Increasing the visual presentation of blackness does not diminish the aural presentation of barking, and vice versa. Presentations of the same kind, however, would oppose each other, and consequently the conjunction of two colors, red and blue, produce a "fusion" (*Versmelzungen*), purple, in which an increase in the strength of the blueness does diminish the redness in the purple of their fusion.

To get a base line, Herbart takes two presentations standing in complete opposition to each other. When these two presentations mutually inhibit each other, the total amount of mutual arrest (*Hemmungssumme*) will be distributed between them in inverse proportion to their strengths—that is, the stronger will inhibit the weaker in direct proportion to its strength. This postulate is, of course, no more empirical than was Newton's concerning the uniform rectilinear motion of a single body; it is simply what Herbart would call a tool for thought.

This reasoning leads Herbart to his basic equation for the statics of mind, expressing the distribution of this "sum of arrest" between two opposing presentation, $a$ and $b$: $a + b : a :: b : ab/(a + b)$. This works out so that the answer for $a$ (or $a$ as a remainder) equals $a - [b^2/(a + b)]$, and the answer for $b$ as a remainder is $b - [ab/(a + b)] = b^2/(a + b)$. Since, then, $b = 0$ only if $a$ is infinite, presentation $a$ can never completely obscure presentation $b$. In other words, if there are only two opposing presentations in mind, the two will always exist in fusion, without the total loss of *b*. But if the equation is expanded to include a third opposing presentation, *c*, then it is possible to work out values which do produce the result $c = 0$ (e.g., if $a = b$ and $a + b = 3c$.) [27]

But the result, $c = 0$, does not mean that *c* has been destroyed; it means, rather, that its force has been temporarily rendered ineffective in the mind in question. "Strictly speaking, nothing in the mind is lost." [28] (This assumption that presentations persist in mind is interesting in view of the fact that the perturbations and self-preservations of the reals, the activities which give rise to presentations, do not persist once the reals are no longer "together." Herbart offers no metaphysical or psychological reason; he simply seems forced to this concession by the brute fact of experience that "ideas" do persist in "mind.") Therefore *c* is not lost, but in Herbart's language has "sunk beneath the threshhold of consciousness." But for a presentation to be "above the threshhold of consciousness" or be "in consciousness" in my mind does not mean that *I* am conscious of it. For Herbart the proposition, "A presentation is in consciousness" is not the same as "I am conscious of my presentation." Herbart is attempting to work not with our vague, subjective inner perceptions, but with the fundamental interactions between our presentations considered as acting, objective forces. Thus if, for example, the solution of the equation given above produces an answer, $c = 1$, presentation *c* is "above the threshhold of consciousness" whether we are aware of *c* or not. Herbart then piles up tables for different values for the various presentations and for more complicated situations with a larger number of presentations.

Since my readers' calculus is probably as rusty as mine, there is little point in going far into the mathematical details. It is, however, important for us to recognize that here and in all the other calculations which constitute the bulk of Herbart's psychological works, he sees these mathematical descriptions as his major contribution because they render psychic phenomena scientific—that is, statable in mathematically expressed

27. *SW* 5:288–90.    28. *SW* 4:409; 5:387; 4:372.

laws. Herbart was convinced that movements of presentations within mind are as subject to law as are the motions of the heavenly bodies; if Newton's laws and the complicated calculations based upon them have organized astronomy, Herbart hopes his laws and computations do the same for psychology.

The process of "sinking" (*Senkung*) already described, in which opposing presentations mutually arrest each other and lose part of their original force in an equilibrium or fusion or perhaps are even obscured so some of them sink below the threshhold of consciousness, suggests certain other fundamental considerations. For these two points we should at least glance at the simplest equations which Herbart offers as stating these phenomena.

The first concerns the "movement" of presentations or the "mechanics" of mind.

> Among the very numerous and, for the most part, highly complicated laws of the movement of presentations the following is the simplest: while the sum of arrest is in the process of sinking, the sinking quantum is at every instant proportional to the quantum as yet unarrested. From this, one determines the entire course of the sinking to the statical point.
>
> Note. Mathematically the above law may be expressed $\sigma = S(1-e^{-t})$, in which $S$ = the sum of arrest, $t$ = the elapsed time, $\sigma$ = the suppressed quantum of the combined presentations within time $t$ [$e$ is, of course, the base of the natural system of logarithms].
>
> If this latter [i.e., the suppressed quantum of the combined presentations] is apportioned among the individual presentations, it is evident that those which lie below the statical threshhold are driven there very quickly, whereas all the rest do not get to their statical point in a finite time. On account of this latter circumstance the presentations of men who are awake, even in the most equitable state of mind, are always in gentle motion. This is also the basic reason why the inner perception never encounters an object that holds it completely still.[29]

29. *SW* 4:372. See also 5:339.

This passage merits quotation not so much for its details (though the formula is basic to Herbart's further development of his mechanics of mind) as for the relatively simple example it offers in small compass of Herbart's general way of working in psychology. He sets up the first equation given in this chapter and by its use finds that under certain conditions presentations can sink below the threshhold of consciousness. He then undertakes to evolve a mathematical statement describing this process of sinking. Trying out this second equation he finds that his mathematical equations tell him that some presentations can never reach their statical point in any finite amount of time—that some presentations are always in motion in mind, sinking through consciousness toward the statical threshhold. As a result, when Herbart says that "the mind is always in motion" he finds his ultimate warrant not in introspection or in observing small boys; this view is, so to speak, thrust on him by his calculations based on the most simple rational postulates he can conceive. To be sure, he cannot accept results which are contrary to experience. In consequence, after nearly all his long mathematical sections we find him making a quick check with experience. So here, our observation of others and our introspection have produced the platitudinous metaphor that consciousness is a stream, not a stagnant pond. Since common opinion is that "thoughts" continually flow through mind, Herbart is reassured about the results of his calculations. One may, of course, criticize Herbart by charging that his tests are rather casual or that he accepts the easy cases which make his results sound plausible rather than seeking the difficult ones which might prove his laws wrong. In extenuation it might be urged that Herbart sees as his chief task the development of a comprehensive body of postulates, and he feels he cannot stop for exhaustive tests of each part. If even a rough-and-ready check indicates to him that he is making general sense, he is content to move on to grapple with the next problem.

This manner of working is in part the origin of a slippery and much debated problem we shall encounter later concerning the relation between Herbart's psychology and his pedagogy. Herbart wrote most of his pedagogical works very early in his career, and many contain rather explicit statements about psychological phenomena. Yet when he eventually conducts his investigations in psychology, the field to which he turned his attention last of all, he never modifies or retracts these educational pronouncements; the statements merely become more complicated and more technical. This fact, among others, has given rise to the suspicion that Herbart developed his psychology out of his pedagogy rather than basing his pedagogy on psychology as he insisted he did.

Several factors interact to produce this situation. One is that Herbart developed the *general* outlines of all parts of his system simultaneously while he was still in Switzerland. Granted that psychology was the last field he worked out in detail and granted that "in general" and "in detail" are rather gross classifications and we cannot know precisely how much detail he had achieved in any field before his first monograph in that area appeared, still Herbart had considerable psychological machinery in hand fairly early, as is evident from his Bremen lecture of 1804 ("On the Standpoint for Judging Pestalozzi's Method of Instruction"), in which he discusses mind, reason, and will as built out of presentations, the mutual arrest of presentations, and similar psychological topics.[30] Certainly not all of his psychology was a late development.

A second factor in producing the problem is the kind of psychological inquiry Herbart conducts. When he says that more investigation is necessary on some topic he does not, of course, mean an experimental attempt to isolate or measure some psychological phenomenon; he means more work with the calculus to achieve a more adequate *mathematical description* of some phenomenon of common experience.

Finally, he often refers to pedagogical examples because psychology, as an application of metaphysics, must begin like all other metaphysics with experience and must return to experience to describe and explain it; and education constitutes a part of experience both relevant to psychology and familiar

30. E.g., *SW* 1:306–7. His own statement (*SW* 9:341) implies the contrary, however.

to Herbart. But the relation between his psychology and his pedagogy is not that to which we are accustomed, though we too believe that psychology can suggest means and hindrances to education. Herbart would be more likely to change his mathematical description than his pedagogical prescription, because he feels that psychological theory should conform to the facts rather than that fictional theory should distort the facts. In this sense those who insist that pedagogy plays the dominant role in the interrelation between the two fields are clearly right. They are wrong, however, insofar as they imply either that Herbart had no psychological theory until he published the *Textbook for Psychology* in 1816 or that his psychological theory was cobbled up simply as a justification for his pedagogy.

The third basic equation concerns recall. As was noted earlier, the fact that a presentation has sunk below the threshhold of consciousness means not that it is destroyed but only that it is no longer active. The further interplay of forces within consciousness may lead to the recall or "rising" (*Hebung*) of presentations previously driven below the threshhold. A suppressed concept may rise simply because the forces suppressing it are in their turn suppressed, and in this "immediate" or "nonmediated" rising the formerly suppressed concept interacts anew with the content of consciousness. Or in mediated recall, the advent of a new presentation similar to the one which has been suppressed may "aid" the suppressed one to rise. The speed of this rising depends on the degree of similarity between the two presentations. Here if $\Pi$ represents the suppressed concept, $P$ the new concept, $r$ the remainder of $P$ not arrested and $\rho$ the remainder of $\Pi$ not arrested, then the help in rising given by $P$, the new concept, to $\Pi$, the old one, is expressed by $r\rho/\Pi$ and the aid $\Pi$ gives to $P$ by the expression $r\rho/\Pi$. Now this aid given by $P$ to $\Pi$ is greater before the union of $r$ with $\rho$ than it is after some arrest has begun; consequently Herbart lets $\omega$ stand for that portion of $\rho$ which has already united with $r$ and been brought into consciousness. Then the equation $(r\rho/\Pi) \cdot [(\rho - \omega)/\rho] \cdot dt = d\omega$ indicates how the influence of $P$ on $\Pi$ to bring up a new part of $\rho$ into consciousness is determined by the amount of that part remaining after subtracting that part which has already passed up over the threshhold $(\rho - \omega)$. Then the equation $\omega = \rho[(1 - e)(-rt/\Pi)]$ shows clearly, says Herbart, how $\omega$ depends on $\rho$, $r$, $t$, and $\Pi$ [31] that is, how the amount of the suppressed $\Pi$ which can be recalled into consciousness depends on the amount of it which can blend with $P$, the amount of $P$ that can blend with $\Pi$, the elapsed time, and the size of $\Pi$.

Since the preceding examples constitutes merely simple fundamentals, what Herbart does when he *really* becomes involved in mathematical psychology can be left to the reader's imagination; or he may consult the *Textbook of Psychology* or *Psychology as a Science* for himself. The preceding sample has been cited at some length merely because it is a necessary introduction to two concepts in Herbart's psychology which are important because of their further relevance, particularly to education: "vaulting" (*Wölbung*) and "tapering" (*Zuspitzung*). When the new presentation $P$ begins to recall $\Pi$, the whole mass of $\Pi$ tends to be pulled up, producing a kind of vault or arch. But with the passage of time, that remainder of $\Pi$, $\rho$, which can most easily blend with $P$'s $r$, is pulled further and further up and into consciousness while the less congruent parts sink back, with the vault now tapering to a point at $\rho$.

A mechanical analogy may serve to suggest the general process. When the beater is pulled from a bowl of whipped cream, at the outset the whole surface of the cream tends to rise with the beater. This is vaulting. But as the beater is pulled farther out, the more distant parts of the surface sink back, but the cream immediately surrounding the beater is drawn to a point (tapering).

These processes are important on several counts. For one thing, they build up out of presentations the more complicated cognitive apparatus such as concepts, categories, and judgments, which are for Herbart not given a priori and are not the products of special faculties like reason or understanding.

31. SW 4:376; 5:369.

For concepts, for example, with repetition of vaulting and tapering the similarities between the various presentations involved are reinforced and the differences further minimized in each new successive fusion. In this way the concept or general notion emerges as a sort of composite photograph of the major similarities among these various particular presentations, a portrait progressively freed from the particularities of each individual presentation. But the concept can never through this process become *entirely* free from all traces of these particular determinations. As a result, a truly adequate logical concept, which ideally should be completely free from any singularity, remains only an ideal.[32]

Vaulting and tapering are likewise involved in making judgments (i.e., formulating propositions), and they have accompanying feelings which also have significant effects:

> Vaulting produces tension; tapering gives satisfaction. As a result there is pleasure in judgment, and hence come premature judgments and nonsense. This harms attention as well as thought. The observer would have noted more had he not gone away satisfied with one kind of tapering; in the case of the thinker, the vaulting would have been more perfect and would have risen higher. Also the pleasure in judgment spoils creativity. Critical minds are seldom productive.
>
> The observer goes from one vaulting to another in succession. Mere perception does not sort out the predicates; it is less precise. Because the vaulting was defective, so is the tapering. From this, incorrect repetition often results. Language, through the ambiguity of words, plays a part here insofar as constant correction does not counteract it.[33]

Herbart is not, however, interested in presentations merely as presentations, since in his view they become transformed into, and hence are the source of, many elements of the "inner"

32. *SW* 4:326, 377, 394; 8:240–41.  33. *SW* 4:329.

life. The feelings, the desires, and the will all have their origin in presentations.

Feelings come about in several different ways. Some arise out of fusions formed by opposed presentations, where the pleasantness or unpleasantness depends on the amount of opposition between them. Other feelings (those properly so called, according to Herbart) have their origin in the strain which the "rising" produced by a new presentation puts on the ties an older presentation has already formed with one or more others. Thus the sight of an object belonging to a dead friend evokes the thought of him, but simultaneous recollection of his death tends to repress the thought and thus by its counterpull produces a painful feeling. Pleasant feelings arise in the contrary situations, when the presentations associated with the older one all facilitate its rising or recall.

The desires are closely connected with the feelings. Let us take a situation giving a painful feeling. When presentation $A$ is lifted toward the threshhold of consciousness by the appearance of a new presentation, $C$, $A$ is simultaneously depressed by its earlier relations to $B$. If $B$ is weak, however, $A$ will be raised above the threshhold of consciousness, but the feelings of effort by which the resistance of $B$ is overcome will be a desire, and $A$ will be active in consciousness as an object of desire.

Both feelings and desires are highly variable as compared with the stability of that circle of thought developed from presentations. "The mature man feels little of the joys and sorrows of his youth; but what the boy learns correctly, the grey-beard still knows." [34] This results because the feelings and desires are not related to presentations in general (i.e., their total mass) but to particular presentations, and as a result they rise and sink with that presentation to which they are attached. There is also the further consequence that different and even conflicting desires and feelings can exist side by side, since they are not directly subject to that unification produced by mutual arrest and recall as are the presentations. In this way

34. *SW* 4:380.

Herbart preserves the general unity of consciousness and yet provides for the experiential fact of conflicting desires and feelings.

The will, in turn, is only a particular form of desire—one whose realization is seen as possible. Thus Napoleon willed as emperor but merely desired as a prisoner on Saint Helena.[35] With the will assimilated to the desires in this fashion, it clearly has definite objects just as do the desires. The act of will is thus a striving for some feasible desired object. This point clarifies certain features of the manner in which the fundamental ethical ideas were stated. One, it is now clear why the idea of perfection was said to be intension, extension, and concentration of the will without regard for its *objects,* and hence how this ideal could be viewed as purely formal (as purged of the material content constituted by the objects). It is also clear why inner freedom is the only freedom of which such a will is capable. Will, to be actually effective in gaining its objects, is dependent on factors outside itself; and if these fail, the frustrated will is no longer a will at all, but only a desire.[36] For this kind of will, then, the only possible freedom is harmony between its subjective and objective aspects—that is, its apparently feasible desires are such as the involuntary moral judgment can approve.

As we saw as early as chapter 1, this effort of Herbart's to develop the will out of the presentations was always a controversial feature of his thought. His reasons for making this attempt in spite of the opposition he must have known it would encounter are quite clear. In many discussions of human action, even in our own day, the will is much talked about, but it remains something of a "black box"; it is the source of many important influences but its inner workings are veiled from our view. Thus, as Herbart never tires of telling us,[37] Kant's "transcendental freedom" taken in a strict sense seems to remove the will forever beyond human understanding and control. Yet ethics, politics, and education, to name only three

35. SW 4:340.   36. SW 2:98–99.
37. E.g., SW 9:290; 1:261; 2:135; 3:151; 10:70.

attempts to improve the human condition, all depend upon the human will and require our ability to do something about the will. Herbart cannot see the human will as divine or innate, though certain congenital factors arising out of the union of the soul with the body are involved. But, as Herbart sees it, the will—strong or weak, good or bad—is largely fashioned out of experience, our contact with people and things. If the presentations are the bearers of this experience, then they are, to that extent, the determiners of the will. At least in the very general sense that Herbart sees the will (or personality, or the drives, or whatever mechanism is seen as performing the operations assigned by Herbart and his predecessors to the "will") as the product of the individual's experience in life, he has more twentieth-century allies than do his nineteenth-century detractors. "The circle of thought" seems at first glance a rather exotic equivalent for "personality structure," but in a good many respects the differences are more apparent than real.

This discussion of Herbart's psychology has to this point ignored a term which later came to be preeminently associated with it—"apperception." As we shall see in chapters 12 and 13, many of the Herbartians saw the theory of apperception as Herbart's great contribution and felt it epitomized his whole psychological and educational doctrine. The prominent American educator W. T. Harris (who was an enthusiastic Hegelian and not a Herbartian) offers a rather typical comment in his preface to the American translation of the *Textbook of Psychology*:

> A careful examination of the pedagogical writings of the followers of Herbart shows that the important thought which has become so fruitful is that of "apperception." . . . It is in fact the central thought from which the author proceeds and to which he always returns.[38]

Yet after listing a half-dozen or so sections in the book where Herbart uses the term, Harris ends by recommending Lazarus's *Life of the Soul* and Steinthal's *Introduction to Psychology and*

38. W. T. Harris, "Editor's Preface" to *A Textbook in Psychology*, trans. Margaret K. Smith [New York: D. Appleton-Century Co., 1891], p. iv.

*Philology* on the ground that "their grasp of this important thought seems to me a great advance in philosophic clearness over the exposition made by Herbart himself." [39] There can be some question whether Herbart "had" the concept in the same sense in which it was later used or perhaps whether he had it in clear enough form for him to be able to recognize the later variants of it which passed under his name.

The issue here can be clarified if we begin by noting some major points of view to which Herbart's theory was generally opposed. First and most obvious among these was the doctrine that the mental life was presided over by a set of faculties—"that presentations are received by the sensibility, preserved by the memory, reproduced and freshly combined by the imagination," and so on.[40] Sense impressions were thus worked over in rather mysterious ways by these faculties thought to be inherent in every human mind. Second, Herbart's general position was also marked off from the doctrine of those sensationalists who saw mind as a passive wax tablet on which impressions scratched their traces. Third, Herbart stood apart from those of the associationists who believed that ideas were linked together as units by the various laws of association.

In other words, whereas the faculty psychologists saw the impressions as worked over by the faculties, Herbart attributed this reworking to the specific fund of presentations already organized in the mind—to the apperceptive mass or circle of thought. Whereas the sensationalists regarded mind as passively receiving whatever was presented to it, Herbart believed that the existing presentational mass actively sorted, reworked, and put into new combinations whatever new presentations it encountered, and that the new presentations in their turn disturbed the existing system. Finally, whereas associationists tended to regard the ideas as mechanically linked together unit by unit, rather like beads on a string, Herbart suggested a much more active interplay between the elements associated,

39. W. T. Harris, "Editor's Preface," p. xviii. M. Lazarus, *Das Leben der Seele* (Berlin: F. Dümmler, 1883–97). H. Steinthal, *Einleitung in die Psychologie und Sprachwissenschaft.* (Berlin: F. Dümmler, 1881).
40. *SW* 4:302.

with greater mutual changes wrought in each element in consequence of this association. (These are insights for which he is still honored.)

If, then, Herbart's general position is loosely defined as the view that the existing content of mind acts upon each new presentation it receives and that this content is in turn restructured by the influence of each new presentation, we have a doctrine distinct from several other well-known views contemporary with it, and probably worthy of a label. Although Herbart took the word (but in a very different sense) from Leibnitz [41] and although he made relatively little use of it himself and never called his psychological doctrine the "theory of apperception" or anything like it, it is understandable that this label was put on his view as a whole and that the general position was attached to his name. Boring summarizes the situation quite correctly: "Herbart is perhaps more famous for his doctrine of apperception than for anything else. . . . Yet Herbart made less use of apperception in psychology than might be supposed." [42]

The label is, of course, a very general one, and a rather wide variety of doctrines can fall under the definition offered above and still differ markedly from Herbart's views at many points. And historically this did occur, though any detailed tracing of psychological developments falls outside the scope of this book. "Apperception" became one of the watchwords of the Herbartians, and Herbart is often praised for fathering the general view, though what is meant by this is often quite different from Herbart's view and sometimes even contradicts it.

Here as elsewhere, however, the Herbartians cannot be charged with making up a doctrine out of whole cloth and then attributing it to Herbart. The following passage is a fairly typical statement by Herbart himself on some matters which were later seen as fundamental in the theory of apperception. It is worth noting as an example of what Herbart meant by apperception, even though some of the terms and processes mentioned in it have not been explained in the preceding

41. SW 5:216–19. For Leibnitz see *The Monadology*, sections 14, 29, 30.
42. E. G. Boring, *History of Empirical Psychology*, p. 245.

pages. Its educational significance will become clearer in the light of the next chapter.

Upon a man's imagination and thought depend his sense-perception [*Anschauen*] and attention [*Merken*], especially his interest. Each man lives in his own world even in the same environment.

Attention is partly involuntary and passive, partly voluntary and active. The latter is not involved here, since it is connected with self-control. The former has its foundations partly in the momentary state of mind during the act of observing, but is also partly determined by the older presentation which what is observed reproduces.

(*a*) Four circumstances are to be observed in the mental state during the act of attention: the strength of the impression, the freshness of the suspectibility,[43] the degree of opposition to the presentations already in consciousness, and the degree to which the mind was more or less occupied previously.

(*b*) As regards the cooperation of the older presentations which are reproduced, these can be unfavorable to involuntary attention by being either too much or too little, inasmuch as in both cases it is impossible for the new perception to adjust to itself the existing state of mind. More precisely, if the new presentation finds too little or nothing old with which to combine, it is usually too weak by itself not to be overpowered by the other presentations which have already collected and combined to a greater extent. If a superabundance of old similar presentations appears, however, the susceptibility for the new is thus weakened. On the contrary, attention is generally favored by two circumstances: first, if the new is in contrast with the old so that the reproduction is strong enough for association without any harm through an excess of susceptibility; second, when a development [44] of old concepts is promoted by the new, something they themselves would

43. By "susceptibility" Herbart means a general openness to sense-impressions, a quality which he sees as at its height in childhood but as declining with age (*SW* 4:384–85).
44. Presentations are often thrust below the threshold of consciousness before they have been completely assimilated, and this "undigested" mass must be reworked when it again arises in consciousness.

have striven for in any event. In this case it establishes new combinations while it simultaneously satisfies a desire, or at least produces pleasant feeling. This happens especially with previously aroused expectation.

Note. Attention and expectation as the two stages of interest also belong to the fundamental concepts of general pedagogy.[45]

Although many of the precise meanings in this passage cannot yet be clear, it does illustrate what Herbart meant by his belief that education would find its means and hindrances in psychology. The way the existing content of mind affects new material presented to it, and vice versa, necessarily has implications for any teaching which seeks to present new materials to mind.

Finally, with feelings, desires, and the will all dependent upon presentations in their interrelations, the proper management of presentations, both their acquisition and their further modification, becomes a determining factor in the development of the human being. As a result, formal education, which is a primary means of controlling these presentations, acquires major importance; and it is easy to see why Herbart is always being led by his other studies back to an interest in education. And within education, particularly an education which seeks to produce a will of the proper sort, the most important part will be that which is most concerned with the ordering and organizing of presentations. This fact accounts for the primary role played in Herbart's pedagogical theory by "instruction." A "scientific" (mathematical) psychology is to make possible a scientific educational theory (one marked by control and prediction):

> The idea of a mathematical psychology . . . does not merely permit us to assume that we can affect the pupil, but also that particular actions produce particular effects and that by continual investigation and proper observation we can approach ever closer to the prediction of this result.[46]

45. SW 4:410.   46. SW 3:151.

# 9

## "Instruction Builds the Circle of Thought; Education, the Character"

The aim of education [1] is virtue, morality. But as was clear from the discussion of the moral ideas in chapter 6, the basis of morality is essentially contained in the idea of inner freedom, the will that wills in accordance with its moral insight. This insight consists of a balanced coordination between all the five basic moral ideas, along with an undetermined amount of knowledge necessary if these ideas are to be applied to human life. [2] This part of the prescription for morality is fairly simple.

The will is a more complex matter. [3] For Herbart, as we have seen, the will is not a faculty to be trained but a structure to be built. The child enters the world without a will of its own, but with only a "wild impetuosity." Since the building blocks with which the will is formed are the presentations, that education which seeks to build a will of a particular kind can do so only by providing the correct kind of presentations. "There

1. Chapter title is from SW 2:169. The quotation continues: "The latter is nothing without the former; herein lies the whole of my pedagogy." See also 3:348; 3:152.
2. SW 1:259; 2:165; 3:343; 10:71.   3. SW 2:165.

is no independent faculty of willing, but the will has its roots in the circle of thought, not in the particulars of what is known, but in the combination and total effect of the presentations which have been had." [4] Education which seeks to build the character must, therefore, control the presentations.

Yet presentations of many sorts flood in upon the child, for to have experience at all is to have presentations. Life both in and outside the schoolroom constantly produces them. Obviously the teacher cannot control them all; but the more of them he can regulate, the closer he can come to doing his job.

> The school cannot be the complete educational institution, at least for individuals. Of the totality of forces which can educate man, it has only a definite part, a particular class, and this is the bodies of knowledge [*Wissenschaften*]. What the world, example, social intercourse, the family and, above all, the silent proper activity of a character [*Gemüth*] working internally can contribute—this the school does not have in its control.[5]

As a result, the aim of Herbart's pedagogical doctrine is to help the teacher utilize effectively those parts of the pupil's experience which the teacher can manage. In the very nature of the situation, the teacher can most readily control such matters as the materials studied and the pupil's relations with his teacher and with his fellow pupils. As a result these areas become the chief concern of Herbart's pedagogy.

"The educability of the child is the fundamental concept of pedagogy." [6] Yet wherever the teacher operates, certain factors limit his effectiveness. "To make or re-make a human being, this education cannot do." [7] Yet Herbart's very awareness of these limitations reinforces his conviction that the teacher must all the more be able to do well what lies within his doing.

From psychology the teacher soon learns two "hindrances"

---

4. SW 10:140–41. See also SW 2:18; 3:152; 1:308.
5. SW 3:291.   6. SW 10:69.   7. SW 9:139.

to his educative omnipotence. The first is the student's previous experience, the presentational masses he brings with him when he enters school. Were the child at birth a tabula rasa, many others would have written on this slate before it comes into the teacher's hands. Masses of presentations, with the desires and the wishes developed from them, have already formed, and the teacher is faced with an existing structure. Like the person remodeling an old house, the teacher can never start completely afresh. He can to a limited extent demolish some of the objectionable features he finds, but for the most part his scope is restricted to alterations and additions, and even these modifications are limited to a considerable extent by the form of the existing structure.

The second tether on the teacher's ambition and power is the pupil's natural endowment. Pupils would vary even if the teacher received them direct from the womb. Herbart is much impressed by these congenital physiological differences. For example, he devotes to them six of his *Letters on the Application of Psychology to Education* and frequently refers to them in his educational writings.[8]

Herbart's recognition of these limitations has several important consequences for his educational doctrine. One is his effort to inculcate a proper professional modesty and even humility in the teacher. The teacher must hope for no more superior a product than his raw material makes possible.[9] A second consequence is Herbart's emphasis on individualized instruction and the procedural flexibilities which must attend it. "Just as any theory in different instances of application must be used now in this way now in that without being changed in its fundamental principles, so must pedagogy wear a very different guise according to circumstances and yet remain true to its fundamental rules."[10] Consequently, when one of his pupils in Switzerland proves unsuited (by reason of faulty previous education, the family's wealth and position, and his personality and habits) to the program which Herbart has

8. SW 9:350–69. E.g., SW 2:86, 120–21; 10:69, 171.
9. SW 10:70; 9:144, 147–48, 350.    10. SW 14:225.

planned for him, the tutor does not hesitate to redesign his plans. "It (psychology) can never substitute for observation of the pupil; the individual can only be discovered, not deduced." [11] Herbart frequently warns, consequently, that plans must always take into account the particular pupil, teacher, and situation. As a result he tends not merely toward individualized instruction, but toward the instruction of individuals and is extremely suspicious of lesson plans and programs devised for whole schools or school systems. Apparently feeling (with some justification, as contemporary and subsequent criticism proved) that his systematic and manipulative procedures will be charged with producing a race of robots, he frequently talks about his care in preserving the pupil's individuality. Actually, in terms of Herbart's own system, this individuality can never be in danger, for the teacher is unable to eradicate it even if he so chooses.

If these are the limitations which the teacher must face in his raw material, what does he have on the positive side to work with? Having observed small boys, Herbart is convinced that two characteristics are widely distributed among them: they are active and they are powerful—a generalization with which few teachers and parents would be disposed to quibble. The educational question for Herbart, then, is how to harness this energy and guide it toward morality.

As was noted in the discussion of the moral ideas, not all of them are equally accessible to the child when he first starts school. "Perfection" in its aspect of extension or the directing of the will toward a wide range of objects is the one which is initially feasible, and its base is manysidedness of interest.

> Consequently the work is to be undertaken in such a way that manysidedness of interest is aimed at. And since the extension of power is produced by presenting to the pupil a throng of objects which stimulate him and set him in motion, if the task is to be accomplished a third something is placed between the master and pupil with which

11. *SW* 2:9; 1:149, 188; 2:39–43, 69; 9:120–21; 14:180–81; 2:16; 3:4; 2:83–84; 2:30–34.

the master busies the pupil. This is to instruct. The third thing is the object about which instruction is given.[12]

In this way "instruction" acquires a chronological priority in education. But this priority of instruction is logical as well as chronological, inasmuch as the choice of this "object" lies within the teacher's power, though his choice is admittedly restricted by considerations of availability, appropriateness, and other factors. When these more particular limitations are added to the general problems of will building, discussions of instruction become almost as long as the process itself. But for Herbart instruction never loses its status as the teacher's most feasible and effective tool for building character.

The other two chief parts of pedagogy, "government" (*Regierung*) and "discipline" (*Zucht*), also help produce the good will within the pupil and are part of the teacher's responsibility. They both cooperate with instruction, but they are less flexible and effective tools.

The government of children—or "classroom management" as it was christened later—is closely akin to discipline, as the common meanings of the words imply. They often use the same means for their rather different purposes, and unfortunately, in Herbart's opinion, can easily become confused in the teacher's mind.[13] As compared with discipline and instruction, however, government is rather low level, a necessary condition for the other two, but little more than a necessary evil. "Moral improvement does not come about through the compulsions of government." [14] But if children are to be instructed, they must at least pay attention; if discipline in its way is to lead children toward virtue, it must be able to count on certain fundamental decencies as instilled by government. The child's "wild impetuosity" and "crude desires" must be restrained and a spirit of order introduced if education is to take place. "Those cannot be allowed to act according to their own minds who have no right desires to put into action." [15]

12. *SW* 2:165; see also *SW* 10:72–73.   13. *SW* 2:111; 10:177.
14. *SW* 10:194.   15. *SW* 2:105; 2:166; 10:177; 2:18–19.

Since a fundamental principle of government is to keep the child busy, occupations, particularly self-chosen ones, are the first resort. Sometimes these occupations can be furnished by instruction and the child is kept busy studying, though this instruction is intended not to suppress the activity of the child but to evoke it in a better directed and more controlled fashion. But because Herbart sees the child as an active being, he stresses the importance of active occupations like handwork or fieldwork, which allow the child to work off his energy.[16] But occupations can never wholly solve the problem, particularly with children whom previous experience has rendered unruly. As a result, supervision, rewards, and punishments must come into play and also constitute parts of government. But "the rigorous and constant supervision of children is equally burdensome to the supervisor and the supervised."[17] Furthermore, the child who is always kept in line by the will and exertions of the teacher never develops a will of his own.

As a result, the contributions and effectiveness of government to education are always minimal, and government should give way to instruction and discipline as soon as the child's state allows them to function efficiently without the aid of the distractive and repressive measures of government. Herbart is never enthusiastic about government and apparently feels that he has little novel to say about it. In fact, he inclines to the belief that anyone who has had much experience in working with children and much success at it will know what to do without being told.

Discipline suffers to some extent from the same limitations as does government. Although the aim of discipline is "moral strength of character," to implant a firmness of will that will persist in the mature man after he has passed beyond the control of the school the educator must rely on the circle of thought which he has built up in the student's mind, chiefly through instruction. "Discipline cannot perform its task except in conjunction with instruction."[18] Consequently, although

16. *SW* 10:136–37, 140–46.   17. *SW* 2:19. See also 1:288; 2:167.
18. *SW* 10:180. See also *SW* 2:35–36, 111, 119; 10:177, 180, 196; 9:140.

discipline by its constant, unobtrusive pressure is an important coadjutor and supplement to instruction for a time, it must, as the boy grows into a youth and his moral judgment is established by its aid, diminish as government did earlier in the case of the growing child.

In the higher forms of government the sources of the teacher's authority are the pupil's love and respect for him; in discipline this relation is the primary factor. The essence of Herbart's concept of discipline is that the teacher should serve as a model. By this he does not mean that the teacher is to be a paragon whose thoughts and actions are slavishly imitated, though in instruction the teacher is to be something of a model of this sort—the personification of how a subject is to be studied, grasped, and linked with other studies. Rather, in regard to discipline the teacher serves as a paradigm or even surrogate for the student's own moral insight. As the boy sees examples of behavior about him or as he reads of actions and characters in history and fiction and begins making moral judgments about them, the teacher is to guide him toward the right judgments. Similarly, in the teacher's approval or disapproval of the boy's own actions he gets a model for his own moral judgments or "subjective will" and for that self-observation and self-criticism which are the necessary bases for achieving the morality inherent in the moral idea of inner freedom. In these and similar ways the teacher conveys to the pupil the proper presentations involved in making moral judgments. By his admonition, praise, and censure the teacher leads the pupil to make his own moral judgments, to make the right ones, to see what they entail, and to abide by them. Obviously then, to be effective discipline must be directed toward an individual pupil, not a whole class.[19]

Whereas government is imposed, discipline is more proposed. Although they both employ rewards and punishments, for example, they use them in wholly different ways and for different purposes. For government, rewards and punishments are simply incitements and deterrents—the stick and carrot for the donkeylike pupil who is not yet in a position to be

19. SW 2:11, 20–22, 23, 123; 10:105.

rational and moral. By the time the pupil comes under the control of discipline, however, he is to see reward and punishment as the workings of the moral ideas of right and requital.

Herbart, with his usual fondness for making classifications, discerns and labels several sorts of discipline, distinguished by their function. As Herbart's own discussion of them makes manifest, however, these distinctions are far from being as neat and clear-cut as his organization implies, and they often seem more elaborate than the subject actually permits. In consequence, he discusses a rather miscellaneous set of topics under each rubric. Nonetheless, the series does illustrate the kinds of function Herbart sees discipline as performing.

For example, "supportive" discipline (*die haltende Zucht*) prevents the boy from forgetting what he is about when he wills or has willed. This aiding of "memory of the will" or the recollection of what one has once willed (the opposite of that heedlessness and forgetfulness which characterizes the actions of young people) [20] provides the minimal base on which moral strength of character can be built. With puns on the compounds of the German word *halten* ("hold") Herbart points out that this discipline does not merely hold the pupil back (*abhalten*) from willing certain things, but also holds him to (*anhalten*) what he has previously willed. With "determining" discipline (*die bestimmende Zucht*) Herbart stresses the role of discipline in helping the pupil learn to choose rightly, for character is formed by making choices. As the boy sees through experience that many of the teacher's prohibitions and commands embody sound choices, he makes these choices his own, as well as adopting the teacher's other injunctions without having to put everything to the test of experience. "Regulative" discipline (*die regelnde Zucht*) comes into play as the moral insight begins to develop in the pupil during the later years of boyhood. Earlier, there is no point in reasoning with boys because they cannot reason, and the commands of government must be their law. But as the boy becomes capable of reasoning about his conduct and begins to do so, then

20. SW 2:91–93; 179.

regulative discipline comes into being as the teacher sees to it that these attempts at reasoning about moral action are persistent and coherent.

Although discipline is more educationally important and effective than government, it is less flexible than instruction. In instruction there is that "third thing," [21] the object studied, and the teacher has a range of choice in selecting appropriate objects. In discipline, however, the relation is a dyadic one between teacher and pupil; and here the teacher is limited as much by his own personality, experience, and intellectual resources as he is by those of the pupil.[22]

In short, government and discipline, though indispensable, are less educative than instruction. Moreover, instruction is the real reason for having schools. In Herbart's opinion education is primarily the concern of the family, and the family would do its own educating did not the demands of instruction for skilled teaching and elaborate equipment compel the family to turn to schools.[23] As a result, though Herbart talks about government and discipline his heart really belongs to instruction, with its power in building the circle of thought. It is the topic that evokes from him the kind of statement frequently quoted during the following century: "One has education in all its power only when one knows how to produce in the youthful soul a large circle of thought closely knit in all its parts"; or "Mankind continually educates itself through the circle of thought it engenders." [24]

For instruction, as was noted earlier, the ethical demand that the will of the active, powerful child should be "perfected" in the dimension of extension gives rise to the educational corollary that in instruction the teacher should present a variety of objects which will arouse many-sided interest in the pupil.

> The ultimate aim of education lies, to be sure, in the concept of virtue. But the proximate goal which instruction

21. SW 2:110–11.  22. SW 2:117, 120–21.  23. SW 2:21–22; 9:137. 24. SW 2:16.

> must especially set for itself in order to reach the ultimate one may be expressed in the phrase "manysidedness of interest." The word "interest" denotes in general that sort of intellectual activity which instruction ought to make possible. For this, mere knowing is not enough. For this latter is conceived as a store of facts which could be lacking without the man's being any different as a result. In contrast, whoever holds fast to what he knows and seeks to extend it takes an interest in it.[25]

Since the ethical criterion is purely *quantitative*, so is its educational counterpart, at least at the outset. Until further considerations enter, the teacher is merely to get the child interested in as many various things as possible—the more, the better.[26] "*Filling the mind*—this is what, before all other, more detailed, purposes, ought to be the general result of instruction." [27] But manysidedness is not to produce a mere scattering or fragmentation of interest, with a resultant threat to the unity of personal consciousness or the personality. The ideal sought is the person "who easily surveys his well-organized knowledge *in all its relations* and unifies it *as his own.*" [28]

To speak of manysidedness or a wide range of interests implies some catalog or classification in order to permit sampling, since obviously interests are too numerous to make possible the inclusion of every single one in the course of instruction. How many "sides" are we talking about when we speak of "manysidedness" of interest? And how are we to classify instructional objects as related to these interests? After looking at some traditional procedures such as cataloging objects of instruction according to the scientific field to which they belong, Herbart feels that these classifications do not meet the particular demands of analysis for educative instruction. As a result he produces a whole new series of classifications, which he believes are more appropriate and which can be combined into two- and three-dimensional grids.

In speaking of interest, however, Herbart reminds us that

25. *SW* 10:142.   26. *SW* 2:28, 35–36; 10:153.   27. *SW* 2:85.
28. *SW* 10:143. Emphasis in the original. See also 2:28–29, 37.

we are already within a fundamental distinction between two forms of human impulse (*Regen*): interest and desire. These are, of course, similar insofar as they both are developed from presentations and both have objects (although interest is directed toward a present object, desire toward one not yet possessed).[29] Each has two stages. Interest has attention (*Merken*) and expectation (*Erwarten*); desire has demand (*Fordern*) and action (*Handeln*). In his *General Pedagogy* Herbart leaves this quartet at this point. Obviously this is one of the topics which he passed over, either because he had not yet completely worked out the psychological theory involved or because he believed that the psychological explanation would be incomprehensible—at least within the space he could give to it in a general book on education.

But the gap regarding "attention" can and must be filled in from his later works, for, as Herbart says, "What is more important to the pedagogue than attentiveness (*Aufmerksamkeit*)?"[30] Unfortunately, in this connection Herbart displays two familiar characteristics: the philosophic urge to make distinctions and his personal habit of failing, once he has made them, to abide by them throughout his discussion of the topic.[31] More specifically, he makes a number of distinctions both within and between *merken, bemerken,* and *aufmerken;* but this discussion, following Herbart's lead, will pay little or no attention to them and speak simply of "attention" and "attentiveness."

Attentiveness [32] is in general a readiness to welcome an increase in the number of presentations available, and this openness to additional presentations may be "voluntary" or "involuntary," as was indicated in the long quotation near the end of the preceding chapter. Voluntary attention requires an act of will on the part of the pupil, which the teacher secures not only by admonitions, threats, and promises, but also

---

29. SW 2:42, 47.   30. SW 9:456.
31. E.g., compare SW 9:456ff. and 10:146ff.
32. This exposition generally follows Herbart's statement in SW 10:146–52.

through the habits and customs of the schoolroom. (This is one of the obvious points where government and discipline relate to instruction and make it possible.) Herbart is not impressed with "voluntary" attention, but he admits it is indispensable—for example, in memorizing, where the more spontaneous operations of involuntary attention produce inaccuracies in the recall.

By and large, however, involuntary attention is what instruction desires, and is of two sorts: "primitive" and "apperceptive." The latter is the more important for instruction, but the former is a necessary condition for it and cannot be ignored. As was indicated above, these varieties of involuntary attention require no effort of will. "Primitive" attention depends chiefly on the strength of the sense impression; we are "attentive" without trying, so to speak, to loud noises and bright flashes. The apperceptive attention is equally involuntary but depends on the spontaneous or free rise of earlier presentations, which is made possible by the appearance of similar new ones. As the passage quoted at the close of chapter 8 indicated, the maximum amount of this apperceptive attention is likely to occur when there is a judicious mixture of the familiar and the unfamiliar: the new presentations find something with which to combine and yet are not overcome by the inertia of too great an existing structure of earlier presentations. To take one of Herbart's illustrations,

> The apperceiving or assimilating attention is, to be sure, not the earliest variety, but it shows itself in very young children when they understand a few words in an otherwise unintelligible conversation among adults and repeat them, or when they name, in their own fashion, objects that they recognize in their picture-books.[33]

This kind of attention has special consequences for instruction which Herbart makes plain in a definition in his *Letters on the Application of Psychology to Education:*

> We denote by the word "attention" that activity pressing up from within through which the object which presents

33. *SW* 10:148.

itself is grasped in preference to all others which also present themselves, so that the perception of it attains greater strength and duration, so that the object is identified as precisely of one sort and not another, and perhaps so that it may be praised or blamed—a possibility which is always present though it may not occur. Thus every change and movement is noted; every deviation of the object from its true nature is perceived with particular clarity; also, comparisons with other similar objects previously observed are not ignored. Such attention is facilitated by previous announcement or description through which expectation [*Erwarten*] prepares the way for attention.[34] All this shows that here the recall of older, similar presentations is at work.[35]

To anticipate, by looking at involuntary, apperceptive attention we have in this quotation implicitly arrived at Herbart's famous "steps" in instruction. But since this is not the path Herbart takes in the *General Pedagogy,* whose scheme we are following, we return to Herbart's examination and classification of interests for instructional purposes.

Beginning with the formal aspect of interests, regardless of their varied objects, Herbart embodies in his first distinction what he considers a fundamental fact, the sort of "intellectual respiration" composed of "concentration" (*Vertiefung*) and "reflection" (*Besinnung*).[36] Herbart says that "anyone who has ever devoted himself to any object of human art or love

34. This emphasis on preparation also appears in SW 10:149 and is of course the basis for Rein's later name and function for the first of his five steps, "preparation."
35. SW 9:157. Herbart made a similar, though less detailed and less "psychological" statement very early in his career (SW 1:160). This is another bit of evidence for those who wish to make the psychology only an embellishment of pedagogical experience.
36. SW 4:409. The use here of "concentration" to translate *Vertiefung* produces ambiguity with "concentration" as a translation of *Concentration* in relation to the moral idea of perfection. Some translators seek to avoid this ambiguity by using words like "penetration" or "immersion" here. But since "concentration" is the obvious English word in both places and since the contexts in which each is used are distinct, I have introduced this minor ambiguity for which (for once) Herbart is not responsible.

knows what 'concentration' means" [37]—the immersing of one's self in something to the exclusion of all thought about anything else. Just as a picture requires suitable lighting and a properly attuned observer, so anything which is worth being observed, thought, or experienced requires a suitable act of attention if it is to be comprehended and absorbed accurately and as a whole.

The importance of these isolating, self-centered acts of concentration runs counter, however, to another demand— that these diverse individual interests must ultimately find their places within the unity of a single consciousness, of a single personality. As a result, concentration must periodically be replaced by "reflection." Concentration excludes all elements of consciousness except itself; reflection allows these elements to come forth, uniting them (especially the results of previous concentrations) insofar as possible. Concentration and reflection cannot be simultaneous because the very exclusivity of any given concentration precludes not only other concentrations but also reflection. Although Herbart sets up these two movements as contraries and apparently thinks that in good instruction the pupil's mind moves back and forth between them, he also views them as the extremes of a continuum between which the "ordinary states of consciousness" lie as mixtures of concentration and reflection. The more concentrations reflection can work on, the richer it will be; the more perfectly it can unite them into a single unity, the better off the individual will be. But the teacher cannot in the time available hope to secure complete manysidedness of interest through successive concentrations on everything, followed by reflections which ultimately combine them all into a single perfect unity. He must be content with approximations.

If not everything can be included, how is selection to be made? Herbart believes the answer is obvious: The pupil's individual circumstances, his horizons as determined by the opportunities which lay open to him, dictated the objects of

37. *SW* 2:38.

his earlier, preschool concentrations. These are, consequently, the sort of thing at which his first concentrations in school should be directed. Yet Herbart is careful to warn that this principle of starting with the pupil's present situation must not be interpreted too narrowly or followed too long. Since "thought travels swiftly," Herbart is still prepared to start with the *Odyssey*, whose hero seems far removed in time and space from the German schoolboy of the early eighteenth century. He is more worried about the "distance" involved in the number and complexity of intervening concepts than he is about distance in time or space. Limitation of concentrations inevitably imposes a parallel restriction on reflection. A "system of systems" which could produce ultimate unity for all reflections is beyond the reach of the schoolboy and even the young man; instruction must leave the more profound reflections to the pupil himself as a mature adult.

Even Herbart feels, however, that the level of the preceding discussion has been too abstract. In order to explain more specifically what he means by saying that "the mind goes out clearly on many sides, one after another" and yet the personality is preserved, Herbart introduces his famous *four* steps of instruction (which the Herbartians were later to expand in various ways into five and to which they were to give different names): clarity, association, system, and method.[38]

Herbart's own example which indicates most clearly and concisely what he means by these steps appears relatively late in his career (1831) in a section of his *Encyclopedia* in which he applies these procedures to the teaching of philosophy.[39]

"If someone wishes to teach philosophy by the application of this series of concepts, he must first of all separate the objects of philosophic treatment from each other and, insofar as possible, look at them separately, for 'clarity' demands the removal of everything which permits one object to obscure another." The name of this step is, of course, taken from logic, where, as we have seen, clarity consists in distinguishing one concept sharply from all others. This first step of focusing the

38. SW 2:38–41; 10:143.   39. SW 9:201–2.

student's attention on a single object involves, of course, the phase of concentration. The student is single-mindedly lost in the observation of some single object of instruction. But he must be brought back from this exclusive concern with one item of consciousness and led to unite it with others in the phase of reflection. The remaining three steps perform this task and thus produce the necessary reflection.

"Then he [the teacher] must mix it [the object] up with everything else so as to bring it into many different sorts of incidental relations until the student is in a position to pass without difficulty from the one to the others, especially until he is certain not to have lost sight of the one in looking at the others." This second step, "association," is a transition point between concentration and reflection: although the object of the concentration is kept clearly in mind, concentration is sufficiently relaxed for the presentations of other objects, with which it is ultimately to be related, to come to mind.

"Only then will systematic exposition enter and only then too will its value in organizing the fluctuating be recognized." This third step, "system," introduces a tentative order and precision among that welter of objects brought into consciousness by association and arrives at that coherence which reflection seeks. But Herbart always stresses that system is not a mush or mixture but an arrangement of distinct elements, with the individual "clarity" of each one preserved. Traditionally in education, Herbart points out, system had been the chief or even sole component of instruction. Even at the outset the pupil was confronted by a systematic organization—for example, a codified grammar of a foreign language, the parts and subdivisions of a science. This emphasis seems understandable to Herbart inasmuch as experience alone gives no system; since experience provides multitudinous presentations but does not organize them, instruction has an obvious responsibility to provide means of organization. But Herbart is seeking by his two preceding steps to emphasize what he regards as indispensible preliminaries to any such systematic instruction: the student must have some units (and preferably, clear units) to organize; and he must see the value of having such organizing structure after having himself faced the problem of organizing an otherwise chaotic array of elements.

"But [system] is not fully tested until finally method comes, which shows to each member of the system the necessity of its place." Thus with "method" the principles on which the system is based are made explicit, and the ground for the unity achieved is revealed and tested.

Through the four steps, in short, initial concentrations are united by reflection into some rationally organized whole. Since the "object" of concentration may be an existent thing or a concept, and since the latter may be at any level of generality, this recipe may be applied at any level of instruction and to small units as well as large.[40]

The names of these four steps are subject to considerable variation in Herbart's writings, even within the span of a few pages. Thus "system" and "method" become "order" (*Ordnung*) and "progression through this order" (*Durchlaufung dieser Ordnung*) or "regular progression" (*regelmässiges Durchlaufen*).[41] Regular progression through the parts of a systematic classification which instruction has developed may well be pedagogically desirable, but it is hardly the same operation as was previously designated by "method"—the understanding of the principles which give structure to that system. For that matter, an additional important feature of this fourth step is application of the system to new materials, a fact which led Rein, a later Herbartian, to assign the name "application" to this last step in his own version of Herbart's pedagogy. Once more, the ability to apply a system or taxonomy undoubtedly constitutes a desirable outcome of the study of any system and a good index of the pupil's comprehension of it. But the three characteristics of the fourth step mentioned so far are hardly exact equivalents of each other.

This variation is further reflected when Herbart, dividing interests into those of "knowledge" and those of "sympathy," paraphrases the four steps in an effort to make them more

40. SW 10:144.   41. SW 2:53, 50.

directly applicable to these two major classes of interest.[42] Here the series as applied to knowledge states that instruction should "point out," "relate," "teach," and "philosophize," whereas that for sympathy asserts that instruction should be "observing," "continuous," "elevating," and "taking hold on reality."

Confusions and uncertainties arising out of this treatment of the fourth step in the *General Pedagogy* are scarcely dispelled by the statement in the *Outlines of Pedagogical Lectures,* written almost at the other end of Herbart's career:

> It is immediately obvious that a many-sided development cannot be created speedily. The "many" can be acquired only one by one; then unification [*Vereinung*], overview [*Übersicht*] and appropriation [*Zueignung*] must follow.[43]

Although the three earlier steps may be translated fairly easily into their previous names, calling the fourth one "appropriation" or "assimilation" only adds to the confusion already created, particularly since one page later he repeats his original four verbatim (clarity, association, system, method).

In part, Herbart's difficulties with this fourth step merely reflect inherent complexities within it, and some of these in their turn are largely consequences of complications within the preceding step, system. Herbart's statement in the *Outlines of Pedagogical Lectures* points out these complications and their interrelations (as well as suggesting some teaching procedures for them):

> What association demands cannot be effected merely by system, and certainly not at the outset. In system each point has its definite place. At that place it is intimately connected with other points which lie adjacent, but it is also separated from other points by a fixed distance and connected with them only through certain links, and the nature of this connection is not everywhere the same. Besides, system is not merely learned but also used, applied, and supplemented by additions made at appropriate

42. SW 2:54.    43. SW 10:143.

places. To do this requires skill in moving in thought from any given starting point, forward, backward, and sideward. Therefore, system is partly devised, partly applied. The preparation lies in association; practice in methodical thought must follow.

Practice in methodical thought will be acquired by the student through assignments, his own production, and the [teacher's] correction of both these. For here it will be evident whether the student has properly grasped the main ideas, whether he can recognize them again in particulars, and whether he can apply them.[44]

The first step also involves certain problems of multiplicity of function, but for the present they may be left to the later ministrations of the Herbartians.

All the evidence, however, drives home the point that Herbart's steps are neither clearly defined nor consistently named. One scarcely needs a crystal ball to peer into the future and predict that any later follower, trying to use the steps himself or to teach them to others with maximum ease and effectiveness, will immediately specify the nature and function of each step more precisely and will clarify and standardize the nomenclature. Herbart is up to his old tricks of mistreating his readers. (Sometimes he seems almost to have sent his first drafts to the printer without bothering to reread them, or at least without pondering whether greater consistency and precision would improve communication.)

At the close of the earlier discussions of "apperceptive interest" it was pointed out that Herbart's analysis of it leads directly toward the four steps and the concentration and reflection they embody. As the quotation from the *Letters on the Application of Psychology to Education* states, through apperception there is a concentration upon one object in preference to all others; the object is identified as precisely of one kind and not some other, although objects previously perceived are not ignored (association and reflection). In other words, Herbart undoubtedly sees his steps as directly related to his

44. *SW* 10:144–45.

psychological theories about spontaneous or freely rising presentations. The steps are the procedures to facilitate such rising.

In this connection a rather long passage merits quotation here; it is taken from his little monograph "On the Dark Side of Pedagogy," which appeared in 1812 as an afterpiece to his "Psychological Investigation of the Strength of a Given Presentation Considered as the Function of Its Duration," a psychological treatise that Herbart considers as necessary as his ethics and his metaphysics for anyone wishing to understand his pedagogy.[45] In this piece, written six years later than the *General Pedagogy*, Herbart makes explicit the relation between his pedagogical doctrine concerning the necessary alternation between concentration and reflection on the one hand and his psychological hypotheses on the other:

> To organize the whole of instruction from its very beginning to its end in the most advantageous fashion, so that each antecedent prepares the disposition of the pupil for the proximate and ultimate consequent, this task was the chief object of consideration in my several pedagogical writings. What was said in my *General Pedagogy* concerning the alternation of concentration and reflection as a continually necessary mental respiration . . . may be expressed as follows: When a series of perceptions has produced a certain sum of arrests, these must be allowed to subside before there can be further progress. This law of the proper punctuation in instruction, as we might call it, does not contain the whole import of these words. For reflection is not merely the process of letting the sum of arrests subside; it is a fusion of what was formerly included in single and separate [acts of] consciousness. This is a subject for another psychological investigation much more extensive than the preceding.[46]

Although Herbart is here explicitly relating his psychology and his pedagogy, the quotation gives some support to the view that he is cutting his psychological goods to fit the pat-

45. SW 3:123.    46. SW 3:150; see also SW 4:408–9.

tern of his pedagogical ideas rather than working out his pedagogy "on the basis of firmly established psychological laws"—as his later followers were going to assert.[47]

In any case, he did not present these psychological arguments in his *General Pedagogy* for reasons with which we are already familiar, and this suggests two important points. First, the reader of Herbart who knows only this book knows the alternation and the steps which embody it only as isolated and rather arbitrary bits of pedagogical machinery. Second, that Herbart chooses to present them in isolation in that book seems to indicate that he felt they would have some utility as rather mechanical procedures even for the teacher unfamiliar with their psychological basis. From these facts some warrant may be found for the tendency of later pedagogues to take the steps in precisely this isolated fashion. Once more, Herbart's difficulties in coping with his system systematically are making almost inevitable some of the sea-changes which will come over his doctrines under the label of Herbartianism.

Turning from his formal and abstract analysis of interest and beginning to consider the possible objects of interest, Herbart warns against trying to classify *things*. Any thing can be an object of interest, and things are innumerable. The educator who struggles in this morass is likely to lose sight of interest amid the interesting. The preventive is to classify not objects but states of mind.

Obeying his own dictum, Herbart begins by distinguishing between "knowledge" and "sympathy":

> Knowledge imitates in an image [*Bild*] that which it has before it; sympathy transports itself into the feeling of another.
>
> In the case of knowledge, an antithesis exists between the thing and its image; sympathy, on the contrary, reproduces the identical feeling.[48]

---

47. E.g., see H. M. Felkin and E. Felkin, *An Introduction to Herbart's Science and Practice of Education* (Boston: D. C. Heath & Co., 1895), p. 106, and their quotations from Lange and Rein.
48. *SW* 2:44.

The two great sources of human development are experience (*Erfahrung*) with the external world and association or intercourse (*Umgang*) with other human beings. Instruction organizes and supplements experience and association by "knowledge" and "sympathy" respectively. The objects of knowledge are thus phenomena, which include both nature and humanity, and the mind's interest in them depends upon their strength, variety, novelty, and varied succession. Once more we are in the presence of his psychological theory of apperception (which Herbart here leaves implicit), but he points out briefly how these four factors have implications for instruction which seeks to arouse interest:

> The strength of a presentation can be partly attained through the power of the sensuous impression (as, for example, through choral recitation by several children, by displaying the same object in different ways through drawings, instruments, models, etc.) and partly through the vividness of descriptions, especially if there are already related presentations in the depths of the mind, which unite with the present one.[49]

Within knowledge Herbart distinguishes three ascending stages: knowledge of the manifold of phenomena, of its regularity, and of aesthetic relations. In contrast to the wider sweep of knowledge, sympathy has as its proper objects only certain manifestations of humanity. Within it too Herbart distinguishes three ascending stages: sympathy with humanity, sympathy with society, and concern about the relations of both to the supreme being.

By this time it is easy to see why the reviewers of the *General Pedagogy* were confused and to wonder how much the contemporary teacher gained from the perusal of Herbart's book. Herbart's remark at about this point in the book, "To apply to practice everything that has been developed up to

---

49. SW 2:53. See also SW 2:144; 10:147. Probably it is because choral recitation contributes to the strength of the presentation ("primitive involuntary attention") that Herbart is so fond of it for the step of clarity, particularly for young children (SW 10:144).

this point, properly interconnected and related to the variegated objects of our world, this is the great and actually immeasurable task of him who would educate through instruction," [50] seems the classic understatement in the history of pedagogy, in view of the fact that several additional distinctions and progressions which Herbart elaborates have been passed over here. But even with these omissions, the end is not yet in sight. At least one other set of distinctions is necessary to produce the tabular form in which he writes his chapter dealing with the "course of instruction."

This distinction classifies instruction as descriptive, analytic, and synthetic. In "descriptive" instruction, the teacher describes something or tells a story as vividly as possible, seeking a strong presentation in the mind of the pupil, often with the use of those devices noted above which help make the presentation strong. This type of instruction is obviously in the service of concentration, an effort to fix the pupil's attention through primitive apperception on the object or narrative. It is also related to the first "step," clarity, insofar as the vivid presentation which the pupil presumably acquires gives him the major characteristics of the thing or of a concept. But clarity is more closely allied with the second type of instruction, the "analytic." In this type, the teacher breaks down complex things or concepts into their constituent parts. This procedure is a natural introduction to any instruction, since the pupil's previous experience (for the schoolboy, his preschool experience in the home and in the neighborhood) has acquainted him with relatively complex things, ideas, and events but has not analyzed them into their interrelated and interacting parts. The third variety of instruction, the synthetic, moves in the contrary direction. It first presents elements and leads the pupil to organize them in some fashion. For example, having seen the linguistic phenomena of the Greek language in reading the *Odyssey*, the boy now codifies these assorted pieces into a system or grammar of the language. (Synthetic instruction, being thus concerned with com-

50. SW 2:58.

bining elements into wholes, involves primarily the last three steps in instruction—association, system, and method.)

Since "descriptive instruction" is so clearly limited to the preliminary stages of education, it will not figure prominently in further elaborations. But by adding the analytical and synthetic modes to the distinctions already made, Herbart evolves a framework (and such schemes were dear to his compulsive heart) within which he can discuss the progression or course which instruction should take.[51] The structure is shown schematically in the diagram below.

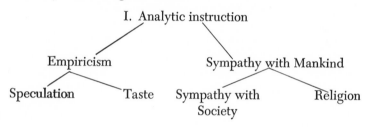

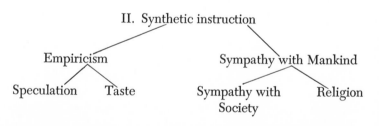

At first glance this chart does not seem to embody the distinctions previously made, but this impression is merely the result of Herbart's unendearing habit of switching his terms. The left-hand cluster incorporates the subdivisions of "knowledge," though that rubric does not appear in the chart. The first of its parts, "knowledge of the manifold" is obtained through the senses and is empirical; consequently in the schema this part is denoted by "empiricism" (*Empirie*). Knowledge of the

51. The later discussion in the *Outlines of Pedagogical Lectures* (SW 10:158ff.) closely parallels that of the *General Pedagogy* (SW 2:58ff), which is followed here.

regularities within this manifold, however, is an affair of reason, the speculative reason, rather than perception; as a result, this section appears in the chart as "speculation" (*Speculation*) rather than "regularity" (*Gesetzmässigkeit*). Finally, "knowledge of aesthetic relations" is transformed in the chart into "taste" (*Geschmack*). (Herbart is here surpassing even his usual standards in making things difficult for his readers.) The right-hand portion of the schema, concerned with sympathy, is less opaque in its derivation; the language of the earlier distinctions is repeated except that the third, "the relations of both [humanity and society] to the supreme being," appears as "religion."

Within this framework, which Herbart preserves even in the typographical arrangement of the pages, Herbart discusses each of the topics. (Ultimately in his late *Outlines of Pedagogical Lectures* Herbart takes these six rubrics—empirical, speculative, aesthetic, sympathetic, social, and religious—as the six classes of interests.) [52] Since both Herbart and his followers give primary emphasis to this process of instruction, the chart must be at least partially filled in.

> In the analytical phase of the empirical part of instruction *pointing* out, naming, and giving permission to handle and move things precedes everything else. It proceeds from the whole to the parts and into the parts of the parts. The parts are associated in that their relative positions are determined. Things are analyezd in detail in this fashion, then the events, which arise in the encounter of different things is developed. The concepts of cause-and-effect and means-and-end, which do not belong here, are appropriately omitted. Empiricism is concerned only with the succession of events, the course of their sequences. In the earlier years the objects of this analysis are, on the one hand, the human body . . . and, on the other, the totality of surrounding things—furniture, plants, animals, etc. Human doing and suffering are associated with human existence and then the closest and simplest natural relations of men. Here presentative instruction comes in; it broad-

ens knowledge about nature and man through elementary study of peoples and places. From this, geography and natural history gradually develop, in which pointing out and associating should always precede teaching. Concurrently the empirical observation of mankind in the immediate surroundings proceeds easily. . . . Analytical exercises in the native language must be carried on to the fullest extent in preparation for spelling, composition, and general grammar and even for the preliminary distinguishing of concepts. What has been pointed out and associated acquires the structure of teaching [*Lehrform*] through definite coordinating recapitulation; and wherever the question arises which place belongs to what in the structure of teaching, there the trace of philosophy appears.[53]

This section has been quoted in full because it illustrates several important points. First, it displays the variety inherent in each stage in regard to both subjects and procedures. Man and nature as phenomenal objects, manufactured objects and tools, human life, human relations, the native language, and the beginnings of geography and natural history are the topics defining the scope of this most elementary level of education for Herbart. The omission of foreign languages, notably Greek taught through reading the *Odyssey*, is only an apparent omission, since Homer and the other Greek authors furnish most of the material for the study of men, places, events, and human relations.

Second, the passage exemplifies the application of the four steps under the labels developed for applying them to knowledge: pointing out, associating, teaching, philosophizing. The primary emphasis at this elementary stage is that of pointing out through presentative instruction. This preliminary focusing of the pupil's attention on various characteristics of things is a necessary prelude to that perception of specific and generic characteristics involved in gaining those clear and distinct concepts which characterize the first step; but pointing out qualities is not the same process as distinguishing similari-

53. *SW* 2:68, 70, 72. Emphasis in original.

ties and differences among them and associating them, the beginning of the second step. These various aspects of "clarity" and then "association" receive the major attention at this earliest stage of instruction. Yet the other steps also appear. The beginnings of system lie in the *Lehrform* ("teaching"), being the label here for the third step, and the discussion of the proper placement of items within this framework introduces a trace of "method" or "philosophizing," the recognition of the principles which underlie the organization or classification.

Third, the analysis of the "encounters" between different things into the changes which each undergoes is already familiar to us from chapter 8, where this model, taken from physics, yields one of Herbart's fundamental psychological equations. Here we find the paradigm apparently extended to the analysis of events of all sorts. Clearly this model seems to Herbart one of the basic tools of thought.

To move on to the second section of analytic instruction, "speculation," analysis through cause-and-effect and ends-means relations (excluded from the preceding empirical section) is now introduced. Even though the metaphysical status of these concepts is not clarified, they are given to the pupil as useful tools in the analysis of experience. Although in this section the relations between man and nature and between man and man receive some notice, the major emphasis is to be put on events of the physical world, and "system" and "method" are taken from physics and ultimately from speculative philosophy.

In the analytic development of the third section, "taste," the effort is "to illuminate the particular without thereby overshadowing the whole." [54] In ordinary experience children see beautiful or sublime things merely as masses like other masses. They must learn to analyze these beautiful objects into their constituent parts and to see how the beautiful parts combine into the complex beauties of a masterwork. (This procedure is, of course, dictated by Herbart's aesthetics, which is based on the simple relations of simple elements.)

54. SW 2:72.

In complement to this progression through "knowledge" stands that devoted to "sympathy." Sympathy with others and an understanding of their feelings presupposes, says Herbart, an understanding of one's own feelings. As a result, analytic instruction in sympathy begins with an analysis of the student's own "soul" to enable him to find within himself these various "movements of the mind." This insight can then be applied to others, and the whole gamut of mutual human attractions and aversions understood. In this process the student profits from working with examples that are larger than life-size and somewhat idealized. For this purpose the heroes of Homeric Greece seem to Herbart to offer the best materials, and this is one of his chief reasons for placing the reading of the *Odyssey* at the very start of his program of instruction.

The next stage, sympathy with society, also begins with the student, in the analysis of his own social relations. Here he is to be made to realize how his own existence is bound up with that of others, with the resultant need and willingness for self-sacrifice. This is the part of instruction which most obviously bears the burden of establishing the ethical ideas,[55] though they are to be involved (at least so Herbart would certainly wish) at all other points in the course of instruction.

The last stage of analytic instruction in sympathy, religion, has its roots in the dependence of man and in his insuperable limitations and those of his society. Thus the pupil is to be led to recognize, on the one hand, such facts as the brevity of human life and the evanescence of pleasure and, on the other, the joys of frugality and of keeping one's wants small. These reflections inevitably lead to teleology or questions of end and purpose; but Herbart wants such considerations confined to the natural world and does not want the pupil to become embroiled in controversy over the ends of human action. At this point Herbart is willing to let education make junction with organized religion, but in a rather restrained fashion, free from all "fanaticism and mysticism."

All the preceding instruction has been "analytic" in that

55. *SW* 10:71–73.

it begins with the complex things, events, and relations of the pupil's experience and breaks them down into their components. The contrasting phase of instruction, the "synthetic," begins with elements (which are usually not found as such in ordinary experience) and shows how they are combined. It "supplies a throng of new presentations and has to work them out." [56] In this process it employs what Herbart calls "combinative operations" and emphasizes the steps of "system" and "method." Thus, in the empirical part concerned with knowledge, emphasis is on such systematic structures as the grammar of a foreign language. In the speculative part problems and concepts like cause-and-effect are to be seen as parts of larger speculative systems. Then in the third part, the child is allowed to evolve his own taste in regard to complex art objects and to create new works of his own out of aesthetic elements, though in both instances narrowness in the child's taste is avoided by presenting him with examples of acknowledged masterpieces in the various genres.[57]

In synthetic instruction relating to sympathy, the shift from the analytic to the synthetic mode does not seem to produce quite the clear parallel which the scheme seems to imply, though there is the constant attempt to develop larger wholes. In the empirical part, since proper sympathy for mankind in general in all its diversity can be felt only by one who himself has in his mind innumerable varied pictures of mankind at its best, as portrayed by the poets and historians, the aim of instruction here is to present these pictures and to make the pupil see the contrast between the actuality of his own times and the ideal of what humanity might be—and to see what he can contribute to improving the situation. In the speculative part, a general theory of society (a sociology, in fact, had it been yet so named) is to be developed, along with a devotion to the best interests of society. The final point, the synthetic treatment of religion, attempts to produce a sound idea of God.

This outline of the "course of instruction" does not constitute a great proportion of the total bulk of the *General*

56. SW 2:97.   57. SW 2:64.

*Pedagogy* and may seem to have been treated at inordinate length here. The present emphasis is justified on the ground that this outline is probably the most important part of Herbart's doctrine, and this opinion in turn has several bases.

First, we have his explicit concluding statement:

> For I demand of the pedagogue above all things that he orient himself in this distinction [among the kinds of interest] most painstakingly and that he practice relating all teaching and learning to it. Whoever fails to do so may be a distinguished empiricist, but never in my opinion a theorist.

Second, as will be evident in the following chapter, this is the part of the doctrine on which Herbart keeps his own eye fixed in conducting his practical operations. In writing general books on education Herbart feels compelled to include a good many topics (e.g., government) simply because readers of such a volume rightly expect to find them treated. These matters are undeniably parts of education. But the amount of space an author devotes to them is not necessarily a valid index of his estimate of their importance. In contrast, in the reports, in which Herbart is trying to convey to the ministry of education what he is doing in his school and to convince officialdom of its importance, his major emphasis is always on this sequence of instruction.

Third, although much that is presented in this outline of instruction was not new even at the time, certain elements of it have some claim to that distinction, at least by being presented in new contexts or with novel emphasis. Obvious examples are the equal emphasis given to sympathy and knowledge, the attention to beauty and taste, the role of religion in a nonsectarian, noncatechetical form, and the effort to combine effectively the personal experience of the student and the "pointings out" of presentational instruction in some sort of organized structure. These points are less bland and abstract than are the four steps and the doctrine of apperception, but they are equally characteristic of Herbart's thought (if not more), and, in my opinion, they are what Herbart himself would be more likely to recognize as his contribution.

Herbart would be likely to see this plan as a contribution because it is specifically directed toward doing what he felt needed to be done—remedying some of what he considered the worst faults of the schools of his day:

> Whoever will continue for himself the reflection here begun . . . will only with difficulty avoid the firm conviction that in the culture of the circle of thought lies the chief parts of education. But let him then compare the ordinary school and the circle of thought which is to be expected from it. Let him consider whether it is wise to treat instruction again and again as the presentation of things to be memorized and to leave to discipline alone the task of making men of those who bear the human form.[58]

Insofar as the teacher needs help, this outline gives him a structuring of the educational "manifold." "The more education appears in the round of daily experience, the more necessary it is to bring our thoughts about it into more definite order and to fix them lest they be lost in the stream of opinion." [59] Like the young pupil becoming acquainted with the diverse elements of some field of knowledge, the teacher, confronted by the chaotic mass of educational procedures, traditions, and problems, is also likely to feel the need for "system" and "method." The sketch speaks to the "combination of studies" because Herbart believes that "what is isolated has little importance." [60] Or to make the same point in different terms, the outline is the result of Herbart's actually applying his theory (the four steps and the rest) to that part of education which he had marked out as his province. As he warns,[61] this scheme is not offered as a universal plan for instruction: he has included too much for it all to be feasible in the education of any given child, and, in any case, an actual plan must take account of the specific experiences and capacities of the

58. *SW* 2:101.   59. *SW* 1:341.   60. *SW* 10:141.   61 *SW* 2:80.

particular teachers and pupils involved. But in the general terms possible in a general book, the outline is Herbart's picture of what instruction should achieve and how it should go about attaining it.

This is the sort of instruction which develops the good will. In terms of Herbart's psychology, "Action generates the will out of desire. . . . The circle of thought contains the store of that which by degrees can mount on the steps of interest to desire and then by means of action to volition." [62]

Important though instruction is, it is unable alone to produce the good will. The contribution of discipline cannot be ignored. The collaboration of these two parts of education produces the desired final product as summarized by Herbart:

> In order to exclude evil, the praiseworthy traits in the objective side of the character [i.e., that formed by the inclinations and desires] must be supplemented by good resolves in the subjective side [i.e., the moral ideas]. These latter demand that aesthetic [i.e., moral] judgment by which the pupil through examples learns to distinguish between better and worse acts of willing. If that judgment is lacking in clarity, strength, and completeness, the resolves have no roots in the character of the pupil and are no more than words he has learned.
>
> On the other hand, if the aesthetic judgment of the will is united with the comprehensive interest which has arisen from experience, social intercourse, and instruction, then a warm feeling for the good appears wherever it is found, which affects not only all the efforts of the pupil but the entire way in which he assimilates what life and learning later offer him. [63]

62. *SW* 2:99–100.    63. *SW* 10:180.

# 10

## "Pedagogy Must Also Be Shown and Practiced"

What did all this theory amount to in the classroom?[1] In answering we are not compelled to draw the longbow of inference or merely to cite activities Herbart suggests, for Herbart presents us with his own example of practical application in the activities of the pedagogical seminar he conducted during his years at Königsberg. Since Taute's "admirably composed and extremely notable statement" for 1831 has the virtues of explicitness and succinctness, it can serve us as a framework here.[2] Its authenticity is unquestionable, since Herbart endorsed this statement both literally and figuratively,[3] and its accuracy is attested by Herbart's more profuse early accounts as well as by the reports of members of the local School Council and the Provincial School Board. Taute's program also closely parallels the procedures more briefly outlined by Herbart in his "Report for 1821–23," in which he asserts that his method is completely developed.

To arouse the six classes of interest, the subjects of educational instruction are also six, though the relation is definitely not one-to-one: languages, mathematics, history, natural sci-

1. Chapter title is from SW 14:9.    2. SW 15:39–63.    3. SW 15:32.

ences, geography, and composition. (Sometimes Herbart combines these into two larger groups, called history and mathematics.) [4] Other subjects may well be included in education generally and even in educative instruction in the strict sense. But these six areas lay special claim to Herbart's attention on two counts: first, they are potentially the most educative in his sense; second, as they were mistaught in the contemporary schools, they had lost most of this educative quality, and hence their teaching seems to Herbart a prime target for reform.

The values and demands of educative instruction, growing out of ethics and psychology, cannot of course be the only determiners. Herbart recognizes that the demands of tradition, the expectations of families, the needs of the state, the structure of the sciences, the relative teachability of certain materials, and other considerations must also effect what he calls the *what* and *how* of instruction; but insofar as possible Herbart seeks to have the "educative" considerations prevail.

His procedures in language instruction reflect the interplay of all these forces. For centuries the teaching of Latin had been the fundamental task of the lower schools, with Greek added in more recent times. Herbart is prepared to accept the inevitability of Latin. The training of candidates for the learned professions and for posts in the state bureaucracy demands it, and he also thinks society should preserve its continuity with its Roman and medieval past. "Latin must be learned and, consequently, Latin grammar too. This is true, and that suffices." But he feels that this is not needed by every schoolboy. For example, he finds far too many pupils in the gymnasium who belong not there but in the *Bürgerschule*, where the teaching of Latin should have no place.[5] In short, Latin has some valid claims to inclusion within the curriculum, but they are limited and do not rest on any inherent educative value of Latin.

4. SW 9:149. He labels them "mathematics" and "ancient languages" in SW 3:297. Compare the "knowledge," "sympathy," and "heterogeneous studies" of SW 2:82.
5. SW 9:148–51.

In educative value, Greek is far superior to Latin, but neither is pedagogically useful simply because it is a *foreign* language. Herbart does not believe that second-language study as such sharpens the brain or trains some (to him) nonexistent mental faculty. The study of language is educative because of the literature to which it gives access, and in this respect Greek is far superior to Latin. Consequently, the study of Greek should come before the study of Latin in order to have its proper effect during the important formative years of early instruction.

Greek has certain other claims. Some rest on pure teachability. Since the general "boyishness" of the Greek epic heroes and their exploits, particularly Odysseus, seems to Herbart certain to appeal to all boys, one should begin the study of classical languages with the *Odyssey*. Similarly the simplicity and naiveté of Herodotus' brand of historiography seems next most likely to appeal to youthful readers, and hence his *Histories* form the second item of instruction. Nonetheless, though Herbart wishes to take advantage of these pedagogical virtues of Homer and Herodotus, the fundamental educative value of these two bits of literature lies in the effect they can have on the youthful heart and soul. Both the *Odyssey*, with its picture of "ideal boyhood," [6] and the *Histories* present clear and simple examples, far removed in time and space, of human character and human behavior, on which the child can pass those fundamental ethical judgments of approval or disapproval; consequently their anecdotes offer the child a practice field for his moral judgment of what is noble, what is base, and all the rest. And with the reading of selections from Plato (the *Crito*, *Apology*, and parts of the *Republic*), which ends the work in Greek, the student passes from the "analytic" to the "synthetic" phase; that is, he no longer uses only the apparatus of moral judgment he already possesses; in these readings arguments are adduced and questions are raised which in all probability have not yet fallen within the scope of his experience, and his circle of thought is thus extended.

6. SW 1:270–71; 2:64–67.

These educative effects cannot eventuate, however, if the boy is deciphering only a few dozen lines a night. He must be able to encompass a whole episode, and it is this requirement which determines the pace, not the problems of vocabulary or syntax. Herbart has no interest in Greek as Greek in a philological sense. The child is started on the *Odyssey* with the barest minimum of linquistic equipment. Since reading is the easiest of the language skills, the student can go relatively far with relatively little. But there are limits to this approach, and, in any case, Herbart's pupils are ultimately to be held to the same standards as pupils who have gone through the more plodding procedures of the gymnasium, notably the requirements for the school-leaving certificate. Hence at the end of the Homer and Herodotus readings, a period of grammatical emphasis is introjected. For this purpose works like Xenophon's *Cyropedia* and *Anabasis* are used. Although these works are chosen primarily on linguistic grounds as being representative models of Attic usage, these accounts of the education of a young prince and of the expedition of the ten thousand Greek into the heart of Persia and safely back again also seem likely to appeal to boys. Then too, the various episodes these books contain also afford fairly simple grounds for the practice of moral judgments.

Instruction in Latin, which follows, simply replicates the Greek pattern. Instruction begins with the *Aeneid* (though Virgil's epic is hardly naive or boyish) and moves to the simple early history of the Romans, Livy's. Linguistic problems are then covered by Caesar's *Gallic War* and the Ciceronian orations traditional in the schools as models of classical Latin style. At the end, Cicero's *On Duties* and his *Tusculan Disputations* introduce ethical issues and arguments parallel to those of the Platonic works, with which instruction in Greek is closed.

Since Herbart is clearly not impressed with any inherent educative value of language study in itself and felt compelled to include in his curriculum Latin (wholly) and Greek (in part) on other grounds, he is prepared to use translations in exceptional instances where the usual pressures for Greek and Latin do not apply or can be ignored; he also welcomes proper passages from the moderns. But he does regard Greek literature, particularly the *Odyssey*, as having a unique value for educative instruction. He holds this opinion, to be sure, within the context of a strong contemporary tradition of instruction in the classical languages. Had this situation been different, it is impossible to say whether he would have had equal inclination to use the *Odyssey* and the rest in translation.

This priority which he undeniably assigns to the *Odyssey* touches two points worth noting here. First, the sequences, Greek-then-Latin and poetry-then-prose, are the actual chronological ones. As we shall see, this fact will give rise among some later Herbartians to the "culture-epoch" theory—the belief that the intellectual progress of the child should recapitulate the intellectual progress of the "race." Herbart himself advances this argument in part; a local professor who examined the work of the seminar reports it and obviously he picked it up from Herbart and his students. But, interestingly enough, Herbart, Taute, and the rest do not mention it in their reports. As a determining factor in curriculum selection and arrangement it seems to have been much less important to Herbart than to the Herbartians. The second point is Castell's opinion, noted earlier, that Herbart's insistence on beginning with the *Odyssey* was only a minor detail which could be disregarded in order to approach more closely the standard procedure of Prussian schools. This view seems clearly erroneous. In Herbart's opinion Greek literature is uniquely fitted to come first, and to teach it in the wrong order (after Latin) and consequently at the wrong time (too late) is to deprive it almost completely of its particular power to work upon the child's soul for ethical ends.

Instruction in mathematics has a more restricted relation to the fundamental ethical ideas; it does not present that array of people and actions which literature offers to the child's moral judgment. Its educative (in the strict sense) justification lies in its contribution to "knowledge"—to the development of many-sided interest in relation to the idea of perfection; and Herbart apparently feels that like Greek, mathematics loses its power for this purpose if it is left until too late. Because the items which form the subject matter of mathematics are potential objects of interest, Herbart particularly dislikes the contemporary teaching of it which disregards and usually destroys interest. Insofar as mathematical instruction in the gymnasium is viewed primarily as necessary preparation for advanced work in mathematics at the university the value of this instruction is completely lost for all those who do not choose to become mathematicians. As Herbart sees it, the chief hope of preserving an extensive interest for the nonspecialist lies in showing its applications, especially to mechanics and astronomy. For this sort of application to be possible, mathematics must cover, in addition to arithmetic and geometry, the simpler parts of integral and differential calculus. Potential interest and potential application then become the criteria for selecting the *what* within the traditional fields of mathematics. The *how* of instruction is modeled on the following sequence used in science.

Educative instruction in the natural sciences, like that in mathematics, is not concerned with moral issues but is educative by virtue of its stimulation of a particular class of interests and by virtue of the kind of knowledge it confers, that knowledge of the world necessary if the good will is to be effective. The nature of the subject matter of both natural science and mathematics suggests the proper order in which they should be taught; and this sequence is essentially the source of Herbart's four steps in instruction, stages not so apparent in the organization of instruction in the languages.

Instruction begins with "exercises in perception." This was a technique Herbart took from Pestalozzi, an indebtedness frankly acknowledged in the *ABC of Sense Perception* and other works. Most simply, the teacher begins by presenting a natural or mathematical object; the student observes it and notes the qualities or characteristics it possesses. Since in logic this determination of what characteristics belong to a particular concept is called "clearness," this process gives its name to the first step in Herbart's terminology. Instruction is primarily "analytic" in Herbart's terms, because the student is bringing a complex concept of something already familiar in his circle of thought and is analyzing out the specific qualities which characterize it. In so doing he comes to see the value of scientific terminology, not as a mere preliminary hurdle and burden to the memory, as often was the case in contemporary education, but as a tool for recording observations precisely and economically: "That leaf is palmate" or "that three-sided, three-angled, closed figure is a triangle." Herbart believes that this Pestalozzian approach is impeccable as a beginning, but thinks that the Swiss master either stopped with it or else proceeded in the wrong way.[7]

Proper procedure is for the teacher to present a series of similar objects. Now the student must see not merely characteristics but distinguishing characteristics. In logical terms this is "distinctness," the determination of which characteristics distinguish between concepts which share other characteristics. "These are both triangles, but that one is equilateral, that one scalene." The concepts thus "associated" on the basis of shared and distinguishing characteristics can then be "methodically" related into a "system." This operation is begun analytically as the student works with what he brings from past experience. But the teacher may start the movement toward a particular accepted variety of system in a "synthetic" way by the qualities of the objects he selects and the qualities he has the children note. That is, "dog," "cat," "sparrow," and "robin" lead to a system different from "robin," "bat," "whale," and "dog." Then too, the characteristics of "bat" which relate it to "whale" and "dog" rather than "robin" are facts that might not occur to the child and be within his circle of thought, though he may in a sense have had experience with all four. "No one expects system from mere experience."[8]

Although the teacher may well introduce standard scientific systems of classification and organization, Herbart feels

7. SW 14:73–74. 8. SW 2:41.

that systems, like technical nomenclature, should be kept in their proper role of servant, not tyrant. Worth noting again is that "method" here is not a fourth step in any chronological sequence; it is involved in system and in fact produces it. Its final position is due on the one hand to the fact that as a principle it is the ultimate generalization, the farthest remove from the particular concept and its particular qualities, and, on the other, to the fact that it must be found and stated *as a principle* before it can be fully applied.

Educative instruction in history is obviously allied to that in languages in several ways. For one, as we have seen, many of the actual works studied for literary or linguistic purposes (such as Herodotus and Livy) are primary sources for the study of Greek and Roman history. More important, in contrast to natural science and mathematics, it involves "sympathy" as well as knowledge. History, like literature, presents a wide range of personalities and events on which the student can exercise and perfect his moral judgments. History supplements literature, partly by preparing for it and partly by filling in the gaps to make the larger picture. As a result, Herodotus must be supplemented by Thucydides and by the more detailed "modern" works of Gillie and Mittford, and Livy must receive similar reinforcement for Roman history.

In addition to Greek and Roman history, medieval and German history also have claims, as Herbart and his staff recognize. These accounts also present instances for moral judgments on the part of the students, but on a less simple and naive scale, for these are histories of more complex societies more closely resembling the kind in which the student lives (and here we have another germ of the later "culture-epoch" theory). The details of this subject matter are, of course, objects of interest in their own right,[9] and again the demands of system and method require that the elements of the historical narratives be organized. As a result, instruction in history closes with some memorizing of chronological surveys and the reading of modern expository works. But as with

9. *SW* 9:121–22.

natural sciences and mathematics, Herbart is concerned lest this scholarly apparatus usurp undue prominence and prove stultifying rather than stimulating and illuminating.

Herbart's treatment of geography is marked chiefly by this same line of thought: he worries about the tendency of instruction to degenerate into a mere cataloging of places and facts, a sin he believes even Pestalozzi is guilty of.[10] Rather, "the world and humanity should appear in luminous outline." [11] The chief difficulty is the inadequacy of the run-of-the-mill teacher in the face of the inordinate demands of the subject, which make the teacher use every bit of wisdom he has (literature, history, science, technology, travel books) to enable the child, who has begun with details from Greece and Rome, to attain an ordered, comprehensive view of the life of all peoples in all times and places. In all the reports on the seminar the procedures followed in geographical instruction are less precise and detailed than those in the other areas. But if one may judge from the comments, Herbart sees geographical studies as something of an integrative and systematizing means for the whole process of educative instruction, though this architectonic use of geography is not explicitly asserted, but only clearly implied.

Finally, in instruction in German composition Herbart combines the demand of generations of composition teachers (that the student have something to write about) with the demands of the moral aims of education. By postponing composition until after the readings from Plato, Herbart secures not merely topics for composition but topics concerning morals, and compositions of this sort force the student to record and make explicit his moral judgments and moral arguments. (In this connection we can recall that one of the earliest works of the youthful Herbart was a comparison of Plato's and Cicero's views of the supreme good—exactly the sort of topic on which Herbart's own pupils would be likely to write.)

This plan is the way Herbart organizes and reports his own practical operations, and it is enlightening to look at this

10. *SW* 14:73–74.   11. *SW* 2:83.

survey in the perspective of his theory. First, the reports concern instruction, and primarily the "course of instruction." Discipline is mentioned explicitly only once by Taute, who merely comments that it cooperates with instruction in producing moral character. Discipline comes in by indirection, however, in Herbart's comments on the personalities of students teaching in the seminar and on how they work with their pupils. Government is nowhere mentioned, and the reasons for this lack are easy to find. First, Herbart probably feels that he is doing nothing novel in this area to interest the ministry and that von Altenstein would assume he knows how to keep school. Second, since the pupils have been individually selected by Herbart, live in his own home, and have probably shown some promise of teachability, the need for government is probably minimal.

Within instruction the six rather traditional fields are undoubtedly those required by the practices and official examinations of the day, but they are here justified by Herbart primarily on the basis of their efficacy in developing manysidedness of interest if properly taught. Three of them (natural science, mathematics, and geography) relate primarily to the idea of perfection, and instruction in them incorporates most obviously the procedure of the four steps: clearness, association, system, and method. Two others, languages and history, are less limited to the single moral idea of perfection and the related manysidedness of interest; the people and events they present give opportunities for judgments based on five of the ideas, though they too make their contribution to manysidedness of interest. In all the foregoing, Herbart's practice of twenty-five years later reflects to a marked degree the "course of instruction" he outlined earlier in the *General Pedagogy*.

Some matters which receive considerable emphasis in the theoretical works are less patent here. Probably Herbart regarded such points as the continual alternation between concentration and reflection and the four steps as built into the program as outlined,[12] and hence their failure to appear more

12. Taute makes this point explicitly in *SW* 15:60.

explicitly should not be surprising. More striking is the lack of psychological explanations and arguments. Granted that Herbart was still working on his psychological investigations during the years of the seminar and also granted that the use of his psychological apparatus would introduce complications into what were, after all, mere yearly reports, still it is curious to find Herbart carrying on practical instruction (which he regards as excellent) without his or his chief assistants' feeling the need to offer explicitly psychological arguments even in passing. One can perhaps argue that, like the other points just mentioned, the psychological necessities are simply incorporated in the program and that "apperceptive attention," "vaulting," "pointing," and all the rest are implicit though not explicit in the structure of the program as presented. This line of thought would lead one to put even greater emphasis on this program of instruction as embodying the application of all Herbart's theories by Herbart himself—the very epitome of what education should be for pupils of this age, provided due allowance is made for particularities of teachers, pupils, and situations. The disquieting facts for this argument are, however, the many points at which this program resembles the schedules Herbart worked out for the von Steiger children long before his detailed psychological investigations. Those skeptical about calling Herbart "systematic" or disliking the system itself have grounds here for arguing that his educational thought was actually much more self-contained and independent of his metaphysics and psychology than Herbart alleges. A definitive judgment here is forever impossible, for reasons noted in chapter 8, though we shall return to this problem again.

Perhaps this course of study was not intended by Herbart to be the precise and comprehensive exemplification of what should result if his theories were applied in a practical situation. Even so, that program would seem to possess considerable importance, if only because Herbart devoted so many of his mature years to the conduct of the seminar. One would expect, therefore, that Herbart's later followers would seek out this program and would find in it, if not a general model, at least a source of various practical suggestions. But this was not to happen. For reasons we shall see shortly, the Herbartians, of whatever kind, will pay relatively little attention to the procedures of the pedagogical seminar except to use the existence of the seminar as proof that the master was no mere cloistered theorist but actually a practical and practicing pedagogue. Beyond performing this function, the work of Herbart's seminar will be of slight use or interest to the Herbartians.

# 11

## "Pedagogy Has Never Been for Me Anything but the Application of Philosophy"

In chapter 4 Herbart's general unpopularity and lack of influence at the time of his death were seen as explicable partly by factors outside the nature and structure of his doctrine—such as his shortcomings as a stylist, the nature of the German gymnasium, or contemporary enthusiasm over German idealism. The intervening chapters have presented the main features of Herbart's educational theory and practice along with those parts of his ethical, metaphysical, and psychological views most relevant to educational concerns. The effort there was directed toward the briefest possible statement of his position rather than toward criticism of it, except for the comment inevitably involved in any attempt at explication. Now it is pertinent to look at Herbart's thought more closely, as a set of isolated doctrines or as a systematic whole, and to inquire into its inherent potentialities as a basis for educational thought and action.[1]

Since the preceding chapters did not attempt an exposition of Herbart's ethical, metaphysical, and psychological theories in their entirety but concentrated on those facets most perti-

1. Chapter title is from SW 15:36.

nent to his educational thought, any critical examination of them must be equally limited. Nevertheless, that admittedly limited survey suggests some judgments concerning these parts of Herbart's doctrine.

The most obvious initial point to note about the ethical theory is its relative (and intentional) isolation from some other parts of the system. Although ethics has immediate bearing on education by defining its aim, the relations of ethics to metaphysics and psychology are far less close than the mutual relations between these last two. Since ethics is part of the independent domain of aesthetics, Herbart's ethical views are not entailed by his metaphysics, or vice versa, whereas psychology is closely linked to metaphysics by being an applied form of it. But this isolation of ethics has consequences for the aim of education. Herbart's ethics can have absolutely no bearing upon reality (which always remains unchanging), but only upon phenomena and true events, which only suggest the relations between reals. These relations are, of course, all we know, and Herbart felt that was sufficient. But the belief that moral or immoral action can make no difference to underlying reality is hardly an incitement to the moral life or to education as a means to morality. Either the importance of reality or the importance of morality is necessarily diminished. There is even some question how moral action can affect the course of "true events." This discontinuity was, as we have seen, taken from Kant, but although Herbart harps on the difficulties Kant's "transcendental freedom" makes for education, he seems insensitive to analogous difficulties in his own doctrine.

If this problem is ignored, then apart from such details [2] as the specifications of the subjective and objective will (matters which do become involved in Herbart's psychology), Herbart's ethical ideals could conceivably be accepted by anyone prepared to talk about "the will" at all—as most of his

2. At the general level, of course, we have only a commonplace, for as Herbart says, that the volitions should be in accordance with the moral law is merely a possible definition of morality.

contemporaries were. In other words, anyone accepting the general concept of the "will" is not debarred from accepting Herbart's ethics, even though he rejects Herbart's metaphysics and psychology. As a result, Herbart's ethical views are less likely to stand or fall with the rest of his system.

This fact is reinforced by another point. Although Herbart underscores the uniqueness of his metaphysical and psychological doctrines, he insists that his ethical ideas constitute no new revelation but are merely a better development and ordering of the funded moral insights of mankind. One need not be the seventh son of a seventh son to forsee likely consequences of this line of argument. If Herbart means by "morality" only what everyone else means by it, anyone can feel that his own views are essentially the same as Herbart's and are merely expressed differently. Thus Herbart's ethics becomes noncontroversial, but also scarcely worth bothering with; and in educational activity, "morality" in this vague sense can be kept as the aim without any impediment from metaphysical, psychological, or even ethical views—Herbart's or another's. Furthermore, at the earliest stages of elementary education, the level at which (as we shall see) the German and American Herbartians chiefly worked, ethical considerations do not seem to be so closely involved in the problems of selecting and organizing materials that more than this vague view is necessary.

In his emphasis on the commonplace nature of his ethics, Herbart possibly falls victim to his own rhetoric. Although he was not as profoundly interested in that field as in metaphysics and psychology, and though he may well have felt that he could make only a limited contribution to it, his ethics is actually more novel than he often implies. This individuality of his doctrine lies not in what he includes but rather in what he excludes and especially in the kind of dominance and subordination he produces among the elements. For example, although he does not exclude the traditional lists of duties and virtues, they are relegated to a secondary and derived position. As a result, anyone taking such a list by itself as an adequate definition of what Herbart means by morality would find himself with an ethics rather different from Herbart's. (And shortly we shall see that occurring.)

If the ethical doctrine is considered apart from its rather neutral position within the other elements of the system, the first thought most likely to occur to the modern observer is that Herbart was overly dependent on his musical analogy. As a lover of Bach, he seems to have succumbed to the belief that God was the ultimate author of the *Well-Tempered Clavier* or (to put the point less figuratively) that the accepted harmony and counterpoint of the early nineteenth century rested on some sort of immutable aesthetic laws. Or if we do not stress his musical model and take his doctrine simply as a form of general ethical intuitionism, saying with Hume that these ethical judgments rest on "the very constitution of our frame and make," the analogous criticism comes to mind: too many intuitionists have taken the moral codes of their particular time and place as statements of the moral verities. Anthropology and psychology have made us highly suspicious of the validity of such intuitive judgments. Yet there has always been a branch of the philosophic and religious tradition which has held that these modes of knowing are valid, and the current popularity of existentialism and Zen suggests that this view is far from dead. Consequently some may find Herbart's ethical and social ideas satisfactory as statements of such direct moral insights. It is only fair to point out, however, that this is not really what Herbart himself intends them to be.

Finally, we can approach Herbart's ethics in the manner of those who see ethical codes as sets of noncontradictory postulates and the further propositions entailed by these postulates. All one then asks is that the code be one coherent set of such propositions among a number of other possible sets. Although Herbart himself would object and though he might be charged with giving "wrong reasons," Herbart's set of ideas may be viewed as constituting a coherent set of possible moral postulates.

In short, Herbart's ethical theory, if not taken strictly, is in many respects viable. Herbart was, as we have seen, able to use it himself in his educational theory, and his educational followers managed to keep it formally, even if they did not emphasize or utilize it. Because it caused the least trouble, it was always the part of his system best preserved by them, and this may contribute some limited testimony to its validity.

Herbart's metaphysical theory is much less bland, as even the partial presentation of it in chapter 8 should make clear. Yet one can argue that even this little metaphysical machinery is more than is actually needed for Herbart's educational thought; that apart from the consequences for psychology in regard to the nature of mind and the origin and nature of presentations, Herbart's educational thought shows little trace of and makes little use of its alleged metaphysical foundations. Sometimes (but only sometimes) Herbart seems to feel that way himself: "I leave untouched the metaphysical difficulties connected with this development. He who understands how to educate forgets them." [3] Or to put the point another way, would the person who had read only the *General Pedagogy* and the *Outlines of Pedagogical Lectures* be able to guess (to say nothing of infer) the metaphysical position of their author? That the answer of this question seems so inevitably no gives rise to a number of reflections.

If Herbart's metaphysics is so dispensable for working with education that even Herbart dispenses with it, then assuredly others will follow suit, if only for the sake of simplicity. Herbart's educational thought is sufficiently extensive and intricate without any unnecessary complications. If the relation of the pedagogy to the metaphysics is so tenuous, we can foresee that is will be passed over and that the acceptance or rejection of Herbart's metaphysical thought will not be important to the acceptance or rejection of his educational views.

But this glance into the future has distracted us from a critical look at the validity of Herbart's metaphysics and its utility as a basis for education. The observer is likely to suspect

3. *SW* 2:29.

that Herbart does not make greater use of his metaphysics simply because it is not useful—possibly even because it is more a hindrance than a help.

Herbart arrived at his metaphysics (as in their different ways did Fichte, Schelling, Hegel, and the others at that time) through trying to improve on Kant's answer to the problem of knowledge. In consequence, Herbart's metaphysics is dominated by epistemological considerations. His reals, his true events as images in mind, and all the rest of his apparatus were developed to secure what he felt was an adequate answer to the question, "What are the relations between our ideas and reality (if such indeed there be)?" Thus his metaphysics speaks to our passive knowledge of events in the external world. But what, for example, of those events in which we are active in causing phenomena to appear by manipulating "objects"—when, say, instead of observing a fire we light one? Granted that we cannot know the nature of the reals in either situation, still if our perceptions rest on the comings and goings of reals, in acting and making we somehow control these comings and goings, since we do make true events occur. "Productive" or "operative" activities receive scant attention and encounter some difficulties in this metaphysics.

Our limited purview of Herbart's metaphysics renders invalid any attempt to judge the doctrine purely as a metaphysics even if time and space were available here. But the difficulties of relating it to education have already been suggested. The teacher cannot affect reality; he cannot change the student's soul. At best he works with phenomena as images in mind, rather far away from the "thingy" world of teachers, pupils, and objects of instruction. And this is a very difficult place for an active teacher to work. As a result, we find Herbart as an educator working not there, but in what is essentially the world of naive realism, not within his more sophisticated realism with its phenomenalistic epicycles.

For Herbart metaphysics becomes involved in education mainly through its application, psychology, in regard to the natures of the soul and mind and the origin and nature of presentations. But in his educational works Herbart does not make much of these metaphysical foundations. As a result, the educators following him were tempted not to pay much attention to them, to take "mind" (in some sense) as somehow furnished with "ideas" through sense impressions, without prying too much into what mind is, why it has ideas, or why these ideas become associated or otherwise react with each other.

In any case, as is stated in the quotation which serves as the title for this chapter, Herbart was not an educator seeking to develop metaphysics (and its applied branch, psychology) as a basis for educational thought or action. Although he had a life-long interest in education, he always saw himself as primarily a professor of philosophy, within which the areas of metaphysics and psychology were much more important than pedagogy. He related psychology closely to metaphysics, partly because psychology afforded what he considered the best answers to some traditional metaphysical puzzles (e.g., continua) and partly because metaphysics, in turn, could give him some fundamental postulates for psychology. But metaphysics, cut off from ethics, is linked to education only through psychology, and this connection is tenuous insofar as the links between psychology and pedagogy are weak or are difficult to assess.

If any judgment on Herbart's metaphysics can be rendered on the basis of that small portion treated here, the immediate reaction is likely to be that it is clever because it gives plausible explanations by some ingenious machinery. But the more one attempts to work with it as a system, the more problems one encounters, and one's more mature judgment inclines to the belief that although the metaphysics is clever and learned, it is not profound or insightful. Despite its apparent neatness, the difficulties encountered by Drobisch, Hartenstein, and others who attempted to carry the metaphysics forward appear to demonstrate its shortcomings conclusively. It was probably a godsend to those who later revived Herbart's educational thought that his metaphysics was not more obviously involved in his educational doctrine. Herbart clearly was not destined to immortality as a metaphysicist, although one suspects that as a child of his times he would have wished most to be remembered for this part of his work.

We need not accept uncritically the judgment of Rudolf Eucken, who was professor of philosophy at the University of Jena when Wilhelm Rein's pedagogical seminar there was making that institution the hub of Herbartianism, but his comment can be considered typical:

> and especially do I share your view of Herbart; according to which he may doubtless be regarded a great pedagogue but not a leader in philosophy. This is the conviction of most learned men in Germany. Herbart's metaphysics scarcely finds a disciple among the younger generation. However, among teachers his pedagogy, owing to its systematic structure and careful elaboration, justly finds many disciples, but alas! these disciples are very apt to fall into the danger of adopting his dry and uninspiring view of the world, owing to the usefulness of his pedagogy.[4]

This comment is remarkable on at least two counts: it charges the metaphysics with nothing worse than being "dry and uninspiring" and suggests that some of Rein's students have at least some knowledge of the metaphysics and some interest in it. Nonetheless, Eucken's general opinion is that of the philosophers during the educational triumphs of Herbartianism.

As for Herbart's psychological theory, it was, as we have seen, a network of hypotheses and the consequences developed from them. Herbart was impressed by the progress of physics and astronomy, which dealt wholesale with what were for his metaphysics "fictions" and yet were able to organize the phenomena with which they were concerned. Therefore he sought to develop a comparable set of fictions for psychology, endlessly elaborating his mathematical formulations of them and, to a degree, testing to see whether they too explained the

4. From a letter to W. T. Harris published in the *Educational Review* 10 (1895): 207. The translation is that of the *Review*.

relevant phenomena. The fatal flaw was, of course, that the phenomena against which he checked his fictions lacked the precision to serve as adequate tests, something physics and astronomy had developed through precise and prolonged observation and experiment. He too suffered from a weakness with which he had charged his psychological predecessors: he lacked an adequate "natural history" of fundamental psychological data. Because his data were crude, his tests were even cruder; and in consequence his empirical testing rarely, if ever, helped him revise, much less question, his theoretical constructions. It is probably his failure to see this need (rather than any want of ingenuity concerning how to supply this lack, once it had been noted) that leaves his psychology at the level of what he would have called in another's work a mythology. Other difficulties are cited at length in the literature,[5] but this very fundamental one suffices for our purposes.

If Herbart's psychology, as psychology, is this inadequate, and if it is as closely related to his pedagogy as he alleges, is his educational theory irretrievably doomed? Clearly, if we take Herbart completely and seriously the answer is yes.

Obviously there are other possibilities. We may "correct" Herbart's psychology and then try to make the corresponding necessary changes in his educational theory. This is essentially the course pursued by some who later called themselves Herbartians, and the results are necessarily psychologies and pedagogies differing in varying degrees from Herbart's. Another possibility is to hold that Herbart was mistaken about the closeness of the relation between his psychology and his pedagogy or about the direction of the flow of influence in his own thought. One then discards the psychology, preserves the pedagogy and, perhaps, evolves a new statement of his psychology from what is inherent in his educational theory. This view amounts to saying that Herbart, the thoughtful and observant pedagogue, was a better psychologist than Herbart, the student of the calculus. These procedures too have been

5. E.g., H. Ströle, *Herbarts Psychologie im Verhältnis zu seinem Erziehungsideal* (Stuttgart: C. Belser, 1903), pp. 20ff.

adopted in varying degrees by later followers or students of Herbart. Needless to say, this is not what Herbart promised and not what was sought by some other Herbartians, many of whom believed that the chief value of Herbart's pedagogy was that it was firmly based on psychological laws. But both Herbart and the Herbartians may have been mistaken.

To suggest the possibility of a psychology implicit within the pedagogy is really to face directly the question, "To what extent do Herbart's educational theory and practice involve a psychology in anything but the very loosest sense of that word, and to what degree is it merely a mixture of contemporary practice, his personal predilections, and his own summary of the distilled wisdom or empirical generalizations of the generations of those who before him had 'kept school'?" The reasons why Herbart may not have offered detailed psychological explanations and justifications for his educational procedures (as he did not) have already been considered in the biographical and historical context. Now we need to look at Herbart's psychology as it actually appears in his educational doctrines.

The classifications and distinctions within his theory of instruction (such as those which give rise to the four steps) are obvious objects for such a scrutiny. Even on rather casual inspection it becomes evident that these need not rest on any very profound psychological principles or detailed research, regardless of the efforts (some of which we have seen) Herbart later made to connect them with his theories. Many of them are age-old logical or commonsense distinctions, and this point should not be dismissed out of hand as a distinction without a difference on the ground that logical or commonsense principles are simply one facet of how the mind works or ought to work and that therefore they are at bottom psychological. Even if this point is valid, the principles are so general that any logic or any psychology will permit them.

To say, for example, that experience presents us with things and events whose characteristics can be noted and which can usually be analyzed into parts or elements is hardly a profound or doctrinal matter. To say further that on the basis of these characteristics groupings and separations of the items can be made and that the resulting organizations embody some principles of ordering is equally commonplace. Then to say that human knowledge consists of this sort of thing (observation of characteristics and classifying them together or apart on the basis of some principle) is not earthshaking. Yet these points give us the four steps, and not on the basis of any recondite theory of "learning" or "mind."

The distinction between knowledge and sympathy is no more profound; the intellectual-emotional or cognitive-affective distinction is no new deliverance. (In fact, though Herbart keeps this distinction in his pedagogy, one might have expected him to abandon or blur it because his psychological apparatus actually links very closely the cognitive-conative-volitive.) The subdivisions within this distinction likewise illustrate the same point. That the recognition of regularities among phenomena, even if such laws are not imposed by the human mind, at least involves something more than the mere perception of a given event was a commonplace in philosophic thought for generations before Herbart; yet this is the source of the distinction between "empiricism" and "speculation." That judgments of worth or value constitute a class different from the preceding two is again a fairly bland philosophic proposition. As for the subdivisions of sympathy in turn, the distinction between the individual and society and between man's relations to his fellowmen and his relations to God are so commonplace that they scarcely merit a label "philosophic," "psychological," "sociological," or "theological." Yet these are the distinctions which determine much of Herbart's pedagogy. All these facts suggest that one reason we get so few arguments that strike us as "psychological" in Herbart's pedagogical works is the kind of "psychology" actually involved.

Here the critical point is probably the difference between what "psychology" meant to Herbart and what it means to us. When Herbart sought fictions as the basis for framing his laws of mind, he was not prepared to accept just anything. He naturally sought categories, criteria, and principles which gave some promise of being relevant and useful in his effort to organize and explain what psychological data he had. In this position, he was neither the first nor the last to turn to the history and structure of "science" in some sense to find clues concerning the acquisition, organization, and utilization of human knowledge. As a result, it is not surprising that his four steps, for example, incorporate precisely the principles involved in building a taxonomy. Since these principles seem basic in developing this form of scientific knowledge, he generalizes the process to all learning. That the zoologist, botanist, and mineralogist of Herbart's day organized his knowledge in this fashion must have seemed to Herbart to suggest that it was a good way. As a result, what does not seem to us very "psychological" is for Herbart the very basis of psychology, for he takes these forms of human knowledge gained through "science" as more or less given by human experience. Starting from this base, Herbart can move to either pedagogical or psychological elaborations. His psychology and his pedagogy are consequently only as good as these rather commonplace bases are valid and appropriate. With the four steps, for example, considerable congruence exists between the principles of building a taxonomy and some principles of learning in general. As a result, as we shall see in chapters 13 and 14, the steps will persist as a technique because they possess this plausibility and cogency; but they have this force because of their original derivation, not because of Herbart's psychological development of the steps from mutual arrests and the like. This is one of the chief reasons that in these favorable cases the psychology appears to be a pompous elaboration of basic pedagogical principles; the pedagogy stays closer to the original data and, being less tightly structured than the psychological theory, can be modified to bring it still closer.

In less happy instances where Herbart found less plausible bases and his recipes seem bereft of all "psychological" or "scientific" underpinnings, what do they become? Largely the prescription of the personal preferences of the educator in question—granted that like all such prescriptions past and present they may rest on experience which the educator has sought to examine. They are, to be sure, better organized and set forth in greater detail than the observations of most of his predecessors. But if this is all that Herbart has to offer as the "father of scientific education," then he was not even a ghost, but rather the figment of various imaginations, of which his own was the first.

If we may emulate Herbart and attempt to put things "in the nutshell," he had, despite his undoubted sincerity and effort, arrived at a set of dead ends by the time he died. That he should ever become more famous than he was at this point seems scarcely conceivable; but such are the surprises of history.

# 12

## Ziller Transforms the Labyrinth

Formerly the great majority of teachers, even among
Herbart's pupils, wondered at the network of abstract
conceptions to be found in his *Allgemeine Pädagogik*
without knowing what to make of them. This apparent labyrinth of concepts was first transformed by
Professor Ziller of Leipzig into a theory which can
actually direct the practice of instruction in the proper
course by means of a series of practical and adaptable
imperatives.[1]

At Herbart's funeral one of the eulogists asserted that the de-
ceased's work would not be properly recognized until a century had passed. If this statement is taken not as merely the
pious testimonial of a colleague but as a serious prediction, it
was in a sense fulfilled within only a quarter of a century. In
1865 Tuiskon Ziller published his *Foundation for the Doctrine
of Educative Instruction* (*Grundlegung zur Lehre vom erzieh-*

1. W. Rein, *Pädagogik im Grundriss* (Stuttgart: Sammlung Göschen,
1890), 3d ed. (1893) translated as *Outlines of Pedagogics* by C. C. Van
Liew and I. J. Van Liew (London: Swan Sonnenschein & Co., 1893),
p. 140. The translation is the Van Liews'.

*enden Unterricht*), and there is almost unanimous agreement that this is the book which started "Herbartianism" on its way. That the beginning of any historical movement can be dated so simply and so precisely is in itself suspicious and proves to be not quite true,[2] but this dating is certainly as valid as most such turning points and can serve.

Ziller was born in 1817 in Wasungen near Meiningen, where his father was a pastor. After graduation from the gymnasium at Meiningen, he entered the University of Leipzig. Family circumstances, however, prevented his carrying his work through to the doctorate, and he returned to teach for a while in the Meiningen gymnasium, thus becoming interested and involved in the practical problems of education. About 1850 he returned to the University of Leipzig, presumably to study jurisprudence. But because of a desire to help humanity [3] he gave up the study of law and devoted himself to philology and philosophy. And here he entered the apostolic succession from Herbart in that his chief mentors in philosophy were Drobisch and Hartenstein. The former was, as we have already seen, probably Herbart's closest student and collaborator during his lifetime. Hartenstein, though slightly less intimately connected with the master, had also remained a friend and correspondent and was, at the very time Ziller returned to Leipzig, beginning his publication of Herbart's *Collected Works*.[4] If anyone was ever likely to hear about Herbart again, it was a philosophy student at Leipzig during this period, and Ziller obviously got the word.

Ziller, after completing his doctorate in 1854, began to lecture on pedagogy at Leipzig, publishing his *Introduction to General Pedagogy* (*Einleitung in die Allgemeine Pädagogik*) in 1856 and his *Government of Children* in 1857. These

2. Note his earlier "Eine Skizze der pädagogischen Reformsbestrebungen in der Gegenwart, nach Herbartischen Grundsätzen," *Zeitschrift für exakte Philosophie* 4 (1864), and his outline in *Berliner Blätter* (1863).
3. See Ziller, *Allgemeine Pädagogik*, 3d ed. by K. Just (Leipzig: Heinrich Matthes, 1892), p. 19, n. 3.
4. G. Hartenstein, *J. F. Herbart's Sämtliche Werke*, (12 vols.; Leipzig: L. Voss, 1850–52; 2d ed., 13 vols. 1883–93).

books possessed only a slight Herbartian flavor, caused little stir, and exerted little or no influence.

In the practical field, however, Ziller was moving along lines similar to those followed by Herbart. In the winter of 1861–62 he established a pedagogical seminar, intended to be truly devoted to the study of education, in contrast to seminars at other universities (Jena excepted), which seemed to him to offer only a little practice teaching and some instruction at what we would call the level of "credentials" or "certification" for students whose main interests were philological or theological.[5] In 1863, in conjunction with Earnst Barth, he organized, a la Pestalozzi, a society for the creation and maintenance of a school for poor children where the students of the seminar could practice. He thus killed the birds of both social and educational reform with one institutional stone.

He did not wish to help the culturally deprived merely by teaching them a marketable skill; he felt that if they could be improved, they could better their own lots in life.[6] And by "improving" them, he meant precisely what Herbart did— enriching and coordinating their circle of thought for the sake of its effect upon character.

Out of these ideas and activities came the publication of the *Foundation* (1865), and it was far from his sole contribution. He had piled up about one hundred pages of revisions in the manuscript, which were included by Vogt in the second edition published in 1883, the year after Ziller's death. In 1876 Ziller published his *Lectures on General Pedagogy*, incorporating a reworking of his earlier *Introduction* and his *Government of Children* with the inclusion of much more material on "special methods" in the various subjects. For this book too he produced voluminous manuscript changes and additions, which were incorporated by Karl Just in his second

5. T. Ziller, *Grundlegung zur Lehre vom erziehenden Unterricht*, 2d revised ed. by T. Vogt (Leipzig: Von Veit and Co., 1865), pp. 207–8, n. 6.
6. So especially the section of the *Grundlegung* entitled "Manysidedness of Interest as an Aid in Earthly Activity," *Grundlegung*, 2d ed., pp. 383–95.

(1884) and third (1892) editions of the *General Pedagogy* after Ziller's death.

Of equal importance with Ziller's publications was his organization in 1869, in collaboration with Senff of Berlin, of the "Society for Scientific Pedagogy" (Verein für wissenschaftliche Pädagogik), with a *Yearbook* and a monthly journal (*Monatsblättern für wissenschaftliche Pädagogik*), which became the first rallying point for converts to Herbartian pedagogy on Ziller's model. By 1894, this organization had more than eight hundred members.[7]

The important fact about Ziller's *Foundation* is, of course, that although he presents Herbart's theories, he presents them with omissions, additions, and changes; and it is these variations which give all later Herbartianism its particular cast and hue and which pose, for ever after, the general problem of the relation of Herbart to Herbartianism.

For the sake of simplicity and brevity three major points can illustrate the kind and degree of change: (1) the four steps are given great importance, and the first is divided into two for a total of five; (2) "concentration centers" are developed as the focus for each year's work; (3) these centers are organized in chronological sequence as "culture epochs" on the theory that in formal education the child should relive the intellectual history of his species. The importance of these three points can be seen in the fact that Wilhelm Rein later notes them as the chief characteristics of Herbartianism.[8]

Just how much emphasis Herbart himself actually intended to give to his four "steps" is open to dispute. Caselmann[9] quite justly points out that the proportion of either Herbart's *General Pedagogy* or his *Outlines of Educational Lectures* which is explicitly devoted to them is extremely minute.

7. Christian Ufer, *Introduction to the Pedagogy of Herbart,* trans. J. C. Zinser (Boston: D. C. Heath & Co., 1894), p. 76, n. 1.
8. W. Rein, A. Pickel, E. Scheller, *Theorie und Praxis des Volksschulunterrichts nach Herbartischen Grundsätzen,* 6th ed., 8 vols. (Leipzig: Heinrich Bredt, 1898 ff.), 1:15.
9. Christian Caselmann, *Der unsystematische Herbart.* (Heidelberg: Quelle & Meyer, 1962), pp. 58–59.

As chapter 9 has suggested, however, the steps are implicitly inherent in or are related to a number of other matters, and on these grounds the estimate of their importance for Herbart may be raised somewhat. Nevertheless, in making any such revision one must admit that a sensitivity to the formal steps engendered by Ziller and his followers may lead us to find them and topics related to them where Herbart himself did not so intend; and in any case the Herbartians undeniably give the steps more prominence than did Herbart. The fact that Theodore Wiget's *The Formal Steps* [10] went through *six* editions tells something about the movement. The steps have become for the Herbartians the foundation of how to teach the subject matter once it was organized by the concentration centers and culture epochs.

In addition to giving greater stress to the steps, Ziller altered them.[11] Most obviously, he broke Herbart's first step, clarity, into two—analysis and synthesis. As we saw, Herbart does use these terms to denote different phases of instruction; but if they are attached exclusively to the first step they, and the first step, no longer mean what they did for Herbart.[12] But as was predictable from Herbart's own treatment of the steps, anyone else attempting to use them would be almost certain to try to reorganize and clarify them. In fact, Ziller's modification of the steps was merely the opening lead of a game in which most other German Herbartians (Stoy, Dörpfeld, Vogt, and especially Rein) were also to play hands.[13] That Ziller's own effort to clarify the steps was not completely successful is

10. T. Wigit, *Die formalen Stufen*, 6th ed. (Chur: J. Rich, 1897). See also Karl Richter, *Die Herbart-Zillerischen formalen Stufen des Unterrichts nach ihrem Wesen, ihrer geschichtlichen Grundlage und ihrer Anwendung im Volksschulunterrichte dargestellte.* (Leipzig: M. Hesse, 1888).

11. Ziller, *Allgemeine Pädagogik*, 3d ed., pp. 257 ff.

12. "From his *General Pedagogy* the author cannot help noting briefly that he finds necessary an analytic and a synthetic thread of instruction, *both simultaneous* except that the former is a few steps ahead." (SW 1:258. Emphasis in original.)

13. Rein summarizes these differences in his *Theorie und Praxis*, 6th ed., 1:110–56.

perhaps attested by the story that his students nicknamed a particularly dark set of cellar stairs in his institute "the five steps." [14]

Ziller's two other changes, his introduction of concentration centers and the culture epochs, were still further removed from the main body of Herbart's doctrine. Since those modifications are closely related to each other and spring from much the same causes, they are best considered together.

The culture epochs concern the vertical *sequence* of studies; the concentration centers govern their horizontal *correlation*. The precise forms which both these undertakings assumed are functions in large part of the general educational situation in nineteenth-century Germany.

Herbart's own practical operations had been largely pointed toward the secondary rather than the elementary level of education with, for example, the students in his practice school at Königsberg being prepared for entrance into the final year of the gymnasium. As we have seen, his theory and practice made little impression on the gymnasiums of his time and were destined to suffer pretty much this same fate forever. Occasional private schools might try to be more or less Herbartian, and gymnasium teachers undoubtedly got "suggestions" from Herbart and the Herbartians. But systematic and large-scale adoptions did not occur despite the efforts of Frick and some other Herbartians [15] to prepare suitable programs. The gymnasium was the conservative institution of the conservative upper classes. In spite of the powerful forces which beat upon it, the changes in emphasis, procedures, and materials which did in fact occur, and the many reformers (including Herbart) who wished to alter it,[16] the gymnasium remained

14. F. H. Hayward, *The Student's Herbart* (London: Swan Sonnenschein & Co., 1902), p. 27.
15. A convenient listing of such materials can be found in Van Liew, *Outlines of Pedagogics,* pp. 188–89.
16. For details, see Hajo Holborn, *A History of Modern Germany 1648–1840.* (New York: Alfred A. Knopf, 1964), pp. 465–76, and J. Roach in the *Cambridge Modern History* (Cambridge: Cambridge University Press, 1960), 10:104–33.

to an astonishing degree unaltered from about 1810 till the reforms of 1932, particularly in prestige and in social function.

On the contrary, elementary education and secondary education in institutions other than the classical gymnasium were much less rigid and much less sacred, and from the seventeenth century onward they had been a matter of public and official concern in Prussia and the other German states. For one thing, Germany suffered from a plethora of types of school, which had grown up for various purposes at different times and places. As Rein was to exclaim toward the end of the nineteenth century, "Have we not now higher and lower burgher-schools, upper real-schools, real-gymnasiums, and real-schools, middle-schools, progymnasiums, real-progymnasiums, etc.?" [17] The ineffectiveness of the total system, the lack of articulation among its various elements, and the lack of concern (compared to that devoted to the gymnasium) which had been bestowed upon the elementary level troubled others besides educators. The Iron Chancellor himself stated, "The ability to read is much more widespread among us than it is in France and England; the ability to make practical judgments about what has been read is much less widespread here than in those countries." [18] By presenting an articulated eight-year program, Rein and the others hoped to revitalize the *Volksschule* and to make some sense out of the eight years of school attendance presumably required by the law of 1869. In these schools, at least, elementary and secondary education could be linked in a unified sequence, and for this reform the place to begin was the elementary school.

With this shift in the educational level to which the doctrine was to be applied, Herbart's own theory and practice became less literally applicable; and for the earlier grades at least Ziller would have had to make his own way to a considerable extent in any case. More important, this change to the elementary level confronted Ziller with the fact that the ele-

17. Van Liew, *Outlines of Pedogogics*, p. 27. For Ziller in a similar vein, see his *Allgemeine Pädagogik*, 3d ed., pp. 140–58.
18. O. v. Bismarck, Speech to the Reichstag, 9 Oct. 1878.

mentary schools of Germany were primarily church-related, either Lutheran or Catholic. In contrast to the situation in many other countries, in Prussia and other German states church and state had collaborated fairly peaceably in elementary education. Herbart was always prepared to give religion what he felt was its due, but he believed that this amount was easily exaggerated and he was always suspicious of religion in its creedal and mystical forms. (After all, even as a boy he had been taught to approach religion in a very rational fashion.) [19] His program for moral education was based, therefore, not on religious insight, tradition, or revelation, but on the fundamental ethical ideas, which he obviously thought more rationally grounded and more universal than any particular religious faith. As a result Ziller faced the task of adapting what was at best a nonreligious theory to the use of essentially religious institutions. As matters stood, therefore, it was probably better for Ziller's purposes that Herbart's doctrines were not more clearly and directly related to the task at hand. Ziller was much more religious in the confessional sense than Herbart and might have given Herbart's doctrine this religious turn anyway: "Herbart in his theory did not emphasize the religious side enough." [20]

Herbart's own procedures in curriculum organizing and planning had always been flexible and even free-wheeling, directed toward the individual student. For better or worse, Ziller eliminated all that in order to achieve a uniform plan. To each of the eight years of his program he assigned a concentration center and ordered these eight centers for the most part on the basis of the culture-epoch theory:

1. Epic fairy tales
2. *Robinson Crusoe*
3. The history of the biblical patriarchs

19. Typical of his view of the role of religion in education is his statement in *SW* 3:296–97. See also W. Asmus, "Glaube und Wissen im Denken J., Fr. Herbarts," *Der Evangelischer Erzieher* 20 (Sept. 1968): 329–37.
20. Ziller, *Allgemeine Pädagogik,* 3d ed., p. 34 and n. 8.

4. The judges in Israel
5. The kings of Israel
6. The life of Christ
7. The history of the Apostles
8. The history of the Reformation [21]

Centers 3–8 are simply based on the sequence of biblical and ecclesiastical history, and religious enthusiasts were very indignant with the Herbartians for failing to start the series with number 3. Ziller and his immediate followers were, however, convinced that this was impossible. Being related to a completely different civilization and language family, the names, customs, places, and other features of the early biblical narrative were simply too exotic to be a sensible starting-point for the education of German six-year-olds.[22] Something more appropriate had to be found for the first two years. Use of German translations of the Greek epics was a pious gesture toward Herbart's devotion to beginning with the *Odyssey*, but the fairy stories of the brothers Grimm seemed preferable for German children just beginning to read and write. As for the second year, no less an "authority" than Rousseau had come out in favor of *Robinson Crusoe* as a text for elementary education,[23] and, to be sure, Crusoe on his island did suggest an Adam in the state of nature and hence a culture epoch previous to that of the biblical patriarchs, in spite of certain technological advantages Robinson possessed. Once these first two, rather anomalous, years were past, then the biblical-ecclesiastical sequence could provide a concentration center for each of the remaining six years.

All this is rather different from Herbart's own program, but Ziller and his followers felt they had warrant for these changes not merely in the situation but in Herbart's own

21. Ziller's *Grundlegung*, 2d ed., where a parallel sequence in the classical authors is hopefully offered for the upper stages (the early years of the gymnasium).
22. Rein summarizes this controversy and restates his own arguments (with extensive bibliography) in his *Theorie und Praxis*, 6th ed., 1:4–10, 164–72.
23. *Emile*, book 3.

position. Herbart's division of instruction into that concerned with "knowledge" and that concerned with "sympathy," as well as the clear differences in the way Herbart treated the historical-linguistic studies on the one hand and the scientific-mathematical studies on the other, seemed to threaten the student not with two cultures, but with several insufficiently related circles of thought.[24] If a mishmash was to be avoided, Ziller felt, it was necessary to build a single, unified circle of thought; and the first step in this process was to concentrate on one focal point each year. By selecting his centers from the historical-religious side, Ziller incorporated his own preference for the literary over the scientific and also made the curriculum appropriate for the existing religious schools. (In this respect, however, he did not go to the extreme of his follower, Thrändorf, who worked out a curriculum sufficiently sectarian for the pupil to be confirmed and received into the Lutheran church at the end of its eight years.) [25]

In setting up the concentration centers, Ziller and his followers undoubtedly saw themselves as merely applying two principles taken from Herbart, one from his ethics, the other from his psychology. In fact, they tend to imply that they are only doing faithfully what the master himself would have done had he fully seen the thrust of his own arguments.

The ethical argument involves the idea of perfection of the will. As chapter 6 indicated, the perfected or efficient will is not merely strong in each of its individual strivings, which are directed toward many different objects; the further criterion of the perfected will is that these multiple, strong strivings be *concentrated*, producing a new unity out of the diversity of many strong strivings. In the opinion of the Herbartians, instruction claiming to educate toward morality could not neglect this third characteristic of the perfected will, especially

24. Ziller, *Allgemeine Pädagogik*, 3d ed., pp. 224–30, 243–44. Interestingly enough, although the Herbartians could have cited Herbart's own warnings about onesidedness in this respect (SW 10:153–54), they do not seem to do so.
25. K. E. Thrändorf, *Die Behandlung des Religion-Unterrichts nach Herbart-Zillerische Methode*, (Langensalza: A. Berger u. Söhne, 1887).

since it is so intimately related to manysidedness of interest, which is also related to perfection, the moral idea with which Herbart said education is primarily concerned. The concentration centers are, consequently, justified as being necessary to produce the perfected or efficient will.

A psychological argument for the concentration centers grows out of the general theory of apperception, and extreme emphasis on apperception, which is only a part of Herbart's psychological doctrine, is another characteristic of Herbartianism and another claimant for the title of the "major modification" or "major distortion" which the Herbartians worked in Herbart's theory. Once more they seem to have felt that the master had failed to face up to the implications of his own principles.

Herbart did believe, to be sure, that the existing circle of thought or apperceptive mass determined what new presentations would be retained in consciousness and be active there and that a new presentation could be assimilated to the degree that it was similar to presentations and combinations of them already existing in that circle. Consequently, the Herbartians argue, since only similarity insures apperception and assimilation, new objects of study must be similar to previous ones if instruction is to be effective; and this similarity can be achieved only if everything centers around a single topic. Here again the Herbartians have emphasized, or overemphasized, a single principle of Herbart. At this *general* level, however, Goethe [26] and a number of others had said something like, "We can learn only what we are prepared to learn." Had Herbart actually wished for this snaillike gradualism in moving through curricular topics, both in developing perfection of the will and in arousing many-sided interest, one would have expected him to enunciate it as a principle and to apply it in his own practical work.

As for the chronological sequence through the culture epochs, the Herbartians justified this procedure on the grounds of Herbart's practice and his theory. In practice, Herbart, by

26. E.g., *Wilhelm Meisters Wanderjahre*, chap. 3.

beginning with the *Odyssey,* did in fact begin with the start
of the literary-historical tradition of Western Europe; and by
following Homer with Herodotus he moved chronologically
within Greek literature as well as recapitulating the Greek
sequence of poetry first, then prose. His use of Xenophon and
Plato later also coincides with the chronology of Greek literature. Likewise, Greek first, then Latin (one of his favorite
themes) also happens to be a historical fact. But, as we have
seen, Herbart's reasons for doing all this are rather different
from any decision to adopt as a general principle the recapitulation of mankind's total cultural history, and Herbart's procedures here seem scarcely to constitute even an implicit
acknowledgment of recapitulation as a principle to be followed.

The Herbartians' second line of argument rests on some
explicit statements Herbart does make in regard to specific
parts of instruction, the synthetic treatment of "sympathy" and
"taste." To give Ziller and his followers their due, we should
look at the whole of a typical statement by Herbart on this
point:

> Only those partially possess it [sympathy] and can to some
> degree impart it who have produced within themselves
> many varied pictures of humanity—only the worthiest
> among the poets and, after them, the historians. In them
> we seek the clearest *perception* of general psychological
> truth. But this truth is *continually* modified according to
> now this, now that circumstance of mankind in times and
> places. And sensitivity to it is continually modified with
> advancing age. It is the duty of the educator to take care
> that both these modifications always properly effect each
> other, progress together. Therefore, a CHRONOLOGICAL
> PROGRESSION FROM THE OLD TO THE NEW! . . . Also the
> distorted and artistically bad, . . . when presented in such
> a sequence with all its oppositions and contradictions will
> lose its attractive influence which it usually exerts on the
> unprepared, who seeking culture without sure direction,
> are so easily deluded and often so dangerously affected.
> Moving forward on the *heights* of human development,
> we, when we have arrived at our contemporary literature,
> will easily pass by its low and boggy places, and with this

is connected a considerable degree of security against everything misleading in the present world. The whole course will end with the contrast between our age and the rational ideal of what man could be.[27]

There is also another briefer passage on the same point:

If one would prepare the youth for spiritual elevation, he should see what the spiritual development of mankind has been. In this way by imitating the track of moral culture in the human race, the educator will see in the progress of his pupil a recapitulation of the great progress of mankind.

Even if we grant that these and similar quotations make out the case for using something resembling the culture epochs in synthetic instruction in sympathy, they hardly seem justification for extending the principle to all parts of instruction, particularly in the face of his statement regarding instruction in the sciences, "It would be absurd to make the pupils' advance in these subjects dependent upon the gradual progress of discoveries." Herbart was undeniably aware of the possibility of progressing chronologically and admittedly did so in devising parts of his theory; but (it seems equally undeniable) Ziller's extension of the principle goes beyond (and, in part, even contrary to) Herbart.

The culture-epoch theory was not, needless to say, invented by Ziller. Even earlier (1836) in what might be called loosely the Herbartian tradition, Herbart's student Brzoska, in his book dedicated to Herbart, *On the Necessity for Pedagogical Seminars at the University,* had said:

The human being, growing from the cradle on, presents a picture perfectly analogous to the development of the entire human race .... But if the rising future generation is to attain its highest goal of furthering human ennoblement with conviction and certainty, then it must see clearly and plainly before it the course which mankind has moved through up to its own time.[28]

27. *SW* 2:75, 77, 79. The italics and small caps reflect similar emphasis in the original. See also *SW* 2:82, 65–66.
28. H. G. Brzoska, *Über die Notwendigkeit pädagogischer Seminare auf der Universität,* 2d ed. by W. Rein (Leipzig: J. A. Barth, 1836), p. 16.

But the recapitulation theory was an intellectual commonplace quite apart from anything the Herbartians did about it. Chronological order is one of the most obvious types of organization and, consequently, one likely to occur to even the most amateur curriculum planners. The German Herbartians were fond of quoting Goethe (just as the American Herbartians later primarily quoted still another non-Herbartian, Herbert Spencer). But Goethe was quoted only because he was the proper man to quote, for the same idea could have been quoted (and sometimes was) from Lessing, Kant, Fichte, Schiller, Schelling, Herder, Schleiermacher, Hegel, and a crowd of other Germans; if foreigners were wanted, there were Spencer, Huxley, and Comte; or one could display classical erudition by citing Clement of Alexandria, Augustine, and others.[29] The basic idea was no more Herbart's than it was the Herbartians', though emphasis on it was a major characteristic of German Herbartianism.

The preceding summary presents the main contributions of Ziller to Herbartianism, but, like many similar ones in the literature, it is misleading in several respects. First, it fails to reveal Ziller's general method of working, which was undoubtedly a major factor in his effectiveness. Where Herbart had been abrupt and disconnected, not only in sentence and paragraph structure, but also in presenting his ideas without adequate introduction or argument, Ziller works painstakingly, making each point with detailed care, meeting possible objections, and garnering supporting arguments from earlier educational thinkers, from religion, or from wherever he can find them. He is determined to be clear and persuasive, since, as Vogt says, Herbart's own *General Pedagogy* was "too obscure to be effective." [30] Since the *Foundation* is over five hundred pages long and on many of them the text is a thin stream trickling over a bedrock of footnotes in smaller type, the book

29. For Americans the most accessible summary (with references) is that of C. C. Van Liew, "The Educational Theory of the Culture Epochs," *First Yearbook of the National Herbart Society*, pp. 72–80.
30. T. Vogt in "Editor's Foreward to the Second Edition" of Ziller's *Grundlegung*, p. vii.

may have seemed too long to some readers, who would prefer the more schematic presentation of Ziller's later *Lectures on General Pedagogy.*

But the *Foundation* is not repetitive or verbose; its length is a consequence of the care with which it covers much ground. For example, the movement toward the elementary level is not an abruptly announced decision, but the conclusion of a gradual argument extending over about one hundred pages. Ziller sees the last years of the gymnasium as devoted to the specialization required for entrance into the universities and into government service. There is little room here for educative instruction even if the teachers were capable of it—which they were not: "In scarcely any other rank is the number of dullards, bunglers, and quacks as great as it is among higher-school teachers and school-inspectors in regard to pedagogic-didactic development, and the result of this is that the art of method has not kept pace with the continuous development of the teachers in their professional disciplines." [31] Prerequisites for the prerequisites for this specialization take their further toll of student's time in the earlier years of the gymnasium. If, then, educative instruction is desirable for everyone—and here Ziller marshals all the arguments for what we would call "general education" as well as for Herbart's and his own "moral education"—this instruction must find its place in the earliest educational years. By this meticulous method of working Ziller undoubtedly carried a conviction which the "naked and puzzling" presentation of Herbart never could. And though Ziller is applying the theory to elementary education—something Herbart did not attempt—Ziller is using arguments which are fundamentally Herbart's.

Second, these summaries with a historical emphasis naturally stress the modifications which Ziller introduced into Herbart's educational scheme. In so doing, however, they necessarily give a somewhat distorted picture of the great extent to which the *Foundation* reproduces Herbart rather faithfully. For example, the particular functions of government, disci-

31. Ziller, *Grundlegung,* 2d ed., p. 210.

pline, and instruction and their interrelations are all set forth with detailed clarity, as are direct and indirect interest. Herbart's arguments for the primacy of instruction are advanced with a cogency and intensity which Herbart never surpassed, if indeed he equaled them. Again and again Ziller echoes Herbart's maxim that character can be developed and made firm only by properly forming the pupil's circle of thought.

Third, as a result of this the modifications which Ziller is making are somewhat overstressed in these summaries, whereas they actually do not loom large in the total span of the book. The formal steps receive very little space, and the same is true of the concentration centers and the culture epochs. For example, the programs proposed for the first two years are introduced only at page 282, through a footnote referring to their publication two years before. (In fact, Ziller himself never worked out in detail anything beyond the plan for the first year.)

The *Foundation* is, in short, a book which must be read if Ziller's position is to be seen accurately. The statement of Hayward, an English Herbartian, is perhaps exaggerated and slightly misleading; yet it does suggest the force of Ziller's book:

> If once the five-hundred-paged *Grundlegung* of Ziller were to appear in English form, the effects of so original and inflammatory a book would probably be considerable; perchance the ranks of the ministry would be depleted and all enthusiasts would rush to be school teachers in the lowest city slums.[32]

Ziller has indeed composed a moving encomium to the power of instruction in forming and reforming human character, and as an educational classic the *Foundation* has merited translation into English more than a good many works which have received that attention. The failure of the American (and English) Herbartians to translate the *Grundlegung* probably contributed in part to the particular shape we shall see American Herbartianism taking, for the greater use of the later Ger-

32. Hayward, *The Student's Herbart*, p. 12.

man Herbartians (especially the psychologists) tended to weaken even more the link to Herbart. In Ziller Herbart had found his first ghost-writer, who, at least in the *Foundation,* transmits the thoughts of the original author with considerably less distortion than we are usually (or at least less than I had been) led to expect. "Herbart's story as told to Tuiskon Ziller" is certainly not Herbart's "very words," but within limits Ziller works as a faithful and competent mouthpiece.

In view of the important changes which Ziller wrought in the doctrine, one may ask why he bothered to see his own work as a revival of Herbart's thought at all. To this question the probable answer is that Ziller saw his efforts as a mere continuation of Herbart's thought, a more careful and extensive application of Herbart's principles. If one then asks why Ziller adopted Herbart's views at that relatively late date, at least three parts of the total answer are fairly apparent in terms of the advantages the doctrine offered Ziller.

The first is Herbart's belief in the formative and even reformative power of instruction. Many educational theories available to Ziller (such as Pestalozzi's) had viewed education as a process of unfolding the pupil's natural capacities and powers, as the developing of those "seeds" of the good, the true, and the beautiful which lie within each child. But Ziller's interest was partially directed toward a group whose capacities and potentials had already been distorted and aborted by social conditions. Educational practices intended to be merely ancillary to an unlikely regeneration of natural capacities were much less appealing to a social reformer than a doctrine suggesting direct manipulations of the learning process as possible positive efforts at rehabilitation. Even if Herbart's program did not claim to make or remake mankind, its direct and active approach was undoubtedly attractive to Ziller, with his interest in remediation.

Second, Herbart's emphasis on morality as the end of education commended his view to Ziller in several different connections. It fitted the political and social feelings endemic in Prussia and the other German states, which, ever since their defeat at the hands of Napoleon, had stressed moral regeneration and "spiritual development" (*geistliche Bildung*). Likewise, morality, if not specified too precisely, was an educational objective appropriate to the church-related elementary schools with which Ziller wished to work. This ethical emphasis was also valuable to Ziller as an educational reformer seeking to make headway on the one hand against the "bread-and-butter" subjects and, on the other, against mere erudition, the two strongest currents in the educational stream of Ziller's time. Herbart's doctrine had a place for learning without becoming lost in the sterile piling up of facts; it was solicitous of the pupil's welfare without falling into sentimentality about the child.

Third, the "systematic" nature of Herbart's doctrine was useful to Ziller even if he did not emphasize the total philosophic system and made changes within the pedagogical part. That the total system was the product of a German professor from the great period of German philosophy conferred on it a cachet of intellectual respectability and profundity important for any cultural activity in nineteenth-century Germany. Moreover, whatever the necessary modification and extensions, the doctrine was sufficiently systematic to provide a basis for a definite and comprehensive program for the *Volksschule;* furthermore, with elaboration of the steps and the concentration centers relating to the culture epochs it could yield a method and a content useful in training teachers along the proper lines for the expanding German school system.

The same advantages would not have accrued to the same degree had Ziller adopted and adapted some other set of educational theories and practices. Those of Pestalozzi were the most likely competitors. Fichte, for example, had recommended them in his *Addresses to the German Nation* as the basis for his proposed system of national education. But the work of Pestalozzi and his followers was too unsystematic, too fragmentary, and too restricted to the most elementary states of schooling to give Ziller the scope he needed; and Pestalozzi never approximated the erudition and academic status of Herbart, who could, in addition, even be viewed as systematizing and expanding Pestalozzi's position.

Securing these and other advantages from the use of Herbart did not, to be sure, compel Ziller to preserve Herbart's thought intact; in fact, extensive additions to some of Herbart's views and a judicious blurring or ignoring of others were required, and Ziller did not hesitate to do what he felt was needed. As a result, we get those qualities characteristic of earlier German Herbartianism: although much is taken from Herbart, the most obvious and important features of Herbartianism involve extensive modifications of the original.

With the publication of Ziller's *Foundation* and the organization of the "Society for Scientific Education" Herbartianism began to spread throughout Germany and ultimately to a large part of the world. Ziller's position has been given considerable attention here because of his role in popularizing Herbart's doctrines as never before and because the changes which he made imparted to Herbartianism much of the general structure it was to have forever after.

Herbartianism was, however, far from a single doctrine; even within Germany a great many professors and teachers got into the act. They too renamed and reorganized the steps; there were controversies about whether to have concentration centers and culture epochs, and, if so, which ones. But for the most part, the controversies seethed about Ziller's changes, not about Herbart; and Ziller was "refuted" not by quoting Herbart but by citing other Herbartians.[33]

In this throng, two Herbartians demand brief mention and a third claims considerably more of our attention. Friedrich Wilhelm Dörpfeld spent most of his career (1849–80) as director of the school at Barmen in the Rheinland. He published about ten volumes on pedagogy in a generally Herbartian mode, one of which, *On Thought and Memory*,[34] was made partially available to English-speaking Herbartians through a very free adaptation by H. T. Lukens. Although he

33. The most extensive summary in English of the various Herbartian doctrines and of the attacks upon them appears in F. H. Hayward and F. E. Thomas, *The Critics of Herbartianism*, (London: Swan Sonnenschein & Co., 1903), 43–208.
34. *Über Denken und Gedächtnis* (Gütersloh: C. Bertelsmann, 1873). (5th ed., 1894).

too tinkered with the names and functions of the formal steps, his chief interests were psychological.

A second major Herbartian was Karl Volkmar Stoy, who had attended Herbart's own lectures and hence had a slightly more direct connection with the master than did Dörpfeld or Ziller. As privatdozent and later professor at Jena (1842–65 and 1874–85), he established a pedagogical seminar there in 1874 (of which we shall hear more shortly). But in the period before Ziller's *Foundation* Stoy's discipleship did relatively little to preserve or revive Herbart's ideas. Once Ziller got the new movement started, however, Stoy's lectures and seminar became the center for what was usually considered the "conservative" or "moderate" wing of Herbartianism, so called on the ground that he kept closer to Herbart's original ideas than did Ziller and especially some of Ziller's followers. To be sure, he rejects as not Herbart's the *Fairy Tales* and *Robinson Crusoe,* which formed Ziller's concentration centers for the first two years; he likewise disapproves of Ziller's total integration of all subjects around the single literary-historical core. But Herbart's ideas did not flow through Stoy as an uncontaminated stream, for Stoy tends to take the principle of cultural recapitulation, the culture epochs, and the theory of concentration centers in somewhat the same way as Ziller.

Whatever the differences between Ziller and Stoy, their advocacy of their respective brands of Herbartianism did put the general movement in a privileged position. Since the positions they occupied were the only two "real" chairs of pedagogy in Germany, Herbartianism enjoyed something of a monopoly, though, to be sure, there was no equally well-organized doctrine based on some other philosophy or psychology to offer competition.[35]

But the third German Herbartian is of vital importance for our purposes, for he was Herbart's second great ghostwriter, Wilhelm Rein of the University of Jena.

---

35. See C. Ufer, "The Attitude of Scientific Thought in Germany toward the Doctrines of Herbart," *Educational Review* 12 (1896): 209–20.

# 13

## Rein Makes the Doctrine Useful

In 1885, when Stoy retired at Jena, Wilhelm Rein, a student of Ziller's, took over Stoy's seminar and practice school there and reorganized them on Zillerian lines. If Ziller did much to revive Herbart's name, Rein is probably the man who did most to make it world famous. For America particularly, "Herbartianism" is Reinism.

Rein's contribution can be briefly summarized by noting the two points of greatest importance. These were the two additions to the total work of the Herbartians which were indispensable if Herbart's doctrine (if such it still was) was to appeal to school people throughout the world.

First, Rein further neatened and tightened up the whole pedagogical theory. This point is most dramatically illustrated by a comparison of Herbart's names for his four steps (and the labels offered by Ziller, Dörpfeld, and Stoy are not much better) with those suggested by Rein: [1]

1. W. Rein, A. Pickel, E. Scheller, *Theorie und Praxis des Volkssehulunterrichts nach Herbartischen Grundsätzen*, 6th ed., 8 vols. (Leipzig: Heinrich Bredt, 1898ff.), 1:131ff.

| HERBART | REIN |
|---------|------|
| Clarity | Preparation (*Vorbereitung*) |
| Association | Presentation (*Darbietung*) |
| System | Association (*Verknüpfung*) |
| Method | Generalization (*Zusammenfassung*) |
| | Application (*Anwendung*) |

Confront any teacher with Herbart's list and inform him that these are the procedures he is to follow in teaching both large and small units of instruction. One will be lucky if one gets nothing worse in return than a puzzled frown. And little will be gained from referring this teacher back to Herbart's own writings for further light on the situation; for, as we have seen, Herbart is far from clear about most of these points. Contrast the situation when that same teacher is given Rein's list. He is almost certain to feel that he understands it, for it seems to speak his language. In fact, he is likely to think that the series is merely a handy checklist of the operations which he or any other experienced teacher goes through whenever he tries to teach something. Rein's list will strike the average teacher as a practical, sensible suggestion; his comments on Herbart's set would probably be unprintable. What Herbart means is not clear to him; what the average teacher would think of Rein's list intends is probably not far wrong, though Rein uses somewhat more Herbartian language in explaining it than would the average teacher.

But if what the list involves is so obvious and if it is so in accord with customary practice, we seem entitled to ask this teacher what he has gained from reading Rein or Herbart. We should probably get an answer something like, "Well, I had never thought it out so clearly or expressed it so neatly." But this was not what Herbart envisaged in his "science of education."

But this talk about the "average teacher" and "usual practice" undoubtedly does injustice to Herbart and the Herbartians. There is always a rich store of literature on how bad teaching in general is, and the supply of such testimony for the nineteenth century is copious; we have seen samples in the comments of Herbart and Ziller. Many teachers merely dumped facts on children for memorization through brute rote learning; languages were taught by gerund-grinding, and all the other sins were undeniably committed. Although reformers may view this with horror, practitioners silently and complacently tend to follow habit and the line of least resistance. If the situation in the latter part of the nineteenth century was actually and generally as bad as it is often painted, then a checklist which even vaguely suggested something sensible that teachers could do was a real contribution; and herein may lie much of the "suggestiveness" and "stimulation" so frequently attributed to Herbartianism.

At the close of chapter 8 we saw how the "steps" possess an inherent plausibility or face validity because they incorporate the necessary principles for making a taxonomic classification. As such they involve only a rather general and widely accepted view of "mind" and are consequently the part of the "system" most easily retailed and exported to teachers generally, despite the increasing tendency of the Herbartians to move away from Herbart's system as a unit. At any rate we owe to Rein the fact that to most modern American educators "Herbart" means "the five steps: preparation, presentation, etc."

Rein's second great contribution to making Herbartianism popular with educators was his demonstration and elaboration of practical applications. The average teacher has neither the inclination nor the capacity to read treatises on metaphysics, ethics, or mathematical psychology. Even those who do are too harried by the pressures of the daily round or lack sufficient ingenuity to work out for themselves what the abstract principles they encounter in this kind of reading could conceivably mean in terms of their work with children in the classroom. As a result, the fairest theory, if it remains only abstract theory, is certain to make minimal impact upon classroom procedures. The teacher much prefers a finished article to a do-it-yourself kit with puzzling directions. As the ubiquity of the textbook has demonstrated for centuries, most teachers want something they can take over with minimal effort. Herbart himself was well aware of this fact, as the specific "practical" exercises he attached to the *ABC of Sense Perception* show.

Rein met this demand once and for all. In collaboration with two teachers in the normal school at Eisenach—Pickel and Scheller—he carefully worked out the full eight-year course of study for his school and published it in eight volumes, *The Theory and Practice of Folk-school Instruction according to Herbartian Principles (Theorie und Praxis des Volksschul-Unterrichts nach Herbartischen Grundsätze)*. Rein's work was not, of course, the only one of its general type, since many of the German Herbartians published practical handbooks for particular subjects such as history, religion, or poetry.[2] But Rein's volumes were comprehensive and detailed. Even where differences in languages and literatures made changes necessary or desirable, the teacher's ingenuity was scarcely taxed by the need to hit upon, say, an English poem which could be substituted for the German one in Rein's book and yet serve the same purpose and be treated in the same fashion. The busy teacher could now buy his Herbartian program ready-made.

Rein, like Ziller before him,[3] always insisted that the various detailed plans published by him and others could only be suggestive and should be modified by each teacher to fit his own milieu; [4] but the very emphasis he puts on this point leads one to suspect that much of the influence the Herbartians actually had on school programs and classroom operations derived from the rather blind adoption (rather than thoughtful adaptation) of these schedules and their accompanying materials—something one would have expected in any case.

2. Rein kept a listing of these materials up to date in each successive edition of his *Theorie und Praxis*. American Herbartians who did not read the German literature had some access through C. C. Van Liew and I. J. Van Liew, *Outlines of Pedagogics* (London: Swan Sonnenschein & Co.; Syracuse, N.Y.: C. W. Bardeen, 1893).
3. T. Ziller, *Grundlegung zur Lehre vom erziehenden Unterricht*, 2d rev. ed. by T. Vogt (Leipzig: Von Veit & Co., 1884), p. 182.
4. E.g., Rein, *Theorie und Praxis*, 6th ed., 1:60–61, 105.

At the same time, it is important to note that Rein clearly attempted to preserve the tradition stemming from Herbart's writings. His *Herbart's Government, Instruction, and Discipline* [5] went through several editions, and he begins each section of the *Theory and Practice* by citing almost completely Herbart's statements relevant to the point at issue, although these quotations are limited to those writings available in Willmann's edition of the pedagogical works [6] and do not refer to the *Collected Works* edited by Hartenstein. Of course Rein's general position, sometimes explicit, is that these statements must be clarified and interpreted along the general lines he and Ziller had suggested. Nonetheless, he is clearly making an effort to appear a transmitter of Herbart's thought.

In chapter 4, four reasons were offered why Herbart's doctrines (regardless of any actual merits or demerits they possessed as theory) made so little impression during his lifetime, and in chapter 11 some difficulties within the actual system were noted. At this point it is illuminating to look at the activities of the Herbartians in the light of these problems. Because of the diversity of theory and practice among the Herbartians, the examination must be couched either in very general terms or in terms of Ziller and Rein specifically; nonetheless some conclusions seem clear and warranted.

In the matter of style it would be hard to find a less winsome writer than Herbart. The admirers of his "lapidary" prose have been overwhelmingly outvoted by editors, translators, and students for more than a century. Both Ziller and Rein, on the contrary, write in extremely clear and straightforward expository styles—and Ziller has somewhat of a literary flair. As a result, the success of Herbartianism sprang in large part from the ability of these two gifted ghost-writers to rework and edit Herbart's unorganized and turgid presentation. Had a writer of Ziller's caliber translated Herbart into

5. W. Rein, *Herbart's Regierung, Unterricht und Zucht. Pädagogische Studien* vol. 1; 3d ed. (Vienna & Leipzig: A. Pichler's Witwe & Sohn, 1881).
6. G. Willmann, *Herbart's Pädagogische Schriften,* 2d ed., 2 vols. (Leipzig: Voss, 1880).

readable prose without altering a single idea, the change would have been enormous. Quite apart from general style, at the more specific level of terms and explanations, Ziller and Rein made Herbart appear comprehensible and usable, convictions Herbart himself evoked from but a few.

But the rewriting done by Ziller and Rein went far beyond selecting some catchier terms and producing more penetrable paragraphs. Confronted with Herbart's numerous interlocking distinctions within pedagogy and pedagogy's ramifications into other parts of philosophy, Ziller and Rein, like Alexander the Great, solved the Gordian knot by chopping. Metaphysics is neatly cut away and—almost literally, I believe—never mentioned. The five ethical ideas are mentioned, but they are not derived or developed beyond the comment that Herbart, like Kant, located morality in the goodness of the will. For example, Ziller himself did a book on ethics [7] which is Herbart's ethics plus some Lutheran piety, but he carefully keeps all ethical detail isolated in this separate volume and does not allow it to complicate the pedagogy. In the *General Pedagogy*, Ziller is content merely to mention that the historical, or at least the ideal, Christ personifies the ideal relations of the will.[8] Rein in his turn refers to Herbart and Ziller, but relies on a very vague meaning of "morality" as the basis of his argument for Herbartian education. In fact, he seems quite careful not to emphasize that morality is defined by these ideas and that they are a form of aesthetic judgment. Similarly, the metaphysical basis of psychology is passed over; within psychology Herbart's mathematical elaborations are completely ignored, and stress is put upon a very few matters; interest, concentration, and apperception.

In this way simplicity is achieved by what would seem to Herbart gross oversimplification. But that anyone could bring large numbers of elementary teachers in Germany, or in any other country for that matter, to adopt a highly complex sys-

7. *Allgemeine philosophiche Ethik,* 2d ed. by O. Ziller (Langensalza: H. Beyer & Söhne, 1886).
8. *Allgemeine Pädagogik,* 3d ed., p. 26.

tem of educational thought and practice is scarcely conceivable. Doctrines are fated to have their edges knocked off when they pass current among groups. Even the simplified versions of Ziller and Rein were not taken over as wholes by many (perhaps most) teachers allegedly "influenced" by Herbartianism. For these teachers "Herbartianism" probably amounted to little more than a set of slogans or catchwords culled from one of the Herbartians. In fact, aside from the effort of Rein to cite Herbart, even in the works of the major Herbartians quotations from the master became relatively few and far between, and tended to degenerate into a standard list of instances where Herbart himself had achieved a succinct or epigrammatic statement: "The supreme end of education is contained in the concept of morality"; "Stupid people cannot be virtuous"; "The main task of education lies in developing the circle of thought"; and two or three others. The points still retained from Herbart's philosophy and even from his psychology are so general that the Herbartians can with equal or greater effectiveness quote Goethe or Kant—and usually they do just that, ignoring Herbart.

The third factor in Herbart's lack of prominence, his philosophic and educational isolation and unpopularity, is partly taken care of by the measures just enumerated. If Herbart's metaphysics is left unmentioned and his ethics reduced to rather bland generalities, his philosophic position can scarcely cause trouble by stirring up controversy. Furthermore, German idealism was no longer the rage; and by the date of Herbart's death, the great German period of metaphysical speculation, controversy, and general excitement had ended. Kant, Fichte, Hegel, and Schleiermacher were dead, and Schelling was no longer active in the field. The Herbartians may well have soft-pedaled Herbart's metaphysics, not so much because it would be considered wrong or unpopular as because metaphysics was no longer as exciting as it had been.

On the educational side, too, the passage of time had helped. Herbart had hoped to reform the gymnasium; even the Herbartians met with a singular lack of success in this venture. In the literature, statements sometimes appear to the effect that many gymnasium teachers were influenced by Herbartianism. For example, "It has been cited by competent authority that more than half the teachers in Germany, especially those in the secondary schools, such as the Gymnasia, Real, higher merchantile, etc., are disciples of Herbart." [9] One naturally wonders who that competent authority was, how he took his poll, and what was required to be "a disciple of Herbart." One suspects that these disciples were largely those who had taken over the five steps and similar "suggestions." The shift of focus toward the elementary level, however, offered a more promising opportunity for Herbart's followers than Herbart himself had found. The German states (notably Prussia) and even the united Germany always tended to legislate far in advance of enforcement. But, with the passage of time, practice usually caught up with hope. Elementary education was finally becoming something more than an introduction to the three Rs before the gymnasium and a subject of uninforced legislation, although in later years Rein was less optimistic about the *Volksschule* than he once was. [10]

Nor did Ziller and Rein only passively take advantage of the greater opportunity. Ziller's selection of concentration centers on the basis of ecclesiastical history and, later, Rein's parallel set based on German history, gave Herbartianism a leverage at the elementary level which Herbart's doctrine in unaltered form could never have exerted. [11] A sales campaign directed toward German Lutherans and German patriots in the Germany of the last quarter of the nineteenth century had a wide potential audience, and this tailoring of the doctrine to meet the demands of the situation was clearly a vital factor in whatever success Herbartianism gained. Herbart was not the sort of man to make extensive concessions, and even a less intransigent philosopher would scarcely have done this much violence to his own system.

9. H. M. Felkin and E. Felkin, *Introduction to Herbart's Science and Practice of Education* (Boston: D. C. Heath and Co., 1896), p. 3.
10. Rein, *Theorie und Praxis*, 6th ed., 1:10.
11. See, for example, the scheme in Rein's *Theorie und Praxis*, 6th ed., 1:108–9.

The solution to the fourth difficulty, Herbart's lack of followers, scarcely requires comment. For better or worse, he now had them in Ziller and Rein, and these were advocates whose personalities and literary gifts were able to win new adherents and to give new status to older disciples like Stoy. In the literature the Herbartians are sometimes described as "zealots." It is hard to conceive of Herbart himself as ever producing one. Indeed, though he would have been pleased to have conviction and devotion to his ideas displayed by his hearers, someone who would have been called a zealot—even though the epithet was hurled inaccurately in the heat of controversy—would probably have made Herbart feel uncomfortable.

In short, by the latter part of the century the extraneous yet important obstacles to the spread of Herbart's doctrines either had ceased to exist because of historical changes or had been surmounted by the skilled efforts of the leading Herbartians.

These same explanations also largely take care of the difficulties raised as intrinsic to the doctrine in chapter 11. Since the total system is no longer taken in its full compass and rigor, any architectonic problems have become irrelevant and certainly are never raised. The virtual elimination of metaphysics, especially as a basis for psychology, removes all ontological issues from the arena of controversy. The same effect is secured by the reduction of the ethical theory to a vague set of moral commonplaces. Like Goethe, like Kant, like everyone else, Herbart is shown to be against sin and in favor of "morality"; and since the trumpet-blast of Fichte in his *Addresses to the German Nation* (1807–8), calling for the moral regeneration of the nation, Germans had been in favor of morality. Within psychology only those parts are kept which bear most directly on the parts of the pedagogy the Herbartians retained. All this pruning obviously removes a great many problems, but it also removes a great deal of Herbart.

The general consequences are admirably illustrated within the pedagogical theory alone. The role of presentations in forming the circle of thought and, subsequently, the functions of that circle of thought in controlling the apperceptions of the external world, are exalted to the status of primary principles. They are admittedly Herbart's ideas and are important to his doctrine. But now these ideas gain entirely new status and prominence, partly by being cut free from subordination to the more fundamental principles (metaphysical, ethical, and psychological) which originally justified and defined them vis-à-vis the original first principles. Taking these new first principles, the Herbartians can then elaborate the concentration centers and the culture epochs as the heart of Herbart's teachings. Did German Herbartianism have anything to do with Herbart? The answer can only be yes and no.

Under Ziller, and certainly with the advent of Rein, Herbartianism of this general sort seems to have flourished. Some points we have already seen in passing indicate how difficult it is to get an accurate assessment of how influential it actually was. Certain facts can be cited. "Herbart Societies" sprang up:

> The first of these, representing the Rhine districts and Westphalia, comprised over 400 members. Later meetings were held in East Germany and then in Bavaria and Würtemberg, for extending the work of the societies. Afterward, an important society was formed for Thuringia, and lastly another for Saxony. The Thuringian society has its headquarters at Jena. . . . The formation of this society for Middle Germany, with many affiliated subsocieties, which send delegates to the annual meeting, is a new proof of the rapidly increasing influence of Herbart's principles. It holds its annual conference at Erfurt, and the first meeting in 1892 was attended by over 2,000 educationists, when Professor Rein was elected president of the council for three years.[12]

The Herbartian literature which came into being across most of Europe is impressive both in its extent and in its variety.[13] Delegates began to arrive even from far-off Japan. Interest-

12. Felkin, *Introduction*, p. 3.
13. Thilo, Flügel, Rein, and Rude, *Herbart und die Herbartianer* (Langensalza: Hermann Beyer & Söhne, 1897), pp, 142–53.

ingly enough, Ziller's school and seminar, which had always operated under difficulties, went out of existence after his death—just as Herbart's died when he left Königsberg. But most important for our present purposes, Jena, with Rein's seminar and school, became the shrine visited by many American educators in the years following 1885 (a period when American scholars in many fields sought their advanced education in German universities); [14] and it was these pilgrims who introduced Herbartianism to America.

14. See, for example, Walter T. Hervey, "The Study of Education at the German Universities," (*Educational Review* 16 [1898]: 220–32) or the account of the fiftieth anniversary celebration of Rein's seminar (*School Review* 3 [1895]: 315–16).

# 14

# "No Subject Was Ever Brought into American Schools That Furnished So Much Food for Thought"

Fundamentally Herbartianism won its initial success in America because it met many expanding social and educational needs. Yet these virtues might have passed unrecognized had it not been for its assiduous advocates, and as a result the history of American Herbartianism is to a considerable extent the record of their personal experiences and efforts.[1]

During the last quarter of the nineteenth century, America's continuing expansion in inhabited area, in population, in technology, and in general level of culture placed new and weightier demands on American education.[2] Not only were schools and teachers at every level from the primary grades to the graduate school increasing in number; at all educational

1. Chapter title is from F. W. Parker, "Discussion," *First Yearbook of the National Herbart Society* (1895), p. 153.
2. Many useful data are collected in Benjamin W. Frazier, "History of the Professional Education of Teachers in the United States," *National Survey of the Education of Teachers*, U.S. Office of Education Bulletin, 1933, no. 10, vol. 5, pt. 1 (Washington, D.C.: U.S. Government Printing Office, 1935), pp. 24–41. See also Merle L. Borrowman, *The Liberal and Technical in Teacher Education* (New York: Bureau of Publications, Teachers College, Columbia University, 1956), pp. 70–122.

levels there was also a demand for improvement. Many factors involved in these developments promoted the adoption and spread of Herbartianism.

The proliferation of elementary schools and the efforts to upgrade the teachers in them further aggravated the usual problems of teacher training. That teachers should be better educated in the subjects they undertook to teach was well-nigh universally admitted. But beyond that, many people believed that adequate knowledge of subject matter was not in itself a guarantee that its possessor was able to impart this knowledge to his pupils, particularly to very young children. Some "professional component," some study of the procedures whereby this knowledge could be most effectively transmitted, was seen as necessary to the general training of teachers.

"Pedagogics" and other manuals for the guidance of teachers had long been familiar. But many of those works then were primarily hortatory or inspirational; others were compendia of practical advice about "how to keep school." The somewhat limited nature of these handbooks was made more obvious by the rise of psychology as an independent science. Certainly it seemed likely that this developing science of mind should have something more profound and useful to contribute to a scientific pedagogy than the empirical folklore of school-teaching.

The various states and cities did not, therefore, continue to set up new normal schools, and universities and colleges did not establish new departments of pedagogy, merely to train more teachers and improve their general education; the hope was that the trainees would also be professionally competent practitioners of the art or science of teaching.

Yet the proper sort of knowledge for this purpose was not easy to come by. What was sought had to meet fairly definite specifications. Clearly it had to be helpful and useful in guiding and informing the day-to-day activities of future teachers in the classroom. To serve this purpose the information had to be simple and definite enough to be taught to trainees with the modest backgrounds, capacities, and even aspirations which characterized many, if not most, of the would-be teachers of the time.

Yet, though simple and practical, this pedagogical theory had to have some intellectual pretensions. Some dash of theoretical adequacy was essential to those who were attempting to establish "education" as a field of study and an area of professional activity in the normal schools and universities. Preferably, too, this theory should bear the cachet of European, especially German, scholarship and should incorporate the findings of "scientific" psychology. These points established a bill of particulars for any educational doctrine which was to succeed at this time, and American Herbartianism met them to a remarkable degree.

Comparison of Herbartianism in these regards with some of its predecessors and contemporaries is enlightening. E. A. Sheldon, as president of the Oswego (N.Y.) State Normal School was among those looking for an adequate pedagogy to impart to teachers and to teachers of teachers.[3] On a visit to Toronto in 1860 he came across the version of Pestalozzianism developed by the British Home and Colonial Infant and Juvenile Society, and he felt that he had found a reasonable approximation of what he was seeking. He imported teachers from England, made the alterations in the doctrine which seemed desirable to him, and thus launched the "Oswego movement" or "object teaching."

As was shown by the general professional interest in Oswego's program and by the brisk demand for its graduates, this movement met many of the requirements outlined above.

3. For this movement see J. P. Gordy, *Rise and Growth of the Normal School Idea,* Bureau of Education Circular of Information no. 8, 1891 (Washington, D.C.: U.S. Government Printing Office, 1891); A. P. Hollis, *The Contribution of Oswego Normal School to Educational Progress in the United States* (Boston: D. C. Heath and Co., 1898); N. H. Dearborn, *The Oswego Movement in American Education* (New York: Teachers College, Columbia University, 1925); Charles A. Harper, *A Century of Public Teacher Education* (Washington, D.C.: American Association of Teachers Colleges of the NEA, 1939); Dorothy Rogers, *Oswego: Fountainhead of Teacher Education* (New York: Appleton-Century-Crofts, 1961).

It possessed some aura of European respectability. It could be reduced to a fairly simple routine easily taught to even the most obtuse of future teachers. Its use of natural and artificial objects as the basic material of instruction facilitated enlargement of the rather restricted elementary curriculum by providing openings for nature study and elementary technology. Its emphasis on exact observation also fitted the rising scientific temper of the times and seemed to suggest (by the way in which it treated individual sense data as combined into general ideas) an underlying associationist psychology. The Oswego movement lost its thrust primarily because of its limited nature—its emphasis on discrete observations. American Herbartianism was to profit because it could be seen as comprehending yet extending object teaching. In this sense the Oswego movement served as a forerunner of Herbartianism.

A brief glance at two contrasting competitors of Herbartianism will indicate why they too were less successful than Herbartianism in meeting the social and educational specifications of the day. William T. Harris, as superintendent of schools at Saint Louis and then as United States Commissioner of Education, did much to popularize Hegelianism. Certainly its theoretical pretensions and its academic respectability were much greater than those of the Oswego movement, and the capacious Hegelian system offered an architectonic within which even more expanded conceptions of the curriculum and of teacher training could easily find a place. But though a teacher who had worked through Harris's writings or those of Rosenkrantz (which Harris did much to publicize through the *Journal of Speculative Philosophy* and the International Education Series, both of which he edited), may have felt that he had become fairly erudite about the history and abstract theory of pedagogy, he probably remained uncertain about precisely what he should do with his first-grade class on Tuesday morning. For this reason, though Harris built an enormous personal reputation and though Rosenkrantz's *Pedagogics as a System* was long used in many classes, Hegelianism as a doctrine made relatively little impact on actual teaching in the schools of America.

Similarly, G. Stanley Hall's "child study" in its early days suffered from much the same difficulty. To be sure, whatever it lacked in Teutonic and philosophic profundity was compensated for by its obvious participation in the new developments in experimental psychology. Still, like Hegelianism, the general "study of the child" did not point toward a specific curriculum for teachers-in-training or offer detailed guidance to the embryo teacher in planning lessons or conducting classes.

About 1890, then, a pedagogy that was academically respectable and scientific and yet simple and practical was a desideratum in the universities and normal schools of the United States, and the adequacy of Herbartianism in these respects gave it an entrée to the classrooms of America.

American Herbartianism, like any other educational movement or innovation, gained its driving force from the strenuous efforts of a small body of devoted adherents. A group of this sort is always the spearhead of the advance, and their names are always associated with the operation. But in addition to these primary figures there must be additional adherents who constitute the "critical mass" necessary for action and who in less conspicuous and dominant roles help carry the movement forward. Then beyond them are the "educational leaders" of the time. Although they are usually at most rather mild advocates of the program and may sometimes even be hostile to it, they do not ignore it. That particular innovation is where the educational action is at the time, and as "leaders" such men must concern themselves with what is in the van. The educational leader who misses a bandwagon may soon find himself trudging at the rear of the educational parade. Through their interest or at least their benevolence, the innovation gets attention in the journals, at the national meetings, and in the general shoptalk of the profession.

Herbartianism in America followed this usual pattern. The vast bulk of the writing, speaking, and organizing was done by a half-dozen or so major figures, of whom the most prominent were Charles DeGarmo and Charles and Frank McMurry. But there were hundreds of "Herbartians" who, though they spoke and wrote little or not at all, gave bulk to the movement. They were the audiences, the buyers of the books, the members of the Herbart clubs and the National Herbart Society. Their primary contribution was spreading some variety of Herbartianism in their classrooms. Finally there were educational figures like William T. Harris, John Dewey, Nicholas Murray Butler, Colonel Francis Parker, and John Williston Cook, who in widely varying degrees encouraged, or at least gave publicity to, the movement. Accounts of movements naturally focus on the activities of the primary figures; but such men are only the visible peak of the iceberg.

Herbartianism came to America somewhat by accident. The oldest of the major American Herbartians, Charles De-Garmo, was a Wisconsin boy whose parents had moved to Illinois, where he graduated from the Illinois State Normal University in 1873. After three years of teaching at Naples, Illinois, he returned to I.S.N.U. as assistant in the Training Department, where three years later he encountered Edmund Janes James.

James had been a classmate of DeGarmo's at I.S.N.U. But after a year at Northwestern University and another at Harvard, he had gone to the University of Halle where he took a Ph.D. in political economy under Johannes Conrad. Then after two years as a teacher in the Evanston (Illinois) High School he had returned to his alma mater as principal of the high school. Since, in addition to his specialization in economics, he had developed an interest in education generally, in 1881 he and DeGarmo founded, as "editors and proprietors," the *Illinois School Journal.*[4]

James, however, had many incentives to return to Europe. His wife had come from university circles at Halle, and she was eager to visit her family and friends and to show off her infant son. Furthermore, James's developing interest in educa-

4. *Illinois School Journal* 1 (May 1881): 16.

tion led him to want to know more about European educational systems, especially that of France.[5]

Before James's departure in 1883 he had already been instrumental in introducing Herbartianism to America by convincing several young men at Normal of the value of European study. For, according to another of the major American Herbartians, Frank McMurry, James persuaded DeGarmo and Charles McMurry to go to Germany, and Frank followed his brother Charles.[6] Thus three of the major American Herbartians became part of the group of American students who, in the last quarter of the nineteenth century, flocked to German universities for advanced work.

At the time none of the three expected to make a career of importing and advocating Herbartianism. DeGarmo came closest to going to look for what he actually brought back. He at least saw education opening up as a field of professional activity and went to prepare for a career in it by studying the history and philosophy of education.[7]

But he was not seeking Herbartianism specifically. In turning to Germany he was merely sharing the general opinion that that country was the best source of pedagogical theory. This view is well typified by the remarks of William T. Harris some years before:

> Inquiries from teachers in different sections of the country as to the sources of information on the subject of Teaching as a Science have led me to believe that a translation of Rosenkrantz's Pedagogics may be widely acceptable and useful. It is very certain that too much of our teaching is simply empirical, and as Germany has, more than any other country, endeavored to found it on universal truths, it is to that country that we must at present look for a remedy for this empiricism.[8]

5. *Illinois School Journal* 2 (Feb. 1883): 323.
6. Letter from Frank McMurry to T. S. Lancaster (6 Apr. 1932). Quoted by Charles Harper, *The Development of the Teachers College in the United States* (Bloomington, Ill.: McKnight and McKnight, 1935), p. 199.
7. *Illinois School Journal* 3 (June 1883): 50; 3 (July 1883): 73.
8. Dr. Karl Rosenkranz, *Pedagogics as a System,* trans. Anna C. Brackett (St. Louis, Mo.: The R. P. Stanley Co., Printers, 1872), p. 5.

Similarly, Frank McMurry, according to his own testimony,[9] went into teaching only because he felt himself as well fitted for that as for anything else, and, finding no theory of teaching in America, he went to Germany hoping that he could discover one there.

Charles McMurry was the least conscious of his future mission as a proponent of Herbartianism. In rather obvious imitation of Edmund James, he originally went to Halle to study history and economics; in addition, if his brother's later memory is to be trusted, he also devoted himself to theology.[10] Although his dissertation, done under Conrad, was on an educational topic,[11] his acquaintance with Herbartianism seems to have begun only when his brother Frank dragged him off for a postdoctoral year in Rein's new seminar at Jena.[12]

In short, DeGarmo and the McMurrys did not go to seek Herbartianism. It was, so to speak, thrust upon them. This result was almost inevitable in view of the German situation at the time. In the traditional academic fields an American student could choose among numerous German universities offering programs of various degrees of distinction. In the newer field of education, however, choice was more restricted. Apart from various teacher-training programs or such permissive situations as Conrad's seminar in economics (which nevertheless permitted DeGarmo and Charles McMurry to write their dissertations on educational topics), there were two main chairs of pedagogy; and both of these were held by Herbartians. Ziller occupied the one at Leipzig; that at Jena was held by Stoy, who was succeeded by Ziller's pupil, Rein.

9. Frank M. McMurry, "Some Recollections of the Past Forty Years of Education," *Peabody Journal of Education* 4 (May 1927): 327; Henry Hugh Edmunds, "The History of the Herbartian Movement in the United States," p. 7. (Unpublished manuscript in the Library of the Illinois State University; I am indebted to Joe W. Kraus, director of libraries there, for a copy.)

10. *Illinois School Journal* 2 (Sept. 1882): 147; Edmunds, "History of the Herbartian Movement," p. 7.

11. "Die Organisation des Höheren Schulwesens in den Vereinigten Staaten Amerikas und in England und die Stellung des Staates zu demselben," *Sammlung nationalökonomischer und statistischer Abhandlungen des staatswiseenschaftlichen Seminars zu Halle a. S.,* vol. 5, pt. 3.

12. Frank M. McMurry, "Some Recollections," p. 328.

As a result, American students were almost certain to be exposed to Herbartianism if they sought out one of the major sites for advanced work in education. Thus the two McMurrys were the first American members of Rein's new pedagogical seminar at Jena, and apparently DeGarmo had had some earlier contact with Stoy there before the latter's death.[13] More important to DeGarmo was the influence of Frick, who was then director of the Francke Institutions at Halle.[14] In addition, all of them were undoubtedly influenced by reading Herbart and the Herbartian books, which then constituted a large portion of the German educational literature. Most notably in this regard, Frank McMurry asserts that he underwent the equivalent of a religious conversion upon reading two of the major Herbartian books, Wiget's *Die formalen Stufen* and Lange's *Apperception*.[15]

DeGarmo, arriving home after taking his degree at Halle in 1886, was first in the field with articles and books on Herbartianism. In addition to his own work, however, he translated from the German G. A. Lindner's *Manual of Empirical Psychology* [16] and was instrumental in getting the Herbart Club to translate Karl Lange's *Apperception*.[17] These were both major psychological-educational works of German Herbartianism. Second, through his connection with Heath's "Pedagogical Library," he apparently was also influential in securing the publication in that series of other important works: Zinser's translation of Ufer's *Introduction to the Pedagogy of Herbart*,[18] the Felkins' translation of Herbart's *General*

13. *Illinois School Journal* 3 (Oct. 1883): 149; 4 (June 1884): 358; Edmunds, "History of the Herbartian Movement," pp. 6–7.
14. Edmunds, "History of the Herbartian Movement," pp. 6–7.
15. Frank M. McMurry, "Some Recollections," p. 329. At this date McMurry forgetfully attributed *Die formalen Stufen* to Ufer, another famous Herbartian.
16. G. A. Lindner, *A Manual of Empirical Psychology,* trans. C. DeGarmo (Boston: D. C. Heath and Co., 1890).
17. K. Lange, *Apperception,* trans. the Herbart Club (Boston: D. C. Heath and Co., 1893).
18. C. Ufer, *An Introduction to the Pedagogy of Herbart,* trans. J. C. Zinser (Boston: D. C. Heath and Co., 1894).

*Pedagogy*[19] and their *Introduction to Herbart's Science and Practice of Education*,[20] as well as Adams' *The Herbartian Psychology Applied to Education*.[21] Third, he was the moving spirit in the organization of the Herbart Club in 1892 and later in the formation of the National Herbart Society.

But it was probably his own writings which did most to give Herbartianism its original impetus in America. These merit examination inasmuch as they exemplify one variety of American Herbartianism and also reveal whatever connection DeGarmo's position had with Herbart's original doctrine.

His first major piece was a series of articles in the *Illinois School Journal*, "Glimpses at German Pedagogy."[22] Although DeGarmo was to rework these ideas in his later important book, *The Essentials of Method*,[23] this early piece is important because it antedates the bulk of the American material on Herbart and Herbartianism. For some readers in the Midwest it may have been quite literally their first glimpse of German pedagogy.

The subtitle of the series was "A Philosophic Base for Order in Instruction," and this base was, of course, Herbartianism. After a plea for something better than mere empirics as a guide for teaching (also suggested, as we have seen, by W. T. Harris some years earlier), DeGarmo analyzes learning into two standard Herbartian topics, "apperception" and "abstraction." He sees apperception as involved in the acquisition of knowledge and ties to this process the first two of Rein's five steps, "preparation" and "presentation." Abstraction is the

19. H. M. Felkin and E. Felkin, *The Science of Education* (London: Swan Sonnenschein & Co.; Boston: D. C. Heath and Co., 1892).

20. H. M. Felkin and E. Felkin, *An Introduction to Herbart's Science and Practice of Education* (Boston: D. C. Heath and Co., 1895).

21. J. Adams, *The Herbartian Psychology Applied to Education* (Boston: D. C. Heath and Co., 1897).

22. Charles DeGarmo, "Glimpses at German Pedagogy," *Illinois School Journal* 6 (Dec. 1886): 80–82; 6 (Jan. 1887): 121–23; 6 (Feb. 1887): 166–68; 6 (Mar. 1887): 210–13; 6 (Apr. 1887): 261–63; 6 (May 1887): 312–14; 6 (July 1887): 405–7.

23. Charles DeGarmo, *The Essentials of Method* (Boston: D. C. Heath and Co., 1889).

means whereby these individual notions are built into larger structures (what DeGarmo calls "thinking"), and Rein's third and fourth steps ("association" and "generalization") move toward it. Finally, the fifth step, "application," is seen as moving from the "knowledge" thus acquired to "power,"—that is, to the utilization of knowledge.

This early attempt to bring Herbartianism to American teachers is interesting on several counts. First, DeGarmo introduces a number of themes which will generally characterize American Herbartianism: abstraction as the movement from particulars to general notions, apperception, and the steps. Second, he publicizes contemporary German Herbartianism without reference to or connection with Herbart himself.

This latter omission was partially remedied by a second series of articles, which he did for the new *Educational Review*, "The Herbartian System of Pedagogics." [24] This is the one occasion on which DeGarmo undertook to present in some detail Herbart as the father of Herbartianism, and the significant thing is the stance which he takes toward Herbart's work. On the one hand, he minimizes Herbart's total system as he and his fellow Herbartians always do. On the other hand, he gives here the most detailed American exposition of Herbart's pedagogy.

DeGarmo does not conceal his belief that although Herbart originally presented his ideas in a total unified system, no one will accept all of them, and that the most fruitful ideas are the pedagogical ones. Having thus cut loose Herbart's pedagogy, DeGarmo disposes of the rest of the system in summary fashion.

Metaphysics is dismissed in a single sentence asserting that contemporary German Herbartians pay little attention to it. Ethics gets little more space. Although the five ethical ideas are listed and are indicated as derived from aesthetic judgments, DeGarmo makes no attempt to relate them to Herbart's

24. Charles DeGarmo, "The Herbartian System of Pedagogics," *Educational Review* 1 (Jan. 1891): 33–45; 1 (Mar. 1891): 244–52; 1 (May 1891): 453–62.

goal for education—morality. (For the American Herbartians
education is to be essentially cognitive, devoted to the development of general notions out of particulars, not to the
formation of the moral will, as it had been for Herbart.)
Psychology, naturally, fares best, and though the space devoted to it is slight, DeGarmo manages to state most of
Herbart's psychological principles, especially those related to
apperception—although, as he says, he does not have space
to comment on them.

In sharp contrast to this treatment of the system, he reports Herbart's pedagogical doctrine in great detail. He presents briefly all the main features of Herbart's "government,"
"discipline," and "instruction." This thoroughness is somewhat
surprising since a great many of these points were ignored by
contemporary German Herbartians and the Americans were
to make similarly little use of them. In short, DeGarmo does
competently discharge his task of giving an accurate account
of Herbart's pedagogy. As an exposition of Herbart, its chief
fault is the distortion resulting from his failure to relate the
pedagogy to morality, a disjunction which renders the pedagogy essentially meaningless as far as Herbart is concerned.
But German Herbartianism had already wrought this change,
and DeGarmo and the American Herbartians were not about
to undo it.

DeGarmo's *Essentials of Method* (1889) was the first
book of American Herbartianism, and it and his later (1895)
*Herbart and the Herbartians* [25] were popular.

The most significant point about *The Essentials of Method*
for our purposes is that it makes no particular effort to appear
Herbartian and, more important, no pretense of reporting the
views of Herbart. About the only early clue that the work is
even vaguely Herbartian occurs in the sub-subtitle: *The Essentials of Method: A Discussion of the Essential Form of Right
Method: Observation, Generalization, Application,* whose last
three words possibly suggest a variant of the Herbartian steps.

25. Charles DeGarmo, *Herbart and the Herbartians* (New York: Charles
Scribner's Sons, 1895).

But throughout the earlier, more theoretical part of this little book, only such details as a chapter on "apperception" hint at Herbartian connections; and even here DeGarmo is careful to state that he is mostly following Wundt, with additional deviation of his own even from that view. Part 3, the last quarter of the book, is devoted to "practical illustrations," and here the author does acknowledge that he is "more or less indebted" to Rein and Frick, the Germans who had done most to apply Herbartianism to the elementary and secondary schools respectively. There is the usual selection from *Robinson Crusoe,* and the materials are organized much like Rein's, as preparation, presentation, elaboration, and application, with analysis and synthesis also distinguished part of the time. DeGarmo certainly does not thrust much Herbart upon the American teacher and student.

In regard to the future spread of Herbartianism in America, a noteworthy characteristic of the book is its technicality. Having defined apperception as "the subsumption of a notion, usually newly given and more or less individual, under a predicate which is more complete in content and extent, and which is usually older and more familiar," [26] DeGarmo necessarily becomes involved in discussions of such matters as the "content" and "extent" of class nouns, the types of propositions, and the laws of inductive inference. In consequence, DeGarmo seems to have aimed this volume primarily at his professional peers; it was not the sort of book likely to become an extremely popular text for teachers or teachers in training, though it was so used. Books of this latter sort were to be the contribution of the McMurrys.

Charles McMurry's major book, as its title proclaims (*The Elements of General Method Based on the Principles of Herbart*), is much closer to both Herbart and German Herbartianism.[27] This note is loudly sounded in the preface, which, after pointing out the importance of the Herbartian school in

26. Charles DeGarmo, *Essentials*, p. 5.
27. Charles A. McMurry, *The Elements of General Method* (Bloomington, Ill.: Public School Publishing Co., 1892).

Germany, states, "The following chapters cannot be regarded as a full, exact, and painfully scientific account of Herbartian ideas, but as a simple explanation of their leading principles in their relation to each other and in their application to our own school problems." He then goes on to acknowledge his debt to Rein for encouragement in writing the book. That McMurry's statement is a fair description of the volume can be seen even from noting some chapter titles: "The Nature of Interest," "Concentration" (with a large subsection on "The Cultural Epochs"), "Apperception," "The Will," and "The Formal Steps." Throughout the book McMurry makes it abundantly clear that he is presenting to American teachers a practical text based on German Herbartianism.

This was precisely the type of book needed to popularize Herbartianism among the members of the teaching profession. All the major points of Herbartian doctrine were covered simply and they were related directly to the concerns and activities of the classroom teacher. Now any teacher who wished to be a Herbartian had the necessary recipes in hand. Its welcome is partly attested by the publisher's proud announcement three years later, "Fifth edition, thirtieth thousand"—a rather remarkable sale for the America of that time.

This effect is reinforced by the third major text, *The Method of the Recitation,* the joint product of the McMurry brothers. It clearly takes its stand in the Herbartian tradition, although, as is usual with the American Herbartians, there is an equally specific disclaimer of any attempt to foist a foreign ideology on the American schools:

> The method of the Recitation is based upon the principles of teaching which were expounded and illustrated in the work of Herbart, Ziller, and Rein. At the same time, the authors hope to have shown in the body of the work that we have to do here with principles recognized by teachers in every land, and that there is no thoughtless imitation of foreign methods and devices. While our debt to German thinkers for an organization of fundamental ideas is great, the entire discussion, as here presented, springs out

of American conditions; its illustrative materials are drawn exclusively from lessons commonly taught in our schools. In fact, the whole book, while strongly influenced by Herbart's principles, is the outgrowth of several years' continuous work with classes of children in all the grades of the common school.[28]

Despite the emphasis on Herbart in the preface, neither he nor his ideas figure largely in the book. The Herbartianism is that of Rein, and the five steps in his nomenclature are used explicitly to organize the middle chapters of the book.

Three other chapters (10, 13, and 15) are also obviously Herbartian. Chapter 13, "The Relation of the Formal Steps of Instruction to Textbooks and Their Use," argues that most texts are dogmatic: they emphasize the generalizations of Rein's fourth step (Generalization) or (particularly in histories and geographies) the presentation of new materials (Presentation). In contrast to this dogmatic method, Herbartian instruction is inductive. That is, it demands the inclusion also of the first (Preparation) and third (Association) steps, requires that they all come in the proper order, and does not permit exaggerated emphasis on only one or two of them. The burden of the argument is that teachers should teach inductively and use textbooks only for summary or review. Chapter 15, "Criticisms of the Formal Steps," defends them against the charge of artificiality and woodenness by pointing out that, if the steps do in fact reflect the way in which the human mind operates, there is no point in complaining about them. Chapter 10, "The Socrates' Method of Teaching," presents a long translation from Xenophon's *Memorabilia*, indicating how Socrates' procedures embody the five steps. In short, the whole book is an extended presentation of Rein's five steps.

Insofar as these are the three books which did the most to bring Herbart and Herbartianism to American teachers (and the probabilities seem great that these texts were more influential in this regard than were the more detailed exposi-

28. C. A. McMurry and F. M. McMurry, *The Method of the Recitation* (Bloomington, Ill.: Public School Publishing Co., 1897), p. viii.

tions of Herbart's thought or the translations of his works and those of the Herbartians), the kind of doctrine transmitted to America is evident. Herbart himself is only occasionally mentioned by name and is even more rarely quoted. That is the extent of the linkage with Herbart. Herbartianism, in turn, means essentially Rein's five steps as procedures for moving from "individual notions" to "general notions" and then back to the individual again through application. Since there is less tendency than in German Herbartianism to emphasize the concentration centers and the culture epochs, the steps are even more important theoretically here than in Rein's work. With the clear linking of the psychological theory of apperception to the steps, American Herbartianism as incorporated in these books almost *is* the steps.

The 1895 *First Yearbook* of the National Herbart Society is another place at which to take the pulse of American Herbartianism. DeGarmo wrote the first article, Frank McMurry the second. The third is by C. C. Van Liew, the translator of Rein's *Outlines of Pedagogy*,[29] and the fourth and last is by Lida Brown McMurry. There are two supplements. The first contains a stenographic report of the discussion of the first three papers held at the Denver meeting and a recommended reading list, as well as a section dealing with the purposes and organizational structure of the society. The second supplement comprises John Dewey's "Interest as Related to Will," an obviously Herbartian topic.

Since the society was plainly firing its big guns as far as the authorship of the papers is concerned, the *First Yearbook* merits close scrutiny as setting the tone and projecting the image of American Herbartianism. Moreover, since the society was following the model set earlier by the German societies in having the papers distributed before the meeting at which they were discussed, even the discussions should reflect the considered rather than the extemporaneous views of those sufficiently interested in Herbartianism to attend the meetings and to comment on the papers.

29. C. C. Van Liew and I. J. Van Liew, *Outlines of Pedagogics* (London: Swan Sonnenschein & Co., 1893).

DeGarmo bases his article, "Most Pressing Problems concerning the Elementary Course of Study" on the contention that the current report of the NEA's Committee of Fifteen, by abandoning "formal culture" or "mental discipline," had arrived at the need for *moral* education in the public schools and consequently demonstrated the soundness of Herbart's conception of the moral aim of education. But though De-Garmo mentions Herbart, he does not further cite him. Nor does he do much with morality. Rather, he considers Ziller's culture epochs, and, while "acknowledging the fruitfulness of many of Ziller's suggestions," he rejects the use of the culture epochs on the grounds that this principle "displaces natural and important relations existing among subjects with relations that are non-essential, fantastic or artificial" and that "his whole work rests on a distorted psychological view of the child and an inadequate conception of the function of studies."[30] He continues, after considering and dismissing Colonel Parker's plan for concentrations in science, by offering his own suggestion to meet the need for correlation rather than concentration—geography. This was an idea of Herbart's,[31] though DeGarmo makes no mention of this and possibly was not aware of it.

To one interested in Herbart rather than Herbartianism, this whole performance by the president of the new Herbart Society and the leading American Herbartian, in his role of introducing the organization's new journal, is little short of astonishing. Nowhere does he use Herbart's own thought or cite his writings. As for DeGarmo's suggesting geography, the situation almost suggests that in backing away from Ziller's position he had backed into Herbart's without knowing it.

Frank McMurry even manages to write his rather long article on "concentration" without ever mentioning Herbart by name, unless a passing citation of DeGarmo's *Herbart and the Herbartians* should be included in such a tally. Although he says many things about concentration, about the subjects individually, and about the relations between them which sound more like Herbart than like Ziller or Rein, he makes no

30. *First Yearbook*, pp. 17–18.   31. Herbart, *SW* 9:119.

point of this similarity and one cannot be sure he intended it.

Van Liew's paper on "The Educational Theory of the Cultural Epochs" had actually been written twelve years earlier (apparently when he was at Jena). He considers its current significance mainly historical, since he sees the function of culture-epoch theory chiefly as posing a problem which must be solved by the findings of child study. In surveying the history of the general idea that the child's intellectual development recapitulates that of the human race, Van Liew calls the usual roll of those who held this theory. When he arrives at Herbart in this progress, he does cite Herbart's statement about the foolishness of following chronological sequence in scientific studies and mentions some other limitations on the use of the idea explicitly imposed by Herbart. Even though he seems to find Herbart more inclined toward the culture-epochs idea than the evidence appears to me to warrant, nevertheless we have here an American Herbartian who is aware of Herbart's own position and familiar with Herbart's writings as well as with those of the later Herbartians.[32]

The fourth and last article, "Correlation of Studies of First and Second Years," by Lida Brown McMurry is in many ways a distillation of the German Herbartianism of the preceding twenty years, with some American flavoring added. The first school year with its fairy tales, nature myths, and Bible stories would have been recognized by Ziller as a close lineal descendent of his first concentration center. Likewise in the second year we find Robinson Crusoe, though he is preceded by that early American, Hiawatha, as representing an even earlier culture epoch. (And who can say that American children are not interested in Indians.) In short, the four articles of the *First Yearbook* are generally Herbartian, but reflect Herbart himself almost not at all.

32. It is regrettable that his *Life of Herbart and Development of his Pedagogical Doctrines* (London: Swan Sonnenschein & Co., 1893) did not find an American publisher.

The same slant is given by the "list of books," which each *Yearbook* incorporates to suggest reading programs for clubs or individuals interested in extending their knowledge of Herbartianism. This feature is apparently [33] the contribution of the secretary and editor, Charles McMurry. The list given in the *First Yearbook,* in the order recommended for reading, runs as follows:

1. DeGarmo's *Herbart and the Herbartians*
2. Rein's *Outlines of Pedagogics* (translated by the Van Liews)
3. C. A. McMurry's *General Method*
4. Ufer's *Introduction to the Pedagogy of Herbart* (translated by Zinser)
5. Lange's *Apperception* (translated by the Herbart Club)
6. Herbart's *General Pedagogy* (translated by the Felkins under the title "The Science of Education")
7. DeGarmo's *Essentials of Method*
8. Luken's *The Connection between Thought and Memory* (based on Dörpfeld's *Denken und Gedächtnis*)
9. Lindner's *Manual of Empirical Psychology* (translated by DeGarmo)
10. Herbart's *Textbook of Psychology* (translated by Smith)

McMurry is plainly under no illusions about the intelligibility and attractiveness of Herbart's own writings, though he does charge the Felkins with not giving us "an English classic" whereas he thinks "In German Herbart's writings on education constitute a classic of rare force and excellence of style"—a comment which makes me wonder whether he ever read them. At any rate, he gives the two books by Herbart low positions in the list, sixth and last. This tendency to minimize Herbart is even more noticeable in the "shorter course" he recommends, which contains only three books (DeGarmo's *Herbart and the Herbartians,* Ufer, and Lange) without any Herbart at all.

33. In subsequent *Yearbooks* he signed this section.

These three volumes merit at least a hasty look, since they obviously incorporate what the leading American Herbartians felt was the core of the doctrine they wished to transmit to their compatriots.

DeGarmo's treatment of Herbart's system is both illuminating and typical. The preface promptly announces that the book "is concerned but little with metaphysics." This promise is more than fulfilled. The metaphysical theory is sketched in about a page, and the discussion concludes with the remark: "It matters little to us and is of small consequence for the ultimate validity of Herbart's educational notions whether this supposed universe of monads, souls included, is a sober reality or a phantasm conjured up by speculation; for his system, after all, depends not upon the constructions of abstract speculation, but upon the verifiable facts of experience." So much for metaphysics.

There is a brief chapter on ethics, stating the five ethical ideas, but this account is included simply because Herbart and the Herbartians talk so much about moral education that DeGarmo feels the reader might like to know what they are talking about. Not that it really matters. "Herbart's theory of the manner in which we arrive at moral judgments may or may not satisfy the mind of the student; yet this is a matter of small consequence, for all ethical systems arrive at substantially the same rules of life, however varied the derivations of these principles may be." This introduction is hardly calculated to whet the reader's interest in the following exposition, but, as we have seen, Herbart himself gave some warrant for this type of treatment.

Herbart's psychology is polished off with almost equal brusqueness and receives a similarly unenthusiastic testimonial: "Much of Herbart's psychology is of mere historical interest, while its more fruitful aspects have undergone important changes since his time." In consequence, DeGarmo devotes most of his space to quoting Lange, Lindner, and himself on apperception. (If Herbart had ever been systematic, his leading American proponent was putting an end to it once and for all.)

Herbart's original educational doctrine fares somewhat better. But even here DeGarmo is free with his opinion that although Herbart talked about principles we must look to his successors for detailed directions. As one of DeGarmo's fellow Herbartians said of him, "President DeGarmo, who is no doubt the best versed in the Herbartian ideas of anyone in this country, and withal one of the most independent and original in modifying them to adopt them to our conditions . . . .[34]

DeGarmo's general position is that although Herbart "laid the theoretical foundations," subsequent developments are really the important contributions. One is inclined to ask, "What foundations?" since DeGarmo clearly considers most of Herbart's principles wrong or irrelevant. DeGarmo's probable answer to this question would be to mention such points as Herbart's denial of formal discipline, his emphasis on "morality" and on the importance of the student's "experience," and his affording some basis for the doctrine of apperception—and very little else. Herbart would have found the ten pages devoted to his "Life and Works" correct but perhaps irrelevant in view of his slight role in the book as a whole.

The second recommended reading, Lange's *Apperception*, is divided into three sections of rather unequal length: part 1, "The Doctrine of Apperception"; part 2, "The Theory of Apperception in Its Application to Pedagogy"; part 3, "The History of the Term Apperception." The third and briefest part portrays in fairly schematic form the attention paid to Herbart's work in the entire book.

Lange begins this historical sketch with Leibnitz, whose views on apperception are given in some detail. Kant and Herbart follow, with Herbart getting slightly more space than his two predecessors, but much of this attention involves criticizing him for such matters as not attributing to the will a greater role in the rise and fall of presentations in consciousness. As a result, Lange closes his discussion of Herbart's view with the comment, "Though after what has been said, it is clear that Herbart's theory of apperception needs corrections and

34. H. T. Lukens, "The Correlation of Studies," *Educational Review* 10 (Nov. 1895): 375.

completion in several points, on the other hand there can be no doubt that it is very well capable of such correction and perfection." [35] Whether Lange's strictures are in fact valid and whether such emendation is necessary and, if necessary, possible are questions we must pass over as requiring too detailed a digression to be appropriate here. For present purposes the important fact is that Lange immediately begins to correct and perfect by discussing the ideas of Lazarus and Steinthal (whose improvements on Herbart we have already seen admired by W. T. Harris) and the suggestions of a few non-Herbartian psychologists ending with Wundt. In short, Herbart appears but he certainly does not dominate the scene and is not taken too seriously.

Herbart receives similar treatment in parts 1 and 2. For example, part 2, which discusses the application of the doctrine to teaching, covers points more typical of Herbartianism than of Herbart. For example, Lange considers the theory of the culture epochs at some length and ends by rejecting this view, which he recognizes as Ziller's, not Herbart's. Lange prefers biblical history, because the principle of following the chronological sequence is the only sound thing about the culture-epochs theory and because, on a number of counts, the Scriptures stand at the heart of German life and thought. He is, however, prepared to supplement the Bible stories with some of *Grimms' Fairy Tales* and the Germanic sagas; but he rejects *Robinson Crusoe* and rules out Herbart's favorite, the *Odyssey*, by using exactly the same set of arguments (the strange names, faraway places, odd customs) with which Ziller and Rein had expelled the Bible stories from their programs of the first two school years.

Lange then moves to the "steps," using Rein's terms ("preparation," "presentation," etc.) but also stirring in Ziller's "analysis" and "synthesis." Throughout all this Herbart, on any basis, gets short shrift. The only point at which Lange seems to reflect Herbart's own views directly (Herbart is actually mentioned only a half-dozen times in the book) is in

35. K. Lange, *Apperception,* pp. 262–63. The translation here is that of the Herbart Club.

agreeing that the moral idea of perfection is the one most accessible to children. Since, however, the moral ideas are not developed and the entire context has been altered, the point has lost most if not all of its original significance.

In brief, Lange's book is not likely to make its readers turn to Herbart's own work, and the eager teacher who did so would receive a nasty shock from finding the *General Pedagogy* or any other book of Herbart's so different from what he had probably expected from reading Lange.

Finally, the third book on the "short" list suggested by the Herbart Society, Ufer's volume, begins by setting forth Herbart's psychology. Although Ufer quotes Lazarus's modifications at some length and though, for simplicity, he explicitly ignores the metaphysical connections, Ufer reproduces Herbart's psychological ideas as accurately as can be demanded from a brief and simplified treatment of the topic. Much the same is true of the following section on Herbart's ethical theory, in which he sets up Herbart's view of the goodness of the will as the summum bonum, shows the aesthetic basis of the ethical judgments, and describes and illustrates the five fundamental ideas and, even more succinctly, the five derived social ones. He even begins the next section (on "pedagogical application") with the same fidelity to Herbart's views on interest, attention, sympathy, and the like. But he soon moves to the culture epochs and the concentration centers, reporting the controversies of Ziller, Dörpfeld, and Rein. Then he once again reverts to Herbart's own position in his section on "moral training" as he discusses the will and the relations of volitions to presentations, only once again to switch to Herbartianism in a concluding section on "special methods." Here he indicates the methods and materials for teaching Ziller's concentration center for the fifth school year and suggests how its varied content (the life of Christ, the history of the voyages of discovery, and the life of Luther) can all be woven into a unified whole.

Ufer's *Introduction* is, then, to a considerable degree an introduction to Herbart rather than to Herbartianism, and as such stands in some contrast to the other books examined here. Half or more of the space is devoted to facets of Herbart's own thought, which is reported accurately. Yet as an "introduction" it suffers from the serious fault that it is not likely to lead the reader to Herbart's own work. It packages so neatly and blandly those ideas of Herbart which it touches that it gives the reader little impression that there is more to get or that it is worth getting. On the contrary, Herbart's psychological and ethical ideas seem to constitute a backdrop before which the more interesting and challenging controversies about concentration centers and culture epochs are played out. Ufer's readers may well have felt that they knew all they needed to know about Herbart.

One wonders about the impression an ignorant but eager and interested teacher got about Herbart and his relation to Herbartianism from reading the whole series of ten volumes in the suggested order. Probably this avid student would have been so knee-deep in Herbartianism that, when he eventually arrived at Herbart's own books, he would more likely be led into making Herbart a Herbartian than into testing the Herbartians' views against the original doctrines. Then too, the varieties of Herbartianism presented must have been confusing.

If impressions gained from the articles and the reading list (with Dewey's supplement omitted) [36] are combined with those from the report of the discussion, the important characteristics of the society and the movement emerge with fair clarity. The society as an organization and its leaders as individuals were making intensive efforts not to appear to force Herbartianism upon American educators—a very sensitive point. As a result, the society was not openly one for the propagation of the Herbartian faith. Its avowed purpose was "to study and investigate and discuss important problems in education. Some members of this society are strongly tinctured

36. The extremely interesting and complicated relations both between Dewey's thought and Herbart's and between Dewey and the activities of the American Herbartians must be ignored here and reserved for adequate treatment elsewhere.

with the educational doctrines of Herbart, others are not, and it is right to expect an honest search for truth." [37] This general effort not to appear doctrinaire may account in part for the lack of emphasis on Herbart and even Herbartianism in the opening papers by DeGarmo and Charles McMurry; the speakers were, perhaps, trying to convince the audience that they were talking sense regardless of the source of the ideas. They were very wary of being charged, as they were by G. Stanley Hall, with regarding Herbartianism as "the consummate formulation of educational theory" and with attempting "to apply its rubrics blindly and without change to the very different material and environment of American pedagogy." [38] Several of the discussants note the mild manner with which the Herbartians answered attacks on their position. Whatever the reason, however, certainly no reader of the *Yearbook* and its *Supplements* could complain of an overdose of Herbart.

Herbart's emphasis on the moral aim of education is sometimes recognized and, as in DeGarmo's paper, seen as a commendable feature of the doctrine. But the "morality" talked about in this connection is what Herbart himself would have considered a vague concept; certainly it is no longer specified by the five fundamental ethical ideas, and it means only what each speaker chooses to make of it. Furthermore, although books like DeGarmo's *Herbart and the Herbartians* list, explain, and illustrate those five ideas, these concepts do not appear in the American Herbartians' treatment of education as determining or even partly guiding decisions in regard to instruction and discipline as they did for Herbart himself. This vagueness set in with Ziller, probably as an effort to reduce conflict between Herbart's ethical doctrine and the religiously grounded moral code. The American Herbartians made no attempt to restore Herbart's original doctrine. For the Americans education was intellectual rather than moral.

Herbart's metaphysics gets even less emphasis. Meta-

37. *First Yearbook,* p. 204.   38. Ibid., p. 200.

physics was obviously a dirty word and a touchy subject.[39] The efforts of the Herbartians to pass over it are therefore understandable. The various "introductions" to Herbart all outline his general metaphysical theory in a paragraph or two, primarily as inescapable background for his psychology, which they did wish to claim in part. But the topic is never given extended treatment, and the questions that arise when Herbart's metaphysics is applied to psychology and education are not mentioned or dealt with.

Even so, one is shocked when Colonel Francis W. Parker remarks, "I never understood that Herbart made any claim to metaphysics. He was a psychologist." [40] (One can picture Herbart spinning in his grave.) Now Parker was not a Herbartian. He characterized himself as "an exponent of advanced ideas in teaching, founded on the theories of Comenius, Pestalozzi, and Froebel," with a rather notable omission of Herbart.[41] But if he was no Herbartian, Parker was also no ignoramus about the theory and practice of education. At this time he was at the height of his career as reformer of the Quincy, Massachusetts, schools and the stormy petrel of the Cook County Normal School. Although he did not take a German degree, his three years of travel and study in Europe should have acquainted him with German Herbartianism. Yet it is hard to see any reason why Colonel Parker should have uttered this statement except his conviction that it was true. This being the case, we get some estimate of how much Herbartianism spread the doctrine of its presumed father. Parker was no Herbartian, but he was probably better informed about Herbartianism than all but a half-dozen or so Americans. If he knew nothing about Herbart's metaphysics, few Americans at that time did.

Colonel Parker was perhaps no worse off than the English Herbartian, Hayward, who is guilty either of equal ignorance or of stating his opinion as if it were a fact. In all the literature

39. E.g., ibid., 143.    40. Ibid., 154.
41. *Who's Who in America* 1901–2, s.v. Parker, Francis W. There is also his statement: "I am neither a Froebellian nor a Herbartian" ("Discussion," *National Education Association Journal of Proceedings and Addresses* [1895], 549).

it is hard to find a statement more literally contradicted at every point by Herbart than Hayward's assertion:

> It is clear, from the foregoing sketch, that Herbart's interests were primarily educational and only secondarily philosophical. Herbart's educational system was no deduction, as many people supposed, from a prearranged and artificial philosophic system; his philosophic system was rather an artificial system thrown around or placed beneath his educational system. He was not, like Kant, philosopher first and educationist afterward; education was his first and last interest.[42]

With this nugget of misinformation (parts of which can be found in the writings of other Herbartians) numerous statements by Herbart such as the following can be compared:

> My *General Pedagogy*, though it appeared earlier than the *Practical Philosophy*, was acquainted with the latter since the complete sketches for both, along with that for the *Metaphysics*, lay side by side, and the choice was open as to which should be worked out first.[43]

> In comparison with my other activities it [pedagogy] was only a side issue.[44]
> My *Pedagogy* was a brief, in part not wholly understandable, compendium. Were pedagogy the chief subject of my official activity, I should long ago have presented my thoughts about it exhaustively. Only, pedagogy has never been for me anything else than the application of philosophy.[45]

Herbart may well have been mistaken as to how systematic his educational doctrine was, as has been frequently noted in the preceding pages, but there is absolutely no doubt about what he at least *thought* he was doing. The quote from Hayward indicates that by this time either the tradition of actual knowledge about Herbart's work was running very thin or,

42. F. H. Hayward and F. E. Thomas, *The Critics of Herbartianism* (London: S. Sonnenschein, 1903), p. 38. There is a similar statement, ibid., p. 65.
43. Herbart, SW 3:153.  44. SW 2:163.  45. SW 15:36.

more probably, the later Herbartians were struggling mightily to avoid the contagion attaching to Herbart's total philosophic system.

To be sure, not all the Herbartians tried to cut the pedagogy and psychology free from the metaphysical incubus. Eckoff, in his translation of *Herbart's ABC of Sense Perception and Minor Pedagogical Works,* states the situation more as Herbart would wish:

> But the reader should understand that he has only passed the outposts. Beyond lie the Outlines of Pedagogic Lectures and the General Pedagogy, whence he may make his way into the Text-Book of Psychology and into the Psychology itself. If beyond these strongholds of Herbartianism he can penetrate the granitic Metaphysics of Herbart in all its stern realism, the main ridge of the Herbartian system, of which all the rest are spurs, he will see something very different from what one familiar only with the idealistic philosophers of Germany means when he speaks of German metaphysics.[46]

But few cared to climb these mountains even if they knew they were there.

Psychology is the only part of Herbart's system the American Herbartians stressed—as Colonel Parker's remark makes evident. But parts even of the psychology were explicitly repudiated, notably the derivative and secondary nature of the will, a point always under sharp attack by Harris and others,[47] though Herbart's position was more akin to modern views than was theirs. And even such psychology as is retained is the psychology of the Herbartians rather than of Herbart. One gross indication of this is that the labor of translation was first devoted to the works of the German Herbartian psychologists (Lange, Lindner, Ufer, and Dörpfeld) rather than to

---

46. W. S. Eckoff, *Herbart's ABC of Sense Perception,* (New York: D. Appleton & Co., 1896), 287.
47. E.g., W. T. Harris, "Discussion," *National Education Association, Journal of Proceedings and Addresses* (1895), p. 345; Parr, "Discussion," *First Yearbook of the National Herbart Society* (1895), p. 151.

Herbart's own psychological works. A second bit of evidence is that "apperception" is a favorite term and topic, and Lange's book by that title was one of the sacred writings of the American Herbartians; yet "apperception" figures so slightly in Herbart's *General Pedagogy* that the Felkins did not even index it in their translation. The American Herbartians were fascinated by the development this concept had received at the hands of the German psychologists, and the word remained a shibboleth even after it meant no more than "What we can now experience depends in large part on what we have previously experienced."

But not even that part of German Herbartianism which was retained was transmitted intact. Luken's *The Connection between Thought and Memory* was, as we saw, number 8 on the list of Herbartian titles suggested in the *First Yearbook* and was noted there as a "liberal rendering"[48] of Dörpfeld's *Denken und Gedächtnis*. But the title page of the book itself is more accurate in that it specifies only "on the basis of Dörpfeld's work," and the preface is even more explicit: "whenever better ideas have been found elsewhere, they have been unhesitatingly substituted."[49] Whether this eclecticism produced a superior product or a hodgepodge lies outside the scope of this volume. The example is mentioned only to illustrate a characteristic feature of the Herbartian movement at this period. The leaders are not trying to transmit Herbart's doctrines, or even those of the saints of the latter days, Ziller, Stoy, and the rest. Each author feels free to go his own way, with the result that any resemblance to Herbart apart from this sturdy independence becomes almost coincidental. De-Garmo insists that the Americans do not "worship their ancestors."[50] He displays scarcely a minimum of filial piety.

In the psychological domain, the great counterattraction was, of course, "child study," which posed two threats. First,

48. *First Yearbook*, p. 200.
49. H. T. Lukens, *The Connection between Thought and Memory* (Boston: D. C. Heath and Co., 1895), p. v.
50. "Discussion," *First Yearbook*, p. 152.

it too had adopted the recapitulation theory of the child's development and thus had appropriated a major distinguishing
characteristic of German Herbartianism. The second threat
was child study's connection with the growing attention to experimental psychology. Chapter 8 presented Herbart's reasons
for believing that psychology as he conceived it could not be
experimental. The Herbartian psychologists had not always
emphasized those parts of the system which imposed these
theoretical restrictions, but they had at least inherited a strong
tradition against experimentalism. The mounting popularity
of experimental work, which might, for example, "demonstrate" the epochs the child "really" moves through as he develops (as we have seen Van Liew suggesting) was a major
threat to Herbartianism and caused some bad blood between
the two schools of thought.

As these early ventures of the Herbart Society indicate,
the educational doctrine was that of Rein, and his five steps
apparently were seen as the pedagogical embodiment of the
theory of apperception. The culture-epochs theory was a more
controversial matter, though there was some inclination to
follow the lead of Rein (who had produced a series from
German history to parallel Ziller's biblical set) by developing
a sequence based on English and American history.

A detailed examination of the four other *Yearbooks* would
be overlong and fortunately is unnecessary, since a general
outline is sufficient and can be briefly sketched. The *Second
Yearbook* preserves a general Herbartian flavor with discussion
of such Herbartian topics as the culture epochs and interest by
DeGarmo, Charles McMurray, and Van Liew as well as by
non-Herbartians like John Dewey; and the *Third Yearbook*
still focuses on another Herbartian commonplace, moral education. The *Fourth Yearbook*, with its papers on history and
geography, including a reprinting of Turner's famous paper on
the "Significance of the Frontier in American History," is, however, only remotely Herbartian. With the *Fifth* (and last)
*Yearbook* of 1899 we have clearly reached the end of the line
in more ways than one. Its theme, commercial education, is

one of which Herbart would have been extremely suspicious and about which most of the Herbartians would have been no more enthusiastic. A volume devoted to what the progenitors of the movement would have labeled *Brotwissenschaft* or a "bread-and-butter subject" was an appropriate tombstone to mark a dead end.

What did the movement accomplish before its early demise? Some impression of the amount and kind of influence exerted by the American Herbartians during their time can be gleaned from the following sales figures for the relevant items of the "Pedagogical Library" made available to me through the kindness of Mr. Charles F. Weden and D. C. Heath and Co.:

| | |
|---|---|
| DeGarmo, *The Essentials of Method* | 33,240 |
| Adams, *Herbartian Psychology Applied to Education* | 18,648 |
| Lange, *Apperception* | 12,302 |
| Felkin and Felkin, *The Science of Education* | 4,441 |
| Lindner, *Psychology* | 4,164 |
| Ufer, *Introduction to the Pedagogy of Herbart* | 2,333 |
| Felkin and Felkin, *Introduction to Herbart's Science and Practice* | 1,863 |

Three points stand out clearly from these figures. First, in comparison with the other books in the series, DeGarmo's was a runaway best seller (though not compared with the books of the McMurry's already noted). This popularity undoubtedly stemmed from its early appearance and its utility as a textbook in normal schools. Second, the books by DeGarmo, Adams, and Lange far outsold the only book of Herbart's on the list, the Felkins' translation of his *General Pedagogy* under the title, *The Science of Education.* Third, the other two books which give the most attention to Herbart's own thought (the *Introductions* of Ufer and the Felkins) are the ones which sold the fewest copies. (Unfortunately, printing and sales figures for DeGarmo's *Herbart and the Herbartians,* Mulliner's translation of *The Application of Psychology to the Science of Education,* Eckoff's *Herbart's ABC of Sense Perception* and Smith's

translation of *A Textbook of Psychology* have not been preserved by their respective publishers and, consequently, these
rough measures of the contribution of these books to the
spread of Herbartianism are not available.)

Many of the leading educators of the period testify to the
influence of Herbartianism on American educational thought:
Francis W. Parker, Nicholas Murray Butler, William T .Harris,
and others.[51] The statement of B. A. Hinsdale of the University
of Michigan is typical of contemporary opinions in general tone,
though it makes its point in more than usual detail:

> Competent judges are not likely to question that the
> most powerful stimulus which is now acting upon Amer-
> ican educational thought bears the stamp of Herbart.
> While this is one of those numerous propositions which
> do not admit of positive proof, and must stand at last as
> matters of judgment, still something approaching such
> proof can in this instance be adduced. Reference is made
> particularly to the recent translations of Herbartian works
> that have been published and circulated, such as Herbart's
> *Psychology* and *Science of Education,* Lange's *Appercep-
> tion,* Rein's *Outlines,* and Ufer's *Introduction* but also in
> a minor degree to original works . . . that have appeared
> from time to time. It will not be claimed that a list of
> educational publications equal in number, to say nothing
> of quality, appearing within the same time, or double the
> time, could be made up that would represent any other
> influence or school of thought.[52]

And Charles Thurber, the first editor of *The School Review*
and a frequent witness to the importance of Herbartianism,[53]
describes another way the Herbartians exerted their influence:

51. F. W. Parker, "Report of the Committee of Ten: Its Use for the
Improvement of Teachers Now at Work in the Schools," *Educational
Review* 7 (1894): 496–97; N. M. Butler, "Discussion," *National Education Association, Journal of Proceedings and Addresses* (1895), p. 348;
"Editorial," *Educational Review* 5 (1893): 508; *Public School Journal* 11
(1891): 85.
52. B. A. Hinsdale, "Review of DeGarmo's *Herbart and the Herbartians,*"
*Educational Review* 9 (1895): 192.
53. E.g., *School Review* 1 (1893): 379; 2 (1894): 113; 3 (1895): 423.

Outside an inner circle of Herbartians, and a very small and select inner circle, too, not much has been known in this country about Herbart, and, to tell the truth, few have cared to know until recently. But the members of this little circle of the elect have been persistent and even obstreperous; they have urged their views in season and out of season; certain that they had the truth in their possession, they have laughed at criticism and been laughed at with equanimity. Now those who came to scoff have remained to pray.[54]

Certainly what popularity and influence Herbartianism did achieve in America was not attained by being a "systematic" doctrine. Undeniably, people differ in the appeal which a systematic doctrine has for them. Frank McMurry possibly spoke for some educators when he claimed that "the beauty of connected thought, of system, tends of itself to win converts."[55] But this "connected thought" of which he speaks is, of course, only the limited pedagogical doctrine of the Herbartians, not Herbart's total system. Nonetheless, educators who knew nothing and cared less about the precise details of the system of Herbart or even of the Herbartians were probably reassured by the vague belief that this pedagogy was somehow "firmly based on psychological laws" or that it ultimately rested on a philosophic system of some kind. But the American Herbartians preserved almost none of the total system. "It is clear, therefore, that in seeking assistance from a former leader we shall not be helped by falling back into any outgrown system of metaphysics or antiquated theories of mind or morals, but that, as already indicated, we shall find Herbart's significance for us to lie chiefly in his organization of the purposes and means of education.[56]

Most of the major non-Herbartian educators who were

54. C. H. Thurber, "Review of DeGarmo's *Herbart and the Herbartians,*" *School Review* 3 (1895): 301.
55. Frank M. McMurry, "Concentration," *Educational Review* 9 (1895): 34.
56. Charles DeGarmo, "The Significance of Herbart for Secondary and Higher Education," *Educational Review* 11 (Jan. 1896): 41.

interested and sympathetic (such as Parker, Butler, and Harris) were prepared to consider the pedagogy in isolation—or with only a dash of Herbartian psychology added.[57] Only occasionally did critics question the validity and usefulness of a doctrine which had been torn from its philosophic foundations because these had been repudiated.[58] Many school people saw the chief value of Herbartianism in its "stirring up" of educational thought.[59] (One often suspects that many educational officials are convinced that educational thought, like medicine, should be shaken well before being administered.) But those whose thoughts had been thus stirred up were more likely to take over bits and pieces than anything systematic. The general "influence" of Herbartianism may well have been little more than acquainting teachers with the use of Rein's five steps and leading them to have opinions, pro or con, concerning concentration centers and the culture-epoch theory.

Herbartianism was obviously slow in crossing the Atlantic. Although Ziller's *Foundation* appeared in 1865, a sizeable gap is apparent between that date and, say, 1889, the year of De-Garmo's *Essentials of Method*. Herbart and Herbartianism were not, of course, unknown up to that time; for example, as early as 1878 Henry Barnard had run in his *American Journal of Education* [60] a biography of Herbart and a brief summary of his educational views reprinted from the *Journal of Speculative Philosophy*. But the writings of DeGarmo and the Mc-Murrys were the first major efforts to spread the doctrine among American educators at large. In other words, German Herbartianism had been available for American adoption for twenty years or more. Why did America wait so long before

57. W. T. Harris, "Discussion," *National Education Association, Journal of Proceedings and Addresses* (1895), p. 345; N. M. Butler, ibid., p. 349; "Editorial," *Educational Review* 9 (1895): 422–23.
58. Arnold Tompkins, "Herbart's Philosophy and His Educational Theory," *Educational Review* 16 (1898): 233; E. E. White, "Discussion," *National Education Association, Journal of Proceedings and Addresses* (1895), p. 346.
59. "Discussion," *First Yearbook of the National Herbart Society*, pp. 143, 144, 153.
60. *American Journal of Education* 28 (1878): 45–49.

some enterprising young educator like DeGarmo or McMurry made a career out of importing Herbartianism?

DeGarmo's own answer is probably valid.

> During the past forty or fifty years we have had enough to do in the effort to extend the benefits of education to all the people. Public opinion for universal education had to be developed and formulated into laws. . . . Houses and implements were to be provided; teachers were to be certified and paid, and to some extent trained for their specific duties.
>
> Having undertaken, therefore, for the first time in history, this vast enterprise, it is not to be wondered at that our chief efforts in the past have been directed mostly to the perfection of the external machinery necessary for its successful prosecution.
>
> . . . We began with the primitive ideas of education that were developed when there were few things to study and but few people to study them. Learning had been confined for the most part to languages, logic, and philosophy, and learners had been restricted to literati, gentlemen, clergymen and a few professionals. But now a double difficulty confronts us—vast increases in available knowledge and multiplication of learners . . . he who still adheres to the ancient course of study, whose strength was its poverty, does so against many urgent protests arising from this growth in knowledge and this extension of education to all children of all classes of men. It is found that the mental food so palatable to gentlemen and literati, has proved to be neither palatable nor valuable to many of the sons of toil. . . .
>
> . . . What shall the public schools teach? That this problem is already being vigorously attacked, witness the efforts of New England to shorten and enrich the grammar school curriculum, the report of the committee of ten, and the report of the committee of fifteen on elementary education.[61]

Social and cultural situations of this sort always bring the problems of educational "method" and "content" to the fore with a

61. *First Yearbook of the National Herbart Society*, pp. 7–8.

vengeance. So earlier, the rise of Protestantism, which required enough reading skill in *everyone* to permit access to the Holy Writ to ensure the soul's salvation, had launched Comenius on his search for an infallible method of teaching. So in our own day, concern over the "culturally deprived" child is spawning vast research programs to discover what and how he can be taught, since current curriculum materials and current procedures have proved ineffective. To these questions of "What?" and "How?" Herbartianism was ready in the 1890s to provide a set of answers in precision and detail.

Not to be ignored either is DeGarmo's point about teacher training. If one agrees with the thesis that Herbart defended in taking his doctorate—that the art of teaching does not depend on experience alone—one must then face the question, "How can teachers be taught how to teach?" The "steps"— whatever their names or number—were a clear-cut answer applicable to both large and small units; similarly, in regard to teaching program planning and curriculum building, the concentration centers and the culture epochs (insofar as the American Herbartians used them) gave the teacher of teachers simple principles and direct applications to teach to his aspiring teachers. A parallel set of problems confronting the European nations as they began developing their national school systems in the late eighteenth and early nineteenth centuries had sent a stream of official delegations to visit the schools of Pestalozzi. Although he could furnish some materials, his resources, both in high-flying "system" and pedestrian practical detail, fell far short of what Ziller, Rein, and their associates now had to offer. DeGarmo's suggested answers to the questions why Herbartianism came only when it did and why it came with such a rush once it did come are probably as valid as most answers to historical questions ever can be.

Even when Herbartianism did arrive, it did not spread like wildfire. In 1891 Smith, in the introduction to her translation of Herbart's *Textbook of Psychology* says:

> In America, it is true, the number of educators who have any useful knowledge concerning the Herbartian system

is somewhat limited; yet in the current philosophical and education literature may be found *occasionally a brief* mention, which is probably an indication of the broader study which is yet to follow.[62]

Since at the time she was writing most of the Herbartian books had not yet been published, this statement is perhaps not surprising. Yet even in 1895 DeGarmo commented, "In English-speaking countries his system of educational thought is for most teachers still in the stage of exposition," [63] although one year later Eckoff was more optimistic:

American teachers are beginning to live, move and have their being in an atmosphere of Herbartianism. It is coming to be the pedagogical spirit of the times.[64]

In fact the year 1896 seems clearly the acme of the movement as a theoretical force in American educational thought; Mossman's estimate [65] in this regard is confirmed by my own independent collecting of the evidence. The bulk of the major books in English about Herbart and of the English translations of his work were published within the short span of 1889 to 1901; beyond either limit of that period, the Herbartian material is relatively scanty. In short, American Herbartianism had a short life, for 1899 also saw the last *Yearbook* of the National Herbart Society, which was eventually (1902) reorganized "to put the work of the Society on a higher plane." [66]

Obviously, in 1903 Herbartianism was not what it once was. The report of this death can also be exaggerated; or rather what is meant by dying must be formulated more precisely. As a lively theoretical movement producing new books and articles, American Herbartianism was pretty well dead by

62. Margaret K. Smith, *A Textbook of Psychology* (New York: D. Appleton & Co., 1894), p. xxi (emphasis added).
63. DeGarmo, *Herbart and the Herbartians*, p. v.
64. W. S. Eckoff, *ABC of Sense-Perception*, p. xiv.
65. Lois Coffey Mossman, *Changing Conditions Relative to the Planning of Lessons*, (Teachers College Contributions to Education no. 147; (New York: Teachers College, Columbia University, 1924), p. 21.
66. "Editorial," *Educational Review* 21 (Apr. 1901): 428.

1905. But the usual lag in educational procedures and operations must not be minimized. There is always someone who doesn't get the word, or gets it late. Macmillan published a new edition of Charles McMurry's *The Elements of General Method* in 1903, very late in the life of the movement. But they printed about 75,000 copies of this edition, which remained in print till 1922, and about 23,000 copies of a new edition of *The Method of the Recitation*.[67] D. C. Heath kept DeGarmo's *Essentials of Method* in print until 1934 and Adam's *The Herbartian Psychology as Applied to Education* until 1936. These books were not kept in print for the sake of sales to educational historians. Somewhere, probably in a good many places, teachers were still teaching and students were still studying this brand of Herbartianism in the 1920s and 1930s.

Another instance of this sort of survival might be discerned in the strange episode in the renaming of the reorganized Herbart Society.[68] In 1901 the new title, "The National Society for the Scientific Study of Education," had been achieved merely by dropping "Herbart" from the last official name of the Herbart Society. Because this label seemed cumbersome, a committee was appointed to canvass the membership for suggestions and to offer an alternative. In 1905 this committee reported that although there was consensus favoring a change, there was no agreement on any specific suggestion, though the committee itself favored "The National Society of Education."

The question was referred back to the committee, which in 1906 again proposed its former preference. But the motion which was passed by a large majority at the annual meeting specified the "Herbart Society," with the executive committee given discretionary power to add "National" or "American" as the first word if they wished. But since this motion had not been made as an amendment to the constitution, the executive

67. I am indebted to Miss June Meyer and the Macmillan Company for the figures on the McMurrys' books published by them.
68. Guy M. Whipple, *Commemorating a Quarter of a Century of Service of the National Society for the Study of Education* (Bloomington, Ill.: Public School Publishing Company, 1926), p. 6.

committee "did not feel authorized nor warranted in making the change." Not until 1909 were a revised constitution and name, "National Society for the Study of Education" adopted.

Since the records are sketchy, any statements about this odd turn of events are at best probabilities. But the following interpretation does not seem farfetched. In the reorganization, "Herbart" was dropped from the name simply because the word had lost its magic for those leaders effecting the reorganization. Since Charles McMurry continued as secretary-treasurer during 1902 and 1903 and DeGarmo served on the executive committee for the same period, this group included several former Herbartians. But apparently the little man in the society did not yet know that Herbartianism was done for; and given a choice he still wanted to belong to "The Herbart Society." One suspects that the members who voted to remain "Herbartians" in name were also those who would continue to buy and use the Herbartian books and to teach their version of Herbartianism for several decades.

Why did Herbartianism fade so rapidly in America? The suggestion of Charles McMurry, made about a decade after the decline of the movement, is familiar:

> In the last twenty-five years we have had a rapid succession of reform movements, such as the kindergarten, natural science and nature-study, the elective system, physical geography, classical English literature, manual training, the Herbartian movement, child-study, and more recently, agriculture and vocational training. None of these propagandas have had any such success as their advocates at first expected. All of them have left permanent influences that have changed to some extent our ideas and practices in the schools.[69]

This statement seems valid, of course, not merely for those instances to which McMurry applies it but for all educational reforms past, present, and future. Almost inevitably every innovation is oversold by zealous advocates to everyone, in-

69. Charles A. McMurry, *Conflicting Principles in Teaching and How to Avoid Them* (New York: Houghton Mifflin Co., 1914), p. 262.

cluding themselves; then disillusion sets in. But, eternally hopeful, the profession avidly embraces the next panacea until it too proves ineffective. This phenomenon is the source of that massive cynicism endemic among teachers, many of whom regard every attempt at reform as a mere fad which they need only "wait out" since it will soon be replaced by another, which will perish in turn.

To say with Charles McMurry merely that Herbartianism fell short of the expectations of its original advocates is not to specify what those shortcomings were; and in any case this approach would focus the analysis on personal viewpoints rather than on the larger educational and social situation. To be sure, the general disaffection of the former leaders was undoubtedly a factor. In any such movement, once its most vigorous advocates have made their reputations by espousing the reform, they often turn to something new—a new career line, a new reform, a new field of interest—or they may simply rest quietly on the professional laurels they have already won. The vitality of the movement was undoubtedly affected when De-Garmo left the field of teacher training to become president of Swarthmore College and when Van Liew first turned to advocating child study and then became president of Chico State College.

But to look at some of the aspects of the general social and educational situation is perhaps more enlightening than to consider what motivation the leaders had for turning to other activities. As we have seen, certain factors seem to have contributed to the initial success of Herbartianism. Persistence of some of these factors in essentially the same form and force acted to preserve Herbartianism; alterations in other factors and the emergence of new forces led to its decline.

Its simplicity and immediate practicality continued to recommend it. These characteristics of American Herbartianism, as it was understood by many teachers, kept it alive in classrooms and normal schools well through the first quarter of this century, long after it had perished as a theoretical innovation. To take the extreme case, the mere mechanical application of the steps in making course outlines and lesson plans had real utility for overworked and unimaginative teachers. They clung to the steps happily until they could, by equal oversimplification, reduce Dewey's *How We Think* to a similar mechanical series or could take over Henry Clayton Morrison's sets from his *Principles of Teaching in the Secondary School.* Simple practicality in the classroom had always been a great virtue of American Herbartianism.

For the most part, however, other factors originally favoring Herbartianism had become less operative. General connection with European thought and scholarship was less of a selling point by the opening of the twentieth century. The attraction which Hegelianism and Herbartianism possessed because of their ties with the golden age of German philosophy and with subsequent academic activity in Germany had waned. By the beginning of the twentieth century, American universities, run on German models and staffed to a considerable extent by German-trained faculty, made the country much less dependent upon and subservient to imported wisdom.

Similarly, the relation of Hegelianism and Herbartianism to major speculative systems had rapidly turned from an advantage to a disadvantage. "Metaphysics" and "system" had become opprobrious epithets. The small, neat, precise scientific experiment was now becoming the model for "real scholarship," not the great speculative system.

This new scientific fervor had particularly devastating consequences for Herbartian psychology, the sole part of Herbart's original system still supporting the pedagogy. As Herbartianism had continuously moved its emphasis from moral education to cognitive development, Herbart's ethics had become irrelevant. Metaphysics had become unpopular, and its bearing on psychology in Herbart's system had been progressively minimized. Psychology was, consequently, the only remaining support—one that had become increasingly important throughout the nineteenth century as the professional conviction grew that psychology was the chief science upon which education depended. As a result, any reason for slackening of interest or loss of confidence in Herbartian psychology was certain to pose a serious threat for Herbartian pedagogy.

The rise of experimental psychology constituted such a threat, for Herbartian psychology did not easily lend itself to that experimental manipulation which Thorndike, Judd, and the like were making popular at the beginning of the present century. The general theory of apperception stated that the fate of any new presentation or idea arising in mind is a function of the nature of the apperceptive masses already existing there, but that this structure of mind at a given instant is itself subject to modification through the influence of new presentations. The calculus involved in Herbart's "statics and mechanics of mind" attempted to plot the consequences of these interactions—but in such simplified situations (even for his most complicated calculations) as to be highly "fictional." "Mind" was an individual mind, and the mind of that person at that moment was unique, the product of the precise kind and sequence of his personal experiences. "Mind" of this sort simply did not lend itself to that isolation and measurement of specific components necessary for neat laboratory investigations. Even the technique for dealing with highly idiosyncratic materials, the case-study method, would scarcely have been equal to the task, even had it then been acceptable as a tool of "scientific psychology."

As a result, Herbartian psychology seemed nonscientific or even antiscientific according to the current acceptation of "science." To deprive Herbartian pedagogy of its basis in a "scientific psychology" was a particularly mortal thrust at a time when Americans generally were becoming ardently scientific and when a scientific psychology was seen as the very lifeblood of an adequate pedagogy.

Of the new factors, two demand at least brief mention. The first is that at about this time American education began its long love affair with "the child," a romance hardly shaken until the blast which orbited Sputnik. Simultaneously, partly for this reason and partly for others such as the expanding work in experimental psychology, professional interest shifted from "teaching" to "learning." Even in Herbart's own doctrine "instruction" had always been the major part of pedagogy; and Herbartianism, particularly if reduced essentially to the "steps of instruction," had had the same emphasis. Consequently, when "child-centered" became honorific and "teacher-centered" pejorative and when "learning" became primary and "teaching" became secondary (if that), Herbartianism appeared not merely out-of-date but actually misdirected.

In short, having within little more than a decade become out of step with its times, American Herbartianism as such faded from the scene except in those situations where the practical utility of its simplest procedures gave it something of a "half-life" for another twenty-five years.

# 15

# Epilogue

The questions with which this inquiry began have been answered with varying degrees of completeness and adequacy in the preceding pages, and there is no need for a long last chapter recapitulating the questions and their answers.

Despite Herbart's early problems with his family and the personality characteristics which resulted from this experience, his underlying integrity did eventually get through to people, and we can only rejoice that he achieved as satisfactory a personal and professional life as he did. His happiness was undoubtedly marred by his feelings that, despite his assiduity and ingenuity, he never achieved the professional recognition he felt he deserved. "Happy is the man who finds his time," and Herbart was as out of season as an oyster in an r-less month.

Under the compulsion incumbent upon the German university student of the time to develop an intellectual "system," he evolved a fairly distinctive one. Quite apart from the fact that its somewhat realistic nature made him unpopular in the floruit of the idealisms of Fichte, Schelling, and Hegel, his metaphysics and his related psychology simply did not prove fruitful in the long run. Educationally he was equally out of step. His first and true love was education within the family through the private tutor—at a time when state and national systems of education with their large schools and large classes were first coming into their full strength. As an educational reformer he confronted such systems in the hodgepodge of schools emerging in Prussia and Hanover. He was not interested in the administrative problem of improving this chaos; he wanted to work with the aim, content, and method of education. In regard to all these points he found the German gymnasium a barren field for the sort of change he wished to effect.

When the last torch went out at his graveside in 1841, Herbart's thought was dead, and it was never truly resurrected. His subsequent appearances were those of a ghost, and a much more pale and unsubstantial wraith than Hamlet's father or Jacob Marley.

Ziller did not succeed in reviving Herbart. With his interest in social reform, he was profoundly impressed with Herbart's conviction concerning the power of instruction to build character, and to this end he took from him what he felt would serve his purposes; but he felt few compunctions about modifying or "improving" Herbart.

In any case, the new shift in emphasis toward elementary education with its religious and nationalistic context would have necessitated changes in Herbart's doctrine, whatever Ziller wished. Ziller undoubtedly felt he could find justification for his modifications in Herbart's own writings, but the changes were profound. As a result, Ziller, skilled ghost-writer that he was, became ghost-writer for a ghost.

Rein, the second ghost-writer, perpetuated Ziller rather than Herbart. To be sure, he worked much harder at documenting the connections of his own Herbartianism to Herbart's thought, and hence his use of Herbart's works was more explicit and extended than was Ziller's. But by and large this effort did not result in an inclusion of more of Herbart's own teachings. Herbart was quoted rather like Scripture to justify the courses of action Ziller and Rein had taken. In Rein's work Herbart materializes as a somewhat clearer ghost, but not as a more lively one.

When Herbart's spirit crossed the Atlantic, its ectoplasm became still more attenuated. His name was invoked as part of the benediction descending from German scholarship, but little more. With even Ziller seen as long ago and far away and in another country, Herbart was necessarily a remote and pale shade.

To say all this is not to charge the Herbartians with a crime in failing to transmit their master's teachings unchanged. Herbart had trouble in working with his system and his educational ideas; several times he essentially gave it up as a hopeless task. Greater effort and better success can hardly be demanded of others. Certainly Herbart himself never managed to cause the stir or exert the influence his followers generated for him.

Moreover, Herbart was convinced that altered places, times, and circumstances irrevocably work their changes; the man who felt free to call himself a Kantian, but a "Kantian of 1828," could hardly take umbrage if Americans developed their own brand of Herbartianism in 1895. But it was probably just as well that Herbart, unlike John Dewey, did not live to see some of the things done in his name.

# Bibliographical Note

The following pages do not attempt to cover the voluminous literature on Herbart and Hebartianism or even to include all the materials used in writing this volume or cited in the notes. These comments are intended merely to introduce the American reader who wishes to go further to the most obvious materials, which in turn will lead him to most of the other literature through bibliographies and notes. The emphasis here is, consequently, upon materials in English and on foreign materials most readily available in the United States.

COMPLETE WORKS

There are two editions of Herbart's complete works: (1) G. Hartenstein, *J. F. Herbarts Sämtliche Werke,* 12 vol. (Leipzig, 1850–52; 2nd ed.; 13 vols.; Hamburg, 1883–93). The arrangement of this edition is topical: vol. 1, introduction to philosophy; vol. 2, *Encyclopedia*; vols. 3 and 4, metaphysics; vols. 5–7, psychology; vols. 8 and 9, ethics; vols. 10 and 11, pedagogy; and vol. 12, historical-critical. Since the volumes are approximately the same size, the number of volumes devoted to each topic gives a rough index of the distribution of Herbart's activity. (Volume 13 of the second edition contains additional material made available after the publication of the first edition.)

(2) K. Kehrbach and O. Flügel, *Johann Friedrich Herbart Sämtliche Werke in chronologischer Reihenfolge* (Langensalza, 1877ff; reprinted, 1964). The references in this book (cited as *SW*) are to this edition. Its general organization is as follows:

*Vols. 1–11.* Primarily books, articles and addresses by Herbart, though some other materials are included (e.g., Smidt's "Recollections," adverse reviews to which Herbart replied). Since, with minor exceptions, the chronological order is preserved, volumes 1 and 2 contain Herbart's works up to his departure from Göttingen in 1808; volumes 3–9, the products of his stay at Königsberg; volumes 10 and 11, the late works produced after his return to Göttingen in 1833.

*Volumes 12 and 13.* Book reviews by Herbart. These contain some specific items of interest and also generally illuminate Herbart's relations with his professional colleagues.

*Volumes 14 and 15.* The history of Herbart's pedagogical seminar at Königsberg, from the requests he made at the time of his original call to the reports of the various commissions considering the future of the seminar after his departure to Göttingen. This detailed picture of Herbart as the practical pedagogue at maturity has been much neglected by the English literature.

*Volumes 16–19. (edited by T. Fritzsch).* Letters to, from, and about Herbart, along with some other biographical material. The arrangement is chronological throughout the four volumes except that the bulk of volume 19 constitutes a supplement to the preceding three, containing earlier materials omitted in them.

Also worth noting are at least two of the older editions of only the pedagogical works: that of F. Bartolomäi (7th ed. by von Sallwürk; Langensalza, 1903–6), and that of O. Willmann and T. Fritzsch (3d ed., Harz, 1913ff.). Since these collections were cheaper and more convenient than the complete editions, they were much used by both German and American educators. Their existence may have contributed to the tendency of those Herbartians who were interested primarily in education to ignore the rest of the system, using only those writings most easily accessible and most obviously relevant. A more recent version in three volumes is that of Walter Asmus, (Düsseldorf and Munich: Küpper, 1964–65).

GENERAL BOOKS ON HERBART

In German there are a number of good works dealing with Herbart's life and writings, and (usually) with Herbartianism. In chronological order these are: Thilo, Flügel, Rein, and Rude, *Herbart und die Herbartianer* (Langensalza, 1897); O. Flügel, *Herbarts Lehren und Leben* (Leipzig, 1907); H. Walther, *Herbarts Charakter und Pädagogik in ihrer Entwicklung* (Stuttgart, 1912); T. Frizsch, *Johann Friedr. Herbarts Leben und Lehre* (Leipzig, 1921); G. Weiss, *Herbart und seine Schule* (Munich, 1928); and B. Schwenk *Das Herbartverständnis der Herbartianer* (Weinheim, 1963). A very detailed biography has begun to appear: Walter Asmus. *Johann Friedrich Herbart: Eine pädagogische Biographie,* vol. 1, *Der Denker, 1776–1809,* (Heidelberg: Quelle & Meyer, 1968).

In English the general treatments are fewer. Among the older books, which were written primarily for educators, the best is H. M. Felkin and E. Felkin, *An Introduction to Herbart's Science and Practice of Education* (London and Boston, 1895). A more adequate view of the total system is James Ward's article (s.v. Herbart) in the eleventh edition of the *Encyclopaedia Britannica*. A briefer sketch by me appears in the *Encyclopedia of Philosophy,* ed. Paul Edwards (New York: Macmillan, 1967) 3:481–84. My *Herbart and Education* (New York: Random House, 1969) sketches the system and the work of the Herbartians in pedagogy.

PARTICULAR FIELDS

For Herbart's metaphysics and ethics, there are no complete English translations or monographs. For those who read French but not German, M. Mauxion's *La metaphysique de Herbart* (Paris, 1894) is a fair substitute for the originals since by translating and paraphrasing it stays close to Herbart's own account. Parts of the ethics are available in English in K. Price, *Education and Philosophical Thought,* 2d ed. (Boston: Allyn and Bacon, 1967). F. Seidenfaden, *Die Pädagogik des jungen Herbart* (Weinheim and Berlin: Julius Beltz, 1967) relates Herbart's ethical theory to Kant's ethics and to Herbart's educational theory; unfortunately it became available to me too late to use in this book.

In psychology, the English speaker is much better off. G. F. Stout's "The Herbartian Psychology" (*Mind* 13 [1888]: 321–38, 473–97) gives a fairly detailed presentation of the doctrine, though he intentionally hurries over the metaphysical basis of the theory and minimizes its postulational nature. Happily, for those who wish to learn about the psychology more directly, satisfactory translations of some of the works are available: M. K. Smith, *Textbook of Psychology* (New York, 1894) and B. C. Mulliner, *The Application of Psychology to the Science of Education* (London and New York, 1898).

For pedagogy there is a more generous supply in English of both monographs and translations. To the former class belong F. M. Felkin and E. Felkin, *An Introduction to Herbart's Science and Practice of Education* (London and Boston, 1895); C. DeGarmo, *Herbart and the Herbartians* (New York, 1895); C. Ufer, *Introduction to the Pedagogy of Herbart,* trans, Zinser (Boston, 1894); G. Compayré, *Herbart and Education by Instruction,* trans. Findlay (New York, 1907). (F. N. Hayward, *The Student's Herbart* [London, 1902] and A. M. Williams, *Johann Friedrich Herbart* [London, 1911] are far inferior to the preceding.)

Translations of all the major pedagogical works are available. H. M. Felkin and E. Felkin, *The Science of Education* (London and Boston, 1892) is the translation of Herbart's *General Pedagogy*. Their *Letters and Lectures on Education* (London and Syracuse, N. Y., 1898) translates Herbart's five extant reports to Herr von Steiger, his long letter to Karl von Steiger of 10 Nov. 1900, and his *Outlines of Pedagogical Lectures*. A. Lange also translated the *Outlines* (New York, 1901), which was clearly the best single volume to offer the teacher who wanted his Herbart in a single, simple dose. W. J. Eckoff provided *The ABC of Sense Perception and Minor Pedagogical Works* (New York, 1896).

The relative distribution of monographs and translations in English among the fields of metaphysics, ethics, psychology, and pedagogy plainly reveals the different degrees of interest on the part of the English-speaking world.

HERBARTIANISM

Since much of the older German literature concerns the wars between the varying sects of Herbartianism or the discussion of the applicability of Herbartianism to various reforms in German education, the person interested in Herbart rather than Herbartianism will find little in it. Those who must content themselves with the rather detailed summaries of some of this material provided by F. H. Hayward and F. E. Thomas in *The Critics of Herbartianism* (London, 1903) should not feel that they are missing too much. Those interested in tackling the rather massive German literature can gain access to it through A. Rude's "Die Litteratur der Pädagogik Herbarts und siener Schule" in Thilo, Flügel, Rein, and Rude, *Herbart und die Herbartianer* (Langensalza, 1910); F. Ueberweg, *Grundriss der Geschichte der Philosophie,* 13th ed. by T. K. Oesterreich (Basel: Bruno Schwabe, 1951), pt. 4, pp. 158–60, 363–73, and J. N. Schmidt's *Herbart-Bibliographie 1842–1963* (Weinheim, 1964), though the last is far less comprehensive than its title implies. The bibliography in Seidenfaden's *Die Pädagogik des jungen Herbart* is particularly useful for its citations of recent German dissertations and periodical literature.

Since the major books of American Herbartianism are treated in detail in chapter 14, they will not be listed again here. Additional early works by American Herbartians are noted in my "Herbartianism Comes to America," *History of Education Quarterly*, 9 (Summer, 1969): 202–33.

# Index